BRITISH MIDLAND AIRWAYS

B. G. CRAMP

Airline Publications & Sales Ltd.

Produced and Printed in England by
INTERGRAPHIC PRINT (UK) LTD.
51 Hounslow Road, Hanworth, Middx.
and Ludo Press Ltd.
Setting by Abbey Typesetters, Cirencester.

Contents

ACKNOWLEDGEMENTS

The author is indebted to all those people, too numerous to mention in their entirety, who provided material for this book, but special thanks are due in particular to Mr. E. W. Phillips, M.B.E., the late Wing Commander H. A. R. Roxburgh, A.F.C., Captain E. W. A. Lines (who first inspired me to start this project) and to Mrs. J. Merritt, Miss P. Blaney and my wife, Mildred, who each typed out the manuscripts as they were written, edited, and re-written.

B. G. CRAMP

DEDICATION

To Mildred and Trevor for their patience.

Introduction

On Saturday 11th November, 1972, Boeing 707-321 G-AYBJ departed London Heathrow Airport bound for Khartoum via Rome and Athens. Nothing spectacular about this, one may consider, for Boeing 707's along with many other aircraft types depart almost daily from London Heathrow bound for Khartoum via Rome and Athens and points beyond, so why the interest in this particular flight? The significance about "BJ" was that although it was painted in the house colours of Sudan Airways, and operating Sudan Airways Flight SD113, the aircraft was owned by British Midland Airways and manned by British Midlands crews, both flight deck and cabin staff (apart from two Sudanese stewardesses on board to make Arabic announcements). British Midland, a non-IATA airline, was operating the first flight for a contract on behalf of Sudan Airways—an IATA airline. The contract, initially for one year, provided for the operation of Sudan's 'Blue Nile' international services radiating from Khartoum and serving Addis Ababa, Athens, Beirut, Cairo, Jeddah, London, Nairobi, Rome and Tripoli, the service catering for both economy and first class passengers. In addition, training was to be given to Sudan Airways own staff including pilots, flight engineers, cabin staff, ground engineers and in such matters as accountancy and other managerial spheres. The contract was late in being negotiated and the whole operation was mounted by British Midland in a little under three weeks—a tremendous undertaking and brilliantly executed, which is in itself a tribute to the staff concerned not only for their hard work, but also for their expertise.

British Midland is not alone among the British independent airlines in having an abundance of expertise in its midst, but it is almost unique in being an independent airline in its own right, without having any shipping or catering interests on which to 'hive off' any financial losses, and it has never amalgamated with any other airline in its history (with two minor exceptions neither of which are amalgamations in the accepted sense). Since 1971, BMA has enjoyed one of the fastest scheduled service growth rates of any airline anywhere.

The departure of "BJ" from London on this day really signalled the arrival of British Midland into the 'big-time'. Great oaks from little acorns grow, and certainly British Midland had been a little acorn. This is the story of British Midland, the story of a far-sighted man in its beginning and of far-sighted men (and women) during its history. However, the weak have fallen by the wayside and only the strong remain. British Midland remains.

B.G. CRAMP

Wing Commander N. Roy Harben D.F.C., Founder of the Company

1936-1956

Few men in Britain in 1936/37 were far-sighted enough to see the growing menace on their doorstep, in the shape of Adolf Hitler, the Wermacht and embryo Luftwaffe. Fortunately some did see with their own eyes and prompted the authorities of the time to get off their backsides and sit up and take notice of just what was going on. Had they not done so it is very doubtful whether this story would even have happened. One such far-sighted man was Captain N. Roy Harben D.F.C., at that time a member of the Royal Air Force Reserve of Officers.

Captain Harben served in the Royal Flying Corps in the First World War, and it was on the Western Front that he won the Distinguished Flying Cross. Whilst touring the Continent in 1936-7 with some flying clubs he saw at first hand the embryo Luftwaffe in Germany, together with the quickly-gathering war-clouds. As a direct result of these encounters, Capt. Harben determined upon his return from one such trip to do something about it, and this he did. Approaching the Air Ministry he made his findings known and suggested that with his instructional experiences and expertise, he set up a flying school, at which Royal Air Force Volunteer Reserve pilots would be trained.

The immediate job now was to look for a suitable airfield in the Midlands, and equally important, for an able and reliable assistant to help set up the new school. Certainly the person appointed had to be a first class administrator and organiser, know aviation, and be able to work on his own during Roy Harben's absence.

Now in the pre-war days possibly the world's best-known and well organised flying displays were the Royal Air Force Flying Displays at Hendon, just outside metropolitan London. At Hendon, as Assistant to Air Commodore Drew who at that time was Chairman of the Royal Air Force Displays Committee, was Mr. E.W. Phillips – "Phil" to his friends – and it was to Mr. Phillips that Captain Harben was directed.

Mr. Phillips, who had seen considerable service in the R.A.F., had been organising the Hendon Air Displays for the past 12 years and was certainly capable of both organisation and working on his own. Roy Harben put the problem to Phil and asked him if he would be prepared to help set up and run the flying school in the Midlands, should the contract be forthcoming, and indeed he asked Phil to help in preparation of the tender to be put before the Air Ministry.

About this time, April 1938, Derby Corporation were in the process of building Derby (Burnaston) Airport and were actively seeking either an airport manager or a commercial undertaking willing to run the new venture, and it was to this precise spot that Roy Harben turned his attention. This was where his new flying school would be based if and when the Air Ministry contract materialised. He approached Derby Corporation and was awarded the contract to operate the new airport.

Being successful in his bid to the Air Ministry, and armed now with a contract, Roy Harben asked Phil to go to Derby and commence setting up the organisation required. It was a very wet and dreary Sunday when Mr. and Mrs. Phillips drew in at Derby railway station. Neither of them had ever been to Derby before and therefore were relying on the local people to direct them to this new airport. Imagine their surprise (and dismay) when each person they asked denied any knowledge of the place. Wet, weary, hungry and thirsty by this time, the undaunted couple decided to have a coffee at a cafe outside the railway station, and thus fortified to try once again to find the by now mythical airfield.

Having left the cafe behind, the first person they saw was fortunately (or so they thought at the time) a policeman. Quite relieved they approached him and asked how to get to Burnaston. However, even this stalwart gentleman had not heard of the place, but living up to his reputation he said he would find out. At long last, the policeman returned from a telephone conversation to give the required directions, with the added information that only two buses a day went past the field and it would therefore be better to go by taxi. Once again the individual encountered did not know of Burnaston, but, armed with the policeman's directions the taxi set off and eventually, rain still pouring, made Burnaston House, a mansion-like building dominating the whole domestic side of this new airport.

Burnaston House (Aero Pictorial Ltd). Note temporary wooden buildings in the background.

Waiting to greet Mr. and Mrs. Phillips on the doorstep of Burnaston House was a retired major who, until a short time previously, had been in charge of refugees from the Spanish Civil War, and who had been accommodated in the House. The place was in a terrible mess as the refugees had torn up floorboards and smashed the furniture, most of it being used as firewood, and the whole place was infested with rats and mice. What a greeting to what was after all, the whole future for Roy Harben and the Phillips. To make matters worse, or so it seemed on this very wet day, the airfield itself was not yet complete. In fact at this point the only apparent connection with an airfield was a newly-erected Belman hangar. However, there was a job to be done and characteristically Phil got down to it straight away.

Apart from the Belman Hangar, Derby Corporation were in the process of building another Hangar, to be known as the Municipal Hangar, attached to which would be the offices and public bar. The Air Ministry liked the whole set-up and confirmed that they would be sending a whole host of people to train as pilots. Apart from the Derby Aero Club which was also being operated by the newly established company, the Air Minstry contract called for the operating of No. 30 Elementary and Service Flying Training School. On loan under the terms of the contract were:—

12 Tiger Moths, 2 Hawker Audax trainers, 1 Hawker Hind trainer.

In addition, the Derby Aero Club operated three Taylorcraft D aircraft (which were later known as Auster 1's). Thus started the forerunner of British Midland Airways: Air Schools Limited, the Directors being Mrs. R. Harben and Mr. E.W. Phillips.

For the next twelve months Air Schools operated very successfully—both the Aero Club and the R.A.F.V.R. training aspects. The standard of instruction was, under the guidance of Captain Harben, very high, both on the ground and in the air. Shortly after the operation began to take shape, Captain Harben wrote "The Complete Flying Course—A Manual of Flying Tuition," published by C. Arthur Pearson Ltd. In this manual he laid down a tight schedule of flying training, and he was to insist that this schedule be maintained. By doing so, the high quality of the output of the training school ensured the ultimate success of Air Schools Ltd., and thus the ultimate being of British Midland.

Now a high-grade flying unit required not only a high standard of flying instruction but also top quality ground instruction and first class engineering. In both of these latter aspects Roy Harben insisted upon, and secured, the best standard possible. To this day, these standards are maintained within British Midland.

In the meantime, Mr. Phillips was hard at it organising accountancy procedures, administration procedures, accommodation, catering, recreational facilities etc., all of which required a great deal of work outside normal working hours and, one suspects, a great deal of cajouling in the right quarters at the right time, but if Air Schools was to succeed (and Phil was as determined as Roy Harben that it was going to succeed) then only hard work would ensure that success, and hard work was one thing that both enjoyed.

9

Although Burnaston Airport was operational in the autumn of 1938, it was not officially opened until Saturday, June 17th, 1939, by His Majesty's Secretary of State for Air, the Right Honourable Sir Kingsley Wood M.P. Members of the airport staff invited to the opening ceremony were entitled to free refreshments up to the value of sixpence, although one suspects that this was not altogether freely given.

In mid-1939 the Air Ministry agreed with Derby Corporation to erect the main hangar at Burnaston, for it was all too evident that the gathering clouds of war were not after all going to disperse. In fact, at the outbreak of war the three Derby Aero Club Taylorcraft D aircraft were immediately commandeered, and were never seen at Burnaston again. The training tempo rose dramatically, and there remained the tremendous task of increasing the training capacity and all the associated problems, including the engagement of more engineers, clerical, navigational and Link Trainer Staff. The accommodation problem itself was a daunting one, and Burnaston House was converted into an Officers' Mess, whilst the stables attached to the House were converted into single cubicles.

In addition the Air Minsitry augmented the accommodation with the installation of wooden huts for dining rooms, sleeping, ablutions and so forth. At the outbreak of war the establishment at No. 30E and AFTS comprised 180 RAFVR personnel (all pilots), of whom 40 per cent were at the solo stage whilst the remainder were all ab initio. Immediate steps were taken to train these weekend pilots to RAF "wings" standard as fast as possible. The esprit de corps in those days can only be described as superb. The Air Minstry sent telegrams instructing all trained pilots to be sent to the airfields surrounding London, including North Weald, Biggin Hill, Hornchurch, Hendon among others obviously with the forthcoming Battle of Britain in mind. Needless to say very few of those early Derby-trained pilots survived the Battle.

Air Ministry building being erected at Burnaston at the outbreak of war.
(Derby Evening Telegraph)

With the influx of pupils the Tiger Moth establishment at Burnaston was increased six-fold to 72, whilst the advanced trainers, i.e. the Hawker Harts and Hinds, were withdrawn.

With a vicious war now raging, the training programme was of necessity a continuous one with night flying commencing immediately day flying had ceased, using goose-neck flares to delineate the runway. Flying would continue until 03-0400 hours. Staff worked a two-shift system, seven days a week.

In 1941 Roy Harben who had by this time been granted a "pro forma" commission in the Royal Air Force as a Wing Commander, was invited to go to Canada by Air Vice Marshall R. Leckie, D.S.O., D.S.C., D.F.C., Director of Training, Air Ministry. Whilst there he met Mr. Link of Link Trainer fame Now, in 1939, Roy Harben had written his "Harben Course on the Link Trainer", in which he advocated the use of the Link Trainer to give visual training exercises as well as the originally intended instrument flying exercises. To achieve this visual training he had the two Link Trainers at Burnaston modified by engaging an artist, Mr. Stan King. He painted a panorama around the complete Link Trainer room, the panorama ranging from half normal country fields and half normal coastline and sea, with clear horizon and a few white clouds, to a blank grey wall simulating flying into nil visibility, a smoky town with only small patches of horizon showing, and finally high mountains. The trainers themselves were modified by fitting extra bleed valves so that the Trainer could take on bank and nose down by the application of rudder alone— the nose would also go down when banking. By this means the further effects of the controls could be demonstrated, and it also became necessary to hold off bank and hold the nose up in a turn. A bleed valve was also fitted to the throttle, so that when it was closed and the Trainer nosed down to a normal gliding angle, the air speed indicator registered normal gliding speed. A false nose resembling as closely as possible that of the actual training aircraft, together with a circular piece of celluloid to give the impression of the airscrew disc, was also fitted. Other modifications were: a tail trimming device similar to that fitted on the pupil's training aircraft, annuli over the airspeed indicator and RPM indicator, calibrated to correspond to the pupil's training aircraft, fitting of aircraft type harness, and arranging for a draught to blow on the pupils face necessitating the wearing of goggles and thus enhance reality and accustom the pupil to some of the minor discomforts suffered during those early war days. It has been stated before that Roy Harben was a far-seeing man; maybe his modifications to the Link Trainer were the fore-runners of today's sophisticated electronic simulator. At a later date during the war Mr. Link visited the U.K. and Burnaston in particular, to see those Link Trainer modifications, by which he was most impressed.

Later on in 1941, the Air Minsitry decided to open a further civilian-run flying school at Wolverhampton and invited Air Schools Ltd. to run it. To accommodate this request a new company was formed but still within the Air Schools group its name being Wolverhampton Flying School Ltd. Mr. R.R. Paine, who had joined Air Schools at Derby in 1940 as Hangar Foreman, transferred to Wolverhampton as Chief Engineer. The new school, based at

Wolverhampton (Pendesford) and known as No. 28 E.F.T.S. in the Royal Air Force, was initially equipped with Magisters and Tiger Moths. Gradually both at Derby and Wolverhampton the Tiger Moths were superseded by Magisters, and altogether at the two units a total of 144 Magisters were operated, of which 72 at any one time were always in full flying trim. At one time there were 108 machines at each of the two units.

A feather in the cap of Air Schools was that it was one of the few schools selected to train Link Trainer instructors, and in fact it trained some twenty to twenty-five who were then posted to various parts of the country.

Another "first" for Burnaston was the choice of the unit to train the first of Britain's flying soldiers, the Glider Pilots. The first course attended at Burnaston in 1941 and were given ten hours flying instruction, including a first solo. Under the command of a Lieutenant Colonel Rock, their discipline was of the highest order, in the tradition of the Guards from which most of them were drawn. As one example, if one were even thirty minutes late in returning from a pass, he would be immediately marked R.T.U.—"Returned to Unit", and that was that. Unfortunately, in the tradition of the Guards they wore highly polished hob-nailed boots, and they caused more damage between them with boots through wings etc., than most of the other pupils put together. Their first action new role was, in Sicily where some 98% were killed in action.

Altogether over 14,000 pilots were trained by Air Schools Ltd. during the war, and it was no mean tribute to be signalled at the cessation of hostilities that the organisation had achieved the lowest accident rate plus the best maintenance record in the whole of Flying Training Command.

With the cessation of hostilities, the Air Ministry terminated the training contract. However, so sudden was the termination that everybody was caught off guard. Whilst no one his his right mind could have thought the intensity of training would continue at the war-time level, one would have though that some reasonable warning would have been given. Air Schools Ltd. was, to coin a phrase, "up a gumtree". Many skilled staff were going to lose their livelihood unless some solution was found, and found quickly. The paper existence of the Derby Aero Club was no help in the matter, since the three Austers had been commandeered at the beginning of the war and so were not available. Money had to be raised from some source to replace these aircraft.

Now at this point the Air Ministry realised that they had acted far too hastily in cancelling the previous contract, as the main pre-occupation of most members of H.M. Forces, and in particular aircrew was to return to civilian life. The situation now was that trained aircrew were very rapidly becoming non-existent in the ranks of the R.A.F., so to counteract this the Air Ministry, in their infinite wisdom, produced a new scheme for training pupil Pilot Officers. The method of providing these pupils was to take volunteers, and provided they could pass both fitness and intelligence tests (aptitude tests as carried out in the latter stages of the war were not re-introduced for this new scheme) then the candidate would be sent to Burnaston not only to do the flying course but also to be kitted out in officer's uniform. However, the Bowler Hat rate among these newcomers to the flying fraternity was extremely high and after some nine months the Air Ministry decided that the scheme should terminate. Once again Air Schools Ltd. was left high and dry and an alternative method of keeping the company in existence was sought.

Fortunately, at this time the Royal Air Force Volunteer Reserve still had a reasonable training commitment, and both Wolverhampton and Burnaston continued on the aviation scene carrying out part of this training as No. 65 Reserve Centre R.A.F.V.R., operating the Tiger Moths and Ansons of No. 16 Reserve Flying School. In fact, at Burnaston, Derby Aviation Ltd. was formed within the Air Schools group to,keep the aviation activities from stagnating, and this company was charged with entering the aircraft brokerage market as well as the civil aircraft maintenance field. Thus was born the true forerunner of British Midland.

On 14th February, 1947 Wing Commander N. Roy Harben D.F.C. died suddenly. At this point in the activities of the Air Schools Group his death could not have come at a more extremely critical time. Under the terms of his wartime activities Roy Harben could not hold any shares or occupy a directorship so Mrs Harben held the shares on his behalf. At the time of his death Mrs. Harben held some 2000 shares, whilst Mr. E.W. Phillips held 100 shares. Not having the expertise in the aviation world that she felt was necessary, Mrs. Harben asked Mr. Phillips if he would take charge of everything, to which of course he readily agreed. Shortly afterwards, in March 1947, Mrs. Harben and Mr. Phillips jointly agreed to invite Group Capt. C.A.B. Wilcock, O.B.E., A.F.C., M.P., to become Chairman of the Group and all its companies.

During the 1939-45 war, Group Captain Wilcock was Deputy Director of Manning at the Air Ministry, and Senior Personnel Staff Officer at Transport Command, and in 1944 was awarded the O.B.E. Two years later, in 1946, he was appointed Chairman of the committee on licencing, recruitment and training for civil aviation, which rendered its report in 1949. It can be seen then why the Group Captain was thought to be eminently suitable to be asked to take the Chair.

Three months after the appointment of the new Chairman, it was decided to further strengthen the Board of Directors by appointing Wing Commander H. A. Roxburgh, A.F.C., A.R.Ae.S., as Director of Aviation. The Wing Commander, who up to this point had been the Commanding Officer of No. 28 E.F.T.S. Wolverhampton, transferred to Burnaston at the same time retiring from the R.A.F. The Board now comprised Gp. Capt. Wilcock (Chairman), E. W. Phillips (Manager), Mrs. R. Harben, and Wing Cmdr. Roxburgh, and the Group being Air Schools Ltd., Derby Aviation Ltd., Wolverhampton Aviation Ltd., and Derby Aero Club Ltd.

Shortly after the above appointment the Board was further re-structured by the appointment to the Boards of Air Schools, Derby Aviation and Wolverhampton Aviation of Mr. R. R. Paine and Mr. Lionel Barley (Manager Wolverhampton). Mr. Paine, up to this point the Chief Engineer at Wolverhampton, had impressed Wing Commander Roxburgh with his ability and enthusiasm as he was playing a valuable part in the build up of the civil activities. His knowledge of aircraft engineering was wide by now, and he already showed a marked talent for the buying and selling of aircraft. Consequently Roxburgh strongly represented that Paine should be made a Director, to recognise his ability and to secure his services.

The restructuring of the Board had not of course made any direct effect on the position the Group now found itself in with reference to the cessation of some Air Ministry contracts. Thus, the new Chairman adopted a policy of no longer relying on such contracts, but of widening the Company's activities. To this end, the new Director of Aviation was briefed to obtain additional work and this was done in two ways.

Firstly, the M.o.S. (Ministry of Supply) at this time were looking for outside contractors to carry out the overhaul and repair of mobile cranes and earth-moving equipment, and a contract was secured for this work. Capital had to be found for the purchase of engineering equipment suitable for this form of (relatively) heavy engineering. Fortunately Coles of Coles Cranes (which were originally made in Derby) were moving north and had for sale a variety of suitable equipment at a very competitive price, and furthermore had available a number of trained staff in this field who were more anxious to stay in Derby than move north, so the problem was solved satisfactorily all round.

Secondly, the M.o.S., were (once again) awarding large contracts for the preservation and packaging of Government stores, tools and other equipment. After one or two inspectional visits, the contracts department of the M.o.S., thought the company ideal for the P.I.P. (Preservation, Identification and Packaging) work of every type of equipment used by the Services, from split-pins to Centurion tanks.

Initially, both of these contracts were operated as divisions of Derby Aviation, but they rapidly expanded to the point where it was expedient to set up separate companies. These were Burnaston Engineering Ltd., and Midland Packaging Ltd. Both of these companies made a modest but useful contribution to the Group finances, but after some three years Midland Packaging was closed down when the Ministry contracts dried up and Burnaston Engineering was finally sold. Meanwhile Derby Aviation's civil aircraft activities were developing and Ron Paine was brought over to Derby to strengthen the team.

At the time Wing Commander Roxburgh was appointed a Director, he was also nominated to the Derby Corporation Airport Committee, an appointment which was to have valuable repercussions at a later date.

Early in 1948, in an attempt to introduce more capital into the group, Dennis Sullivan, an underwriter at Lloyds, joined the Board as Commercial Director. His introduction was made by Group Captain Wilcock who, besides being Group Chairman, was also Chairman of Bowman & Sons, (Insurance) Ltd., on whose board Dennis Sullivan sat. Thus the new Board was now complete, and was to remain in that form until the Group Captain's sudden death in 1962.

Up to this point in time, no serious thought had been given to the Group entering the airline business of aviation, and although it was realised that diversification was essential, the real effort was to concentrate on the light aircraft activities. However, airlines as such had not yet begun to blossom in the sense we know it today, although the Berlin Airlift, at its height in 1948-50, had made itself felt in this respect, but mainly in the field of cargo. Certainly the public were not yet ready for short-haul domestic services, and as a result of all these factors Air Schools began to look around for other areas of expansion. In the meantime the club activity expanded and the R.A.F.V.R. schools both at Wolverhampton and Burnaston continued, providing much needed revenue for the group.

Burnaston was re-equipped during 1951/52 with Percival Prentice aircraft, replacing the Tiger Moths for R.A.F.V.R. pilot training. The serial numbers of these Prentices were:

Number	Delivery date
VR 198	1-8-51
283	9-4-52
284	28-7-51
286	28-7-51
288	1-8-51
VS 381	20-7-51
638	20-7-51
645	20-7-51(Written off 5-3-52)
650	1-8-51
685	1-8-51
698	30-7-51
755	22-11-51
758	30-7-51(this aircraft was the last Prentice built)

The Anson pilots, apart from flying navigators of the R.A.F.V.R. around the sky, also undertook Army co-operation exercises in their stride, all part of contracts to keep the Company going and themselves in work. Such work consisted of Royal Observer Corps spotting exercises or searchlight exercises with the Army in the Uttoxeter, Stafford and Birmingham areas.

In June 1948, an eight-seat De Havilland Rapide, G-AIUK, was acquired from Kenning Aviation Ltd., part of the Kenning Motor Group, and was based at Wolverhampton. In 1950/51 this aircraft began to be used for ad hoc charter work on a fill-up basis, i.e. charters were flown when Air Ministry contracts would allow them to be done. In August 1950 a second Rapide G-AKOV was acquired from Inter-City Air Services Ltd. and put into service for charter work. This kind of operation continued for another two years. At the same time a Miles Messenger G-AILL (C/N 6341, built 1946) and a Miles Gemini G-AJZJ (C/N 6465, built 1947, scrapped Biggin Hill 1967) were used for the same work. In point of fact the first truly commercial flight of this nature was flown by Captain Bill Wooden (now Chief Flight Operations Inspector of the Civil Aviation Authority) in the Messenger on 21st August 1947. This was from Derby to the Isle-of-Man and return for the Isle-of-Man T.T. races, and was chartered by a Mr. Turner and two colleagues all of whom were motor cycle enthusiasts. It is also interesting to note that at the time of the acquisition of G-AIUK from Kennings, Sir George Kenning tried to purchase Air Schools for

Kenning Aviation Ltd., but E. W. Phillips would have none of it and was instrumental in blocking the deal.

Whilst on the subject of Miles Gemini's and Messengers, it is of interest to note that Wolverhampton Aviation Ltd. actually built five Gemini's in 1950 on behalf of Miles Aircraft, and also at about the same time converted a number of Messenger I's to Messenger 4A's, all this work being carried out at Wolverhampton.

Here are details of this work:—

Messenger I's converted to Messenger 4A's

Service Serial No.	Civil Registration	C of A	Remarks
RH377	G-ALAH	6-9-48	Preserved in non-flying condition by Northern Aircraft Preservation Society.
RH421	G-ALAE	10-2-49	Damaged beyond repair at Epping 2-8-58.
RH422	G-ALAG	1-5-50	Crashed Germany 30-12-57.
RH423	G-ALAI	18-2-49	W.F.U. 1970
RH425	G-ALAR	26-11-48	To New Zealand Feb. 1954 as ZK-BED.
RH429	G-ALAJ	15-10-48	Wrecked Christchurch, Hants. 29-7-56.

Gemini 3A's built by wolverhampton Aviation Ltd.

C/N	Registration	C of A	Remarks
1002	G-AMDE	1950	Crashed Sibson, Warks. 24-9-67.
1003	G-AMGF	1950	Broken up, Heathrow 1963.
1004	G-ALMU	1950	W.F.U. 1967
1005	G-AMKZ	1950	SE-CMX August 1961.
1006	G-AMME	1950	W.F.U. 1971

One other interesting point worth noting here, but this time concerned with Burnaston and Derby Aviation Ltd., was an incident involving the Avro Tutor now in the Shuttleworth Trust Collection at Old Warden airfield, Bedfordshire. The Tutor, registered G-AHSA (manufactured in Manchester 1937 serialed K3215, civil C of A issued 23-10-51) landed at Burnaston, and, in order to calculate accurately the landing fee involved, the controller requested the Certificate of Airworthiness from which to obtain the aircraft's maximum authorised weight. Unfortunately for the owner (name unknown) it found that the C/A was out of date and therefore the aircraft was grounded. At the time there was no doubt that it was in a beautiful condition.

Avro Tutor G-AHSA now in the care of the Shuttleworth Collection (T. Topps).

Eventually, in order to clear the owner's outstanding debts, the Tutor was sold for £44 to a local man, Mr. Hayward. Derby Aviation engineers carried out a C of A renewal and the test flight was carried out on 17th June, 1953 by R. Death, Chief Flying Instructor at Derby Aero Club at the time, accompanied by Tony Topps.

After a period of time with its new owner it was found that a connecting rod had broken, although it was still flying quite satisfactorily, albeit 100 R.P.M. down. Unfortunately this ruined the engine and as it was impossible at the time to locate a spare one, the aircraft was presented to a local A.T.C. Squadron, at Lichfield, Staffs.

Some time later a request was made for the Tutor to be used as an "extra" in the film on Douglas Bader, "Reach for the Sky" starring Kenneth Moore. Derby Aviation engineers transported the aircraft on a Company "Queen Mary" trailer to the film studios and assembled it. At this point the film people decided that they would like the engine running (just idling they said) if possible. Unfortunately the crankshaft broke and the propeller came off. At least the engineers had a good time sharing meal-tables with Kenneth Moore and other stars. The aircraft of course eventually found its way to the Shuttleworth Trust.

The obvious success of the charter side of the Group's activities led to the application for, and granting of, a scheduled service licence from both Wolverhampton and Derby to Jersey, the route being flown via Birmingham in both directions, for Customs clearance. Thus, on 18th July 1953, began the first of the Company's scheduled services, with Capt. E. W. A. Lines in command, the aircraft being Rapide G-AEAL (obtained from Hunting Surveys Ltd. in April 1953).

The new service was an instant success and led to the acquisition of a fourth Rapide, G-AIUL, from Keale Street Pottery Company in June 1954. The navigation equipment on the aircraft was, even by the standards of the early fifties, somewhat sparse to say the least. All four had S.B.A. (Standard Beam Approach) as a landing aid, but only one, 'UL', had an en-route aid in the form of A.D.F. (Automatic Direction Finder). The other three had to rely on the pilot's map reading ability plus the V.D.F. (V.H.F. Direction Finding) equipment then in use at many ground stations. Fortunately the aircraft were equipped with V.H.F. sets.

In 1954, with the final shut-down of the Volunteer Reserve schools, both Wolverhampton Aviation and Derby Aviation were merged together to form Derby Aviation proper. Up to this time the Jersey service had been operated by both companies, but although only Derby Aviation remained, Wolverhampton continued to be served on the Jersey service. In addition, in 1954 a new service was commenced from both bases, once again via Birmingham for customs clearance, to Ostend, and all four Rapides were used.

It was now obvious that public demand for services was such that larger aircraft would be required, and a Dakota 4 was purchased from C.E. Harper Aircraft Co. Ltd., of Exeter Airport. The aircraft, G-ANTD, was virtually ex-R.A.F. as Harpers had purchased it from the service, converted it to civil standards and then offered it for sale. TD, with thirty six seats, plus two pilots and a hostess, was to be the mainstay of the Company's fleet for some time and finally departed in October 1968. TD was named "Dove Dale" following the decision to name all of Derby Aviation's aircraft after the Derbyshire Dales, and was flown to Derby (Burnaston) by Captain Lines on 16th April 1955. It flew its first commercial service on 3rd May that year, carrying a party of seamen from Manchester to Amsterdam. Three days later, on the 6th May, the inaugural DC3 service to Jersey was flow, from Derby to Wolverhampton, Birmingham (Customs) and Jersey. Flown by Captain Lines the First Officer was Brian Henderson (now a Trident Captain with British Airways) and the Stewardess was Audrey Lines, Capt. Lines' wife. On board was the Mayoress of Burton-on-Trent, the Mayor and Mayoress of Derby, the Mayor of Wolverhampton and Group Captain Wilcock M.P., Company Chairman, accompanied by Mrs. Wilcock.

The dress for the air stewardess was a lapelled jacket with four black buttons, matching midi-length skirt, all in dark blue, plus R.A.F. style forage cap in same material, together with a white blouse.

The end of May saw "TD" in Blackbushe, operating newspaper flights during a rail strike which lasted until 15th June, 1955. During this time 84,000 newspapers per night were carried to Exeter and Cardiff.

Business by the autumn of 1955 was really beginning to boom and it became increasingly obvious that if Derby Aviation Ltd. was going to be able to indulge in the by now firm policy of entering the scheduled service field, then more aircraft would be required for the 1957 season. Besides, there was so much good charter work available that the DC3 capacity was being fully taken up on such work, leaving nothing with which to develop the schedules. As a result of this

Dakota G-ANTD at Birmingham just after its delivery in 1955 (W. H. Blunt).

Air Hostesses wearing the original style uniform.

19

decision, Ron Paine left for Lagos, Nigeria, in late 1955, to inspect some Miles Marathons being put up for sale at a good price by West African Airways Corporation. The result was the delivery in October by some West African Airways ferry crews of two Marathons, VR-NAN and VR-NAR into Burnaston. These two aircraft assumed their original registrations of G-AMGW and G-AMHR respectively, and were subsequently named "Millers Dale" and "Monsal Dale".

Marathon 1 A G-A MHR in its West African Airways Corporation Colours, as VR-NA R (College of Aeronautics, Cranfield).

Having been delivered to Burnaston, a great deal of engineering work had to be undertaken before the new acquisitions could be put into line service, as the aircraft were not up to United Kingdom standards. It was now that the high quality of the Engineering Division, so insisted upon in the beginning by Roy Harben, really came into its own. Both aircraft were stripped completely, all bracketry inspected, spars modified and a new lease of structural life taken. By moving the rear bulkhead further aft, passenger accommodation was increased from eighteen to twenty. The nose-wheel frames were strengthened (a necessary modification in view of the by now rough state of Burnaston airfield), and many other modifications embodied. One "marathon" task undertaken was the complete rewiring of the aircraft electrical systems, made necessary by the fact that the original wiring was plastic covered. In West Africa, it had not been unknown for this insulation to melt and hang in long festoons in front of the

20

pilot's bewildered eyes. If this happened to the electrically actuated fuel shut-off cocks (which it frequently did) the hapless pilot would find the tank shut off was sometimes full of fuel which he was now denied. Obviously this state of affairs could not be tolerated, so all the looms were replaced with rubber-covered wires, the looms being made up on the hangar floor. Quite a feat.

When the Marathons were finally put into service (G-AMGW flew first on 27th March, 1956, Captain T. H. Pike in command, G-AMHR entering service on 13th July, 1956) the crew consisted of one pilot and one hostess. Every flight was handflown as no auto-pilots were fitted, neither were heaters. At the end of a two hour flight, having been plied with hot coffee or tea for most of that time in order to keep some semblance of warmth in the pilot, the poor soul would be bursting to spend a penny and vied with the passengers to see who could get into the terminal buildings first. More than one pilot ended up with a weak bladder as a result. Rain was another hazard, and regular passengers were known to bring umbrellas along, for if they were unfortunate enough to occupy the seats adjacent to the rear starboard emergency hatch in the roof, any rain invariably found its way in there, and the sight of passengers sitting there with raised umbrellas was a sight to behold. Pilots also suffered from the rain, for if left standing overnight it would seep in via the very large plastic canopy and collect inside the overhead electrical panel. When the aircraft started taxying the following morning the water would surge forward, run down the feathering buttons and pour onto the luckless pilots knees. At least one plastic mac was purchased to prevent soaked trousers under these circumstances.

Inside an ex WAAC Marathon. Note that the Hostess (Olive Jones) and all the passengers are still wearing their scarves and top-coats.

However, in spite of all their drawbacks the Marathons worked extremely well and it is true to say that they were responsible for establishing the company in the scheduled service market in the very early days, for they alone at one time flew these services, whilst the D.C.3's were busy on charter and inclusive tour work. To qualify these points it must also be said that Engineering Division worked on the Marathons every night to ensure their availability the following day.

Thus dawned 1956, but it was still realised that having just one DC3 gave insufficient capacity in view of the relatively large amount of work that was becoming available, and so the purchase of another example was sought. At that time an aircraft with a rather famous background was offered for sale by the R.A.F., and so it was that on the 24th February 1956 V.I.P. C-47B (as the military version of the DC3 was known) KN628, now civilianised as G-AOGZ, was flown by Capt. Lines from R.A.F. Silloth to Burnaston for re-furbishing before joining the rapidly expanding fleet. During its Air Force career KN628 had been the personal transport of Field Marshall Montgomery.

Dakota G-AOGZ (ex KN628 Field Marshall Lord Montgomery's personal aircraft) shortly after its delivery.

On March 16th 1956, an R.A.F. Marathon T11 Navigation Trainer XA253 landed at Burnaston, with Flying Officer B. G. Cramp at the controls. Met by Wing Commander Roxburgh and Captain Lines, now the Chief Pilot, the Service pilot was escorted into the main office block and interviewed as a prospective pilot. At this time no Derby Aviation pilots had flown the Marathon, and here was a pilot not only with the type endorsed on his civilian licence, but who had some two hundred hours on type. Although still in the R.A.F., Flying Officer Cramp had been given Air Ministry permission to "fly civil" prior to joining an airline as his chosen career, and thus the future Operations Manager flew for the Company for the first time. The departure of XA253 that afternoon for R.A.F. Thorney Island was the first take-off of a Marathon from Burnaston.

Due to the rapid expansion of all the activity at Derby, one major problem facing the staff was accommodation. The original flying club-house, with its welcome bar and balcony at the head of the stairs, was serving as charter office, reservations office, pilots office, check-in bay—infact, you name it, and the activity was conducted in that block. Also housed in the block, besides Wing Commander Roxburgh and A.C. Felts, the Commerical Manager, was Denis Aldridge. Denis was a real "Jack of all trades", being Charter Manager, Air Traffic Controller (at a later date, for in 1956 there was no air traffic control at Burnaston), receptionist and Steward. If any activity was abounding, Denis was there, in the midst of it all.

The original Company premises at Burnaston Airfield, comprising Head Office, Accounts, Charter Office etc. and bar (Derbyshire Advertiser).

On the 7th May, 1956, following the policy now fully adopted of operating scheduled services instead of relying on ad hoc charter flights, a new service inaugurated from Derby via Birmingham (for both traffic and customs) to Ostend. "TD" the Dakota, together with Marathon "GW", were used to implement the service.

On the 19th May Flying Officer Cramp commenced his first commercial flying whilst "on loan" from the Royal Air Force, flying from Derby via Birmingham to Jersey and back twice, amounting to ten sectors in the one day. When one considers the navigation equipment on aircraft in those "early" days, i.e. A.D.F. and S.B.A. plus V.H.F. radio, and the sometimes appalling weather in the Channel Islands when aircraft could be "stacked" up to 9000ft at 500ft separation, all the time listening (as opposed to looking) to the Standard Beam Approach, followed by a landing in cloud bases as low as 100ft then one cannot but marvel at the regularity of schedules together with the lack of accidents.

The Burnaston airfield of 1956 was not equipped with any control tower, radio, or beacon, neither were any night-flying facilities available. That year saw the introduction by Derby Aviation of a Derby to Isle-of-Man service, and whilst operating this service on the 10th August, Captain (Flying Officer) Cramp took his wife along with him just for the ride. Upon arrival at Ronaldsway in the Isle of Man an urgent request was made for the return flight to be delayed to await the arrival of two unfortunate holiday makers who had been called-up as reservists in anticipation of the invasion of the Suez Canal. To delay too long would mean arriving after dark and there were no night flying facilities. However, Cramp waited as long as he dare and at the last moment the two luckless men arrived and the Marathon was soon airborne. Following the U.K. airways system back as far as Lichfield, the procedure adopted in those days was to leave the airway by descending over the Lichfield beacon to 1500ft, then steer 045° magnetic and follow the River Trent, together with the railway and canal as far as Burton-on-Trent. At this point, the railway only was followed until the "Hilton Gravel" sign in red neon lights was seen, when the Burton-Derby road (the A38) was picked up and followed until the airfield was reached. This was the procedure adopted on this night, but on descending over Lichfield Cramp found, to his dismay, 4/8 cloud below him and that it was getting dark. After leaving the Hilton Gravel sign, descent was made to 600ft. and he hoped he would find the airfield. Fortunately, people on the ground had anticipated the predicament, and Captain S. D. Fenton had driven his car to the hedge bounding the approach end of the field and put his head-lights on to assist. Needless to say, a successful landing was made, and Cramp was grateful (as was his worried wife) to join Wing Commander Roxburgh along with some other pilots and Denis Aldridge at the "Spread Eagle" pub, which adoined the south west corner of the field.

Flying those days was far more personal affair than it is today, and as (normally) all flying at Burnaston had to cease by dusk, it was a common sight to see a convoy of cars leave the airfield at the end of a day's flying and proceed to the "Spread Eagle" where crews and engineers would enjoy a well earned pint in relative peace and quiet. Unfortunately the "Spread Eagle" has now been demolished to make way for the A38 improvements.

The closing months of 1956 saw two major international events in which Derby Aviation were involved. On 11th December Dakota "TD" with Captain Lines in command was engaged in bringing troops back from Malta to Blackbushe after the Suez debacle. The troops told the crew how disgusted they were with the United Nations for making them stop and finally pull out. The other event was the Hungarian crisis in which both Dakotas "TD" and "GZ" were engaged in bringing refugees back from Linz in Austria to Blackbushe. One pregnant refugee said if the baby was a boy she would call him Eric and if a girl Audrey, after Captain and Mrs. Lines.

At the end of 1956 the Company fleet was as follows:

Dakotas	G-ANTD,	G-AOGZ
Marathons	G-AMGW,	G-AMHR
Rapide	G-AIUL	

1957

One point made very obvious during 1956 was the fact that the policy of operating scheduled services was beginning to pay off, and so a good look was taken at the possibilities of operating more such services. If possible these routes should be capable of supporting a year-round operation. Fortunately (for Derby Aviation), Rolls Royce had found it more practicable to transfer a large proportion of both their overhaul and manufacture of aero-engines from their main factory in Derby, to their Scottish base at Hillington, just on the outskirts of Glasgow (Renfrew) Airport. A Glasgow service would suit Rolls Royce very well and an agreement was reached whereby in the first year of service they would guarantee sixteen seats per day, the guarantee decreasing on a sliding scale over five years to nil, by which time it was anticipated that the route would be self-supporting. Thus it was that on the morning of Friday the 22nd March, 1957 the Lord Mayor and Mayoress of Nottingham, the Lord Mayor and Mayor and Mayoress of Derby and the Mayor and Mayoress of Burton-on-Trent boarded G-ANTD for the first Derby-Glasgow scheduled service. Commanding the aircraft was Captain E. W. A. Lines, and the cabin service was provided by Air Hostesses Jean Merritt and Olive Jones. Also on board were Group Captain Wilcock (Chairman), Wing Commander Roxburgh (Managing Director), Councillor Tom Earnshaw (Chairman of Derby Airport Committee and destined to play a big part in the Company's future, but indirectly so), and Mr. E. W. Ives and Mr. J. Britland, Chief Administration Officer and Transport Officer respectively of Rolls Royce Ltd.

The party were received by the Lord Provost of Glasgow and the Provost of Renfrew, followed by a civic luncheon at Glasgow Guildhall. This service, besides being the first "businessman's" service to be operated by the Company, also marked the beginning of a long association with Rolls Royce Ltd. The Glasgow service remains to this day one of the Company's main routes, and operates twice daily throughout the week.

One interesting point about the new Glasgow service was that no handling agency existed at Glasgow (Renfrew) Airport except B.E.A., and they were not interested in handling the new service, presumably, in the light of later experience, because they had no wish for the service to succeed. In view of all this Wing Commander Roxburgh approached Mr. Warden of Scotia Travel in Glasgow, and asked if he would like to handle the new service. Thus it was that Scotia Airport Services came into being, and the company still operates at Glasgow (and Edinburgh) Airport to this day.

In March 1957, a freelance journalist was writing an article on charter flights for "The Club Secretary" magazine, and in order to obtain the latest information on his subject contacted Derby Aviation in the person of Wing Commander Roxburgh, who was only too delighted to help. One condition was imposed by the Wing Commander, and that was a copy of the completed article. Having received the letter, the "Wingco" asked the journalist if he would like to do Public Relations Advertising work for Derby Aviation, and thus there began not only the first P.R.O. in the Company's history, but also a life-long friendship between the "Wingco" and Eric Sample, which lasted until the sudden death of Eric on 4th August 1973. Eric Sample not only wrote articles, but designed time-tables, brochures, etc., arranged inaugural flights, travel agents' receptions, co-ordinated advertising from 1957 until March 1965, when his employers (he was Derby area Customs Surveyor, but part-time journalist on the side) informed him that he was becoming too involved and should cease the connection.

The radio equipment, fitted in those now far-off days was not very sophisticated by today's standards. The main approach aid in use on the Marathon was S.B.A. (Standard Beam Approach) which required the pilot to listen to a series of A's (dot-dash) and N's (dash-dot) in Morse code, telling him if he was left or right of the correct approach path. A steady note (comprising the joining of the A's and N's) indicated the correct path. However, as most people will appreciate, it is much easier to see a maximum signal deflection than to accurately hear it. The replacement for the S.B.A. then was the I.L.S. (Instrument Landing System) which incorporated not only a needle to show the pilot whether he is left, right, or on centre, but also another needle to show whether he is on the correct descent path, or above or below it. This equipment is fitted to all modern airliners either in its basic or a much more sophisticated form. In May 1957, Derby Aviation decided to fit I.L.S. to its Marathons (they were already installed in the D.C.3's). The first flight using the new installation was flown by Captain Cramp in Marathon G-AMGW on the 17th May 1957, from Derby via Manchester to Lille, and the following day from Manchester via Jersey to Bordeaux with a Rugby Football team on board.

During 1957, the Channel Islands service was flown in ever-increasing frequencies, with landings in both directions from Derby being made at Birmingham for Customs clearance. This was a bind for both passengers and crews, not to mention expensive for the Company in terms of wear and tear on the aircraft, although of course no landing fee was charged for these landings which were for Customs purposes only. It was during 1957 that the Wolverhampton-Jersey service was dropped. The Derby to Isle-of-Man service commenced in 1956 was continued and a new Derby-Birmingham-Ostend summer scheduled service was commenced. Charter flying still played a big part in the total operation of course, and on one flight from Shawbury to Swanton Morley in Norfolk for passengers visiting the Royal Show one crew had the party leader slip £5 note into the Captains breast pocket!! Oh for those good old days again.

The Dakota fleet was of course working very hard at this time, and on 18th May 1957 Captain Lines flew the very first Birmingham-Palma Inclusive Tour service for M.A.T.O. (Midland Air Tour Operators), and this was in fact Derby Aviation's first I.T. flight on its own behalf, and was also the beginning of a long association with M.A.T.O.

Dakota charters were also of course in evidence and included the carrying of engines to Aden, Bahrein and Karachi, to name but a few stopping-off points.

Early in the year Mr. E. W. Phillips, prevailed upon the Chairman to let him move back to his "home" territory, and so it was that he went to look at Luton Airport (then still an all-grass field) and Elstree. The report on Luton was very satisfactory, backed up by a recommendation from Mr. Phillips that Derby Aviation should take immediate steps to commence commercial services from Luton Airport as soon as practicable. This report and recommendation were well received by the Board, and as a result Derby became the first airline to operate scheduled services from Luton. In addition, the Board were pleased to receive a report and recommendation from Mr. Phillips that Air Schools Ltd. should take steps to purchase the London School of Flying at Elstree, and this recommendation too was implemented, thus not only prolonging the company's interest in training pilots, but also providing a ready-made source of pilots for any further expansion.

One other undertaking purchased during 1957 in order to carry out a policy of diversification was Photo Flight Ltd., then renamed Derby Aero Surveys Ltd. The Company were fortunate to retain also the services of Colonel H. C. Butcher D.S.O. Contracts were secured for this new activity for new works in Scotland, planning of new town developments. A big contract was also drawn up with Canadian Aeroservices Corporation, itself an offshoot of the Aeroservices Corporation of Philadelphia, a well-known aero-survey organisation specialising in geophysical surveys using airborne mag-netometers. The effects of this particular contract were felt in 1958.

Due to the ever-expanding route network, more capacity was required, and it was discovered that the Ministry of Supply now had for sale a Marathon at Handley Page's Woodley factory which had been used as a modifications aircraft. A successful bid was put in, and on 27th August 1957 a team headed by

Mr. R. R. Paine, and including Frank Marshall, George Lester and Johnny Everett, travelled to Reading to get the aircraft ready to fly again for the first time in eighteen months. Sharing one corner of a huge hangar at Woodley Aerodrome with many other activities was the new acquisition G-AMEW, and right alongside, was the original Handley Page Herald Mark I being fitted with two Rolls Royce Dart engines in place of the original four Alvis Leonides piston engines. Once again a foretaste of the future, for in 1965 and again in 1973 the Company were to operate the Dart Herald. So it was then that in the late afternoon of the 28th August 1957, Captain Cramp bounced across the grass airfield of Woodley in "EW" (total time flown to date only 19 hours since its delivery flight to Burnaston), although the aircraft did not enter service until the summer of 1958. Many modifications were required to fit it for civil use but the 25g military pilot's seats were retained, much to the amusement of the pilots who flew it!

In late October 1957, on behalf of Pirelli the tyre manufacturer, Derby Aviation started a tyre airlift designed to help agents who were unable to supply unusual sized tyres from stock. This was a true use of air cargo whereby air transport was used to obviate the need for expensive warehousing of little used stock by agents all over the continent. Using airlift facilities cut down both the cost of the operation and the delivery time of the tyres to the customer.

Finally, for the year 1957, the lady readers will be interested to know that the air hostesses uniforms were a dark blue midi-length pinafore dress with white blouse, pillbox hat in the same material, with both brevets and hat badges being of miniature type bearing the initials "DA" worked in gold wire in the centre.

The fleet at the close of the year was:—

Dakotas	G-ANTD	G-AOGZ	
Marathons	G-AMGW	G-AMHR	(G-AMEW under conversion from military variant)

1958

The year 1958 was yet again a time of expansion. This expansion appeared not only in an extension of the scheduled service routes, but in other activities, as well. Two more aircraft were put into service, a greater participation in Inclusive Tours emerged, the Company's name was changed and a greater emphasis laid on its public image. At the same time, the Survey Company expanded.

The winter of 1957-58 saw the introduction of skiing holidays in Austria, when in January 1958, on behalf of Sigma Tours of Manchester Ltd., Derby Aviation Dakotas (the Marathons were laid up each winter as they were not cold-weather equipped either for passengers or for airframe icing problems) would depart each Friday night at midnight for Munich via Brussels, arriving at 0600 in Munich, where the crew would retire to bed and carry out the return flight that night departing Munich at midnight. On some of these flights the weather was appalling and the cold on the Dakota flight decks in those days is well-remembered by the crews who participated.

In March, whilst Cramp and Pike had been away in Sierra Leone, Captain E. W. A. Lines had resigned his position as Chief Pilot for personal and medical reasons. Captain Ron Milsom took over the appointment of Chief Pilot, with Captain S. D. Fenton becoming Operations Superintendent, an appointment previously not in existence.

In the Spring of 1958 a Board decision was made to name the operating element of Derby Aviation "Derby Airways". This decision was implemented immediately and made itself manifest on each aircraft as they went through the hangar on routine maintenance, emerging with the name "Derby Airways" on their sides.

For airlines the Spring is recruitment time for pilots and cabin staff, but up to this point in time Derby had never made any attempt at all in the technical training of its crews. This was changed in 1958. Upon his return from Sierra Leone, Captain Milsom asked Cramp to accept the position of Chief Training Captain, which he agreed to do. Most pilots in 1958 could easily obtain Dakota information on which to base their study for the Air Registration Board technical exam, and in addition Dakota-qualified pilots were readily available. With the Marathon however, this was not so as technical information was difficult to come by and Marathon qualified crews were virtually non-existent. Cramp therefore made the technical qualifications for the Marathon his first priority and set up a training syllabus based on this. Thus there came about, the beginning of the airline's training school, which of course continues up to this day in a more sophisticated form at the East Midlands Airport.

Commensurate with the pilots' technical training, Cramp laid down, in conjunction with the Chief Hostess, a proper syllabus for new-intake cabin staff instead of, as in previous years, putting a girl in uniform and virtually teaching her the job on the spot. Today the training of Cabin Staff is much more sophisticated and takes a minimum of four weeks at the Training School at East Midlands.

One major step forward made available in 1958 was the withdrawal of the requirement for aircraft from Derby to land en-route to the Channel Islands at Birmingham for Customs clearance, although the return flight still had to clear inbound from Jersey and Guernsey at Birmingham. Nevertheless this concession was a most welcome one indeed and the first non-stop service from Derby to Jersey operated on 31st March, when the Mayor of Derby gave clearance on the newly-installed V.H.F. radio at Derby for G-AOGZ, commanded by Captain Fenton, to take-off for Jersey.

In this present day and age when air/sea cruises may be seen to be advertised in all leading magazines and newspapers, it may be of interest to note that Derby entered this kind of Inclusive Tour Business as far back as 1958. In that year one could obtain an air-sea crusie on the Royal Mail Lines "Highland Chieftain" leaving London to Vigo (Spain) and Leixos (Portugal) with five days ashore at

Mirimar, returning by Derby Airways Dakota for an inclusive price of 32 guineas. Or how about a cruise on the Union Castle Line "Dunnoltar Castle" to Genoa and return by Derby Airways Dakota?

1958 was also the Lourdes Centenary year, and the Company participated in eight-day pilgrimages to Lourdes. On board each flight to Tarbes Airport was a spiritual leader who accompanied each party throughout. The eight days including coach transfer from Tarbes to the Florida Hotel near the grotto at Lourdes. Cost 35 guineas. Many such flights were operated by the Dakotas that year.

On the 9th May, a third Dakota, G-APBC was added to the fleet. Named "Derwent Dale" (the other two Dakotas were G-ANTD "Dove Dale" and GAOGZ "Darley Dale") the new aircraft was acquired from Transair Ltd. of Gatwick. "BC" differed from all other Dakotas flying in having a "square-cut" wing fillet from the fuselage to the mainplane instead of the usual nicely rounded fillet. The reason for this was that the aircraft had been built up from various airframe components by Transair and included a fuselage from Italy recovered from a wreck! Nevertheless "BC" was a delightful aircraft to fly, even if it did stall some 5 knots higher than the rest of the fleet.

The first service "BC" flew was on the 10th May to Jersey from Derby, and on the 20th May it flew the inaugural service from Northampton (Sywell) to Jersey with Captain Milsom in command and Captain Cramp as his co-pilot. On board were the civic dignitaries of Northampton and officials of Sywell Airport, and a civic reception was accorded them at Jersey on arrival. The first public service from Sywell to Jersey was flown on 21st June.

The new service was very welcome for the Northampton residents, and the airport staff went out of their way to make the service go and Derby Airways welcome. Derby put in its own "Manageress" at Sywell, Mrs. M. Bray, who in spite of having no previous experience, and with ample assistance from the crews, managed the station very well. Sywell was, in fact, the first of the Company's outstations with its own staff (albeit only Mrs. Bray).

Another new service introduced in 1958 was an Oxford-Jersey service, the inaugural of which was flown by G-APBC with Fenton in command and Cramp as his co-pilot on the 23rd May. The next day Cramp commanded the first public service on this route in Marathon G-AMHR "Monsal Dale."

Both the Northampton and Oxford services flew direct to Jersey but landed at Southampton (Eastleigh) northbound to clear customs.

Continuing a stated policy of building up scheduled services at the same time as remaining in and developing inclusive tour services, Wing Commander Roxburgh, Managing Director, the Director responsible for the company's development policy, announced yet another new service for 1958, a Birmingham-Ostend service. Operated four times weekly, both the Dakota and Marathon were used on the service.

With regard to the inclusive tour business, it was decided in the summer of 1958 to build up the traffic on I.T.'s originating in the Bristol and Cardiff areas, and where it was the intention to entrench the Company in 1959. Consequently a retired Royal Engineers transport Officer, Captain T. Mayo, at that time managing a farm in Gloucestershire, was appointed South West Region Manager operating from both Cardiff and Bristol. This was the first serious attempt by the Company to organise the commercial aspects of the operation outside of the Derby area, using its own staff for selling.

On 7th July, another aircraft joined the fleet in the shape of the re-furbished Marathon G-AMEW. Unlike the two sister aircraft obtained from West Africa which had a dark green upholstered interior, "EW" had a chocolate and cream decor which was much more acceptable to the passengers. The flight-deck retained the original military seats for the pilots, each stressed at 25g (it was to be hoped heavy landings were not that bad!). From an operating point of view, "EW" was an improvement on "GW" and "HR" in that it was equipped with a cabin heater of the Janitrol combustion chamber type (no more cold feet and weak bladders), an auto-pilot, plus Goodrich de-icing boots. Whilst not a complete auto-pilot in the accepted sense, it was at least an attempt to take some of the load off the pilot. Even so, in view of the constant pitch corrections necessary due mainly to the hostess walking up and down, many Marathon Captains preferred to hand-fly the aircraft anyway. Due to the popularity of "EW" among the pilots, and the remarks made by the passengers who welcomed the heaters, both "GW" and "HR" were retrospectively fitted with heaters. The first service of "EW" was a Derby/Jersey service, and the honour fell to Captain Cramp as he had flown this particular variant in the Royal Air Force (it was different in instrumentation from the purely civil version in that it was equipped with duel-indicating R.P.M. counters and boost gauges, and boasted a synchroscope), and it was he who had collected it from Woodley the previous year.

Wednesday 10th September was the date of an inaugural flight with a difference. A party of civic dignitaries, press and travel agents joined with Directors of the Company on a flight from Luton to Jersey. The guests were from Cambridge as well as Luton and the flight was a foretaste of the service it was intended to operated in 1959. For the record the aircraft was G-APBC commanded by Captain Milsom with Captain Fenton as his co-pilot. Helen Memory, a native of Paris, was the air hostess.

It had been announced during the year that the second prototype Dart Herald was to be leased from the manufacturers during 1959, making Derby Airways the first airline operating the type. Unfortunately, whilst en route from the Handley Page field at Woodley to the Farnborough Air Show, the aircraft suffered a severe in flight engine fire. Squadron Leader Haseldine managed to land the aircraft successfully at Farnborough quite literally on one engine—the failed engine had fallen out of the aircraft. Derby were therefore unable to operate the aircraft in 1959. Indeed, it was not until 1965 that the type saw service with the Company.

The year 1958, then, was one of controlled expansion, both in aircraft fleet and the number of routes being operated, with a firm policy now of operating both in the scheduled service and inclusive tour fields as well as ad hoc charters. Already an eye was on 1959 and all looked well for the future.

31

The fleet as at the close of the year was:—

| Dakotas | G-ANTD | G-AOGZ | G-APBC |
| Marathons | G-AMGW | G-AMHR | G-AMEW |

1959

1958 had certainly witnessed a dramatic increase in the demand for services from the Midlands area, whilst the signs were already very apparent for services from the South West, i.e., Gloucester and Cheltenham areas, together with South Wales. In order to take advantage of these trends it was obvious that more aircraft were required, and so it was that on the 24th April 1959 two more Dakotas were added to the fleet. G-AMSX and G-AMSW were both acquired from Cambrian Air Services of Rhoose Airport, Cardiff. "SW" was named "Fern Dale" and "SX" "Peak Dale". It was ironic that the two aircraft were acquired from an ailing carrier who was later, through a cruel twist of fate (cruel that is, to Derby Airways) to oust the Company from South Wales, but more of that later.

Another significant step taken early in 1959 was the installation of the Decca Navigator Mark 8, with Flight Log, in the Dakota fleet. It was anticipated that the new aid would allow for better navigation and thus cut down the flying time on any given sector, achieving substantial economies. At Derby Airport, with only a very low powered M.F. beacon "DBY" on 270 Khz, the production (and acceptance by the authorities at that time) of a Decca let-down chart for Burnaston allowed a much more positive approach to be made on many occasions when it is doubtful if a beacon approach would have achieved a safe landing. The let-down chart for Derby using Decca was, it is believed, the first such Decca approach given minima approval in the country.

In 1959, the Marathons were still going strong, and it will be remembered that they had now been in service since 1956. The Certificate of Airworthiness clearly state that the minimum crew was one pilot, and thus they had been operated. During the early part of 1959, however, the Ministry of Civil Aviation (or whatever title it reposed under in those days—the name changed so often with political changes in the country that one forgets just how many titles it has had) decided that aircraft of this calibre were too much for one man to handle and so was born a crew category new to aviation—Captain's Assistant. These crew members were usually holders of a Commercial Pilot's Licence but without an Instrument Rating, or were Private Pilot's Licence holders but with aspirations leaning towards professional licences (who said anything about a P.P.L. holder flying for hire and reward?). The intention was that these gentlemen would serve coffee and barley sugars (ah the good old days) when required, but would also "navigate" the aircraft, keep the engine instrument reading log, do the R/T and generally "assist" the hapless Captain when requested so to do. Unfortunately, in practice these new apprentices to the trade, for that is what they were, were so new to the aviation game, that the workload on the poor old Captain was not eased, but increased. For the Captains' Assistants the apprenticeship was an invaluable one, and the majority are still in civil aviation, most as Captains. Captain Ron Hardy, now Boeing Fleet manager, Captain Dave Moores, and Captain Roger Wise, now DC9 Fleet Manager all commenced as Captain's Assistants, and remain with the Company.

April 8th, 1959, saw the commencement of the new Staverton (Gloucester/ Cheltenham) Channel Island service. Previously operated by Cambrian Air Services with Heron aircraft, the route had been dropped when Cambrian's financial dificulties had forced that company to withdraw many of its services. Marathons were used in the main, with the Dakota filling-in on the odd occasion. Captain Terry Mayo was "posted" to Staverton to set up the new company station and to develop the new service. Yeomans Miller and Company of Cheltenham were appointed as Sales Agents for the Company. Staverton was without Customs facilities, so a landing had to be made at Hurn (Bournemouth) Airport for customs clearance. The same procedure also applied to Channel Islands services from Luton and Cambridge (both commenced in 1959, Luton on 25th April and Cambridge on 5th June), and Oxford and Sywell (Northampton).

In deep contrast to the lack of facilities for Customs clearance mentioned above, Derby (Burnaston) was granted Customs facilities and the first inbound aircraft to be cleared was on the 28th March, 1959. For this purpose a new Customs clearance room had to be built.

Due to the large increase in services being offered for the summer of 1959, it was necessary to recruit and train more cabin staff. Miss Hilary Laverick-Steeple had only just joined as Chief Hostess, having previously worked as an air-hostess with MacRobertson Miller Airlines in Australia, and, together with Miss Edith Johnson, ex-BEA, she set up a hostess training school where such items as elementary navigation, meteorology, aircraft heating systems, bar procedures, bar stock control, health requirements, etc. were crammed into the girls' heads in a three week course. Even BBC TV got to hear of the effort being put in and came to the airfield to film the work. In this present day and age this may not seem so extra-ordinary, but it must be remembered that in 1959, for a small undertaking such as Derby Airways undoubtedly was in those days, the effort being applied was quite stupendous and gave the general public an insight into the standards being set. The standards were, for those days, quite high.

Parallel to the hostess training school, Captain Cramp was running the pilots' training school again, to cater for the new intake of pilots necessary for the two Cambrian Dakotas coming along, and at the same time converting some of the Dakota crews onto the Marathons. In those days crews were allowed to operate more than one type. Today, with the greater complexity of aircraft, a pilot may only operate one type of aircraft.

By late Spring, the summer schedule services were beginning to get into their stride. During the winter months, the only scheduled service had been the Glasgow route, flown only by the Dakotas, the Marathons being unsuitable for winter use since they lacked heaters or de-icing equipment. However, with the advent of summer, the Marathons were once more put into service, "GW" starting on 27th March, thus releasing the larger and more economical Dakota for inclusive tour work on routes ranging much further afield. The usual scheduled service routes were flown, the destinations being the Channel Islands, Isle of Man, Ostend and of course Glasgow. One innovation for the Glasgow service, introduced on the 29th May, 1959, was an agreement signed that day by Wing Commander Roxburgh and Mr. R. R. Paine on behalf of Derby Airways, and Mr. E. H. Humphries and Mr. John Terry on behalf of K.L.M., for a Derby via Glasgow to New York service. Passengers could leave Derby at 0800 for Glasgow (Renfrew), thence by special coach to Prestwick, to join the K.L.M. DC7C service KL647 to New York arriving at 2120 New York time. It is doubtful whether very much traffic was generated for KLM by this new scheme, but it certainly gave some much appreciated publicity to Derby Airways.

The 8th June witnessed a very near-miss overhead Oxford Airport involving Marathon G-AMHR en-route Sywell-Jersey, and an R.A.F. Beverley, Abingdon-based but working Weston-on-the-Green without control. As a direct result of this incident the Oxford-Jersey service was discontinued, much to the relief of the crews.

Whilst the scheduled services were progressing nicely, inclusive tour services were also doing very well. It was the Company's policy in those days to progress along two parallel paths, i.e. scheduled and I.T. services. I.T. licences were being applied for not only for 1959 but for two or three years ahead. In March a provisional licence was granted for scheduled services from Cardiff and Bristol to Nice, Palma, Perpignan and Luxembourg (although the approval came too late for the 1959 season). A Derby/Luxembourg I.T. service was commenced in June; for Whitehall Travel I.T. services were operated from Gatwick to Perpignan, Calvi, Zagreb; Derby and Birmingham to Perpignan, Birmingham to Nice, were flown for Midland Air Tour Operators (MATO), and Gatwick to Palma and Barcelona were operated for Wenger Airtours Ltd.

Derby Airways in 1959 was a member of the now-extinct British Independent Air Transport Association, and via this organisation a suggestion had been put to member airlines that in order to bring about an increase in reservations efficiency the Independent carriers should integrate their reservation services. What was hoped would be the first step in this dramatic new innovation was taken on 10th July 1959, when Derby Airways appointed the then Jersey Airlines as General Sales Agent, on behalf of Derby in the Channel Islands. It was hoped that further agreements being negotiated at that time would extend the service to all parts of the U.K. Alas, as we shall later see, this was not to be. Nevertheless the conception was a brilliant one, and who knows what the developments might have been had it succeeded.

Another possible first for Derby took place on 11th August, 1959, when a Dakota flew via Helsinki to Warsaw carrying delegates to a conference of the Esparanto Speaking Union. It was believed to have been the first occasion on which an independent carrier penetrated the Iron Curtain into Poland.

Earlier in the year, a licence had been granted to operate a scheduled service from Cardiff and/or Bristol to Ostend and/or Rotterdam (if only Amsterdam had been added—this was to have later repercussions). In order to show good faith, and although hard-pressed for aircraft for aircraft during the busiest month of the year, the first service was flown on Sunday 16th August and would operate for six weeks so that "we can show the public it can be done, before a full service starts in May 1960".

In September, it was announced that the Company had made application for scheduled services between Luton and Amsterdam and Luton and Brussels. In addition, an application was made for a vehicle ferry service between Luton and Le Touquet and Luton and Calais using Bristol 170 Freighters carrying passengers and freight as well as vehicles, at an initial frequency of four flights daily, increasing later on demand, for a period of seven years. Needless to say the service was never operated.

Another successful 'Passenger raising' scheme thought up by the Company were cheap charter flights for schools, whereby school children could undertake exchange schemes with school children of another country with the returning aircraft carrying the visitors to Britain instead of coming back empty, thus keeping down the seat costs. One such flight on 12th August took Milford Haven Grammar School students to Tarbes and back at a cost of only £15 per head.

In October, and in readiness for the 1960 season, more licence applications were made, this time from Swansea to the Channel Islands, Luxembourg, Nice, Palma, Perpignan and Barcelona, all but the Channel Islands application being extensions of the Bristol/Cardiff service. There could be no doubt about it now: in a few short years Derby Airways had proved the need for services from the Midlands and in particular from the Derby/Nottingham area. Scheduled services were a reality, albeit only summer services to date, with the exception of the Glasgow service, and now the summer Inclusive Tour services were providing as much income as the schedules.

With the advent of these services and the accompanying greater increase in the number of take-offs and landings at the grass field that was Derby (Burnaston) Airport, it was becoming more than apparent that the airfield surface was breaking up rapidly, and that either that surface would have to be stabilised, or another airport would have to be found. As the vast majority of the passengers originated in the Derby/Nottingham area, a simple move of base to say Birmingham would not suffice, as then there would be insufficient traffic to support the Company. The answer would have to be found in the immediate vicinity.

Initially tests were made to see if the soil could be stabilised at Burnaston. These proved reasonably satisfactory but, in order to provide for modern equipment, the available distance would have to be increased.

This would involve closing one or both lanes at either end of the existing take-off path, and legislation would have to be made to allow this to come about. In addition, the existing drains at Burnaston would have to be strengthened as the continued pounding was beginning to break them up. In any event if the River

Trent nearby was in flood, then the water draining from the airfield could not find a way out and the result was a water-logged airfield which only made matters worse. Often in a rainy spring, crews could quite literally feel the Marathons decelerate as they hit soft patches on the airfield. The Dakota did not suffer from this effect very much as they were fitted with large main wheels, whereas the Marathon had small twin-wheel units, in which the mud would be forced between the two wheels and really increase the drag. To really add coal to the fires, the Central Electricity Generating Board decided to construct a new power station, Willington, along the banks of the River Trent, but *INSIDE* the circuit pattern of Burnaston. From an airport point of view however, the writing was on the wall—Burnaston was out and a new airport had to be found and possibly built as well.

Various sites were investigated by Derby Corporation Airport Committee, including Ashbourne and Darley Moor, both deep inside Derbyshire; and Hucknall, then the Rolls Royce development airfield, but the proximity of the control tower to the runway ruled this airfield out on civil safety standards requirements. Finally, the old R.A.F. Station at Castle Donington, just over the River Trent in Leicestershire was looked at, particularly as the Air Ministry was putting the site up for sale. This military airfield was at one time a Wellington Operational Conversion Unit, and was now "surplus to requirements".

On October 8th 1959, it was formally announced that Derby Town Council had agreed "as a matter of policy" to develop Castle Donnington.

There were "teething snags" at the committee stage, but at least the project itself was under way and would eventually come to fruition. When one reflects upon the decision to develop Castle Donington, and comes to realise that such a mammoth undertaking, financially as well as constructionally, was brought about by the energy and foresight of one private company, it gives real food for thought.

Saturday the 10th October saw the commencement of a new type of winter inclusive tour service—the "Winter Sunshine Cruise". Derby Airways were the first company to carry out this type of service, operating on behalf of Lord Brothers Tours. The aircraft used were Dakotas, in which four seats had been removed and replaced by a table, colloquially known as the "Captain's Table". The operating crews were delighted at the flights for the aircraft were away for two weeks departing Birmingham on the Saturday morning, routing via Gatwick and Jersey as traffic stops, thence via Biaritz to refuel, and on to Madrid where passengers and crews stayed in the Emporado Hotel. Monday morning saw departure for Marrakesh where two nights were spent, enabling the Atlas Mountains to be visited, as well as Churchill's famous casino. Wednesday morning at dawn saw departure for Agadir (refuelling) and on to Teneriffe, where seven nights were spent, the passengers at Puerto de la Cruz and the crew in Santa de la Cruz. The following Wednesday Tangier was made, via Agadir for refuelling again. Many a boisterous night was had in Tangier, where the passengers stayed in the Hotel Fez, but the crew in the Velazqueth Palace Hotel. Visits were made to Hercules caves and to the nightclubs of

Tangiers. One First Officer is known to have been a better belly dancer than the girl giving the show at the Koutoupier Palace Night Club, but was sent flying into a corner by a quick flick of her posterior when he was congratulating himself for having beaten her at her own game. (Incidentally, she came from Manchester). Friday morning saw the return flight back to Derby and home.

In November it was annouced that a Luton-Derby-Dublin licence had been issued to Derby Airways, to be operated from 1960. At the same time, the Company announced its intention of commencing a Winter Service to the Channel Islands from Derby and Birmingham. Thus a new winter schedule was started on 4th December, and that service continues to the present day.

To close a highly eventful year in the Company's history, on the 3rd December a cocktail party was given in the House of Commons to celebrate the 21st anniversary of the founding of the Company. Group Captain Wilcock M.P., was, as Chairman, host to 100 guests, including Mr. Geoffrey Rippon, Parliamentary Secretary to the Ministry of Aviation. If only Captain N. Roy Harben, D.F.C., could have been present to see how his brainchild had progressed. Twenty-one years is quite a long time for any undertaking to be in business, and particularly so in aviation. The Company had come a long way since 1938, and to progress further a great endeavour had to be made to retain the high standard of aircraft operation and maintenance for which the Company were justly proud.

21st Anniversary line-up of crews and aircraft at Burnaston in 1959 (W. W. Winter Ltd.)

The aircraft fleet in 1959 numbered ten, and their maintenance formed the major responsibility of the Engineering Division. In addition, a large number of training aircraft used by the Derby Air Centre and Elstree School of Flying were maintained and overhauled by the Company, which was also entrusted with the maintenance and overhaul of Royal Air Force Chipmunks on the strength of the Leeds and Nottingham University Squadrons.

The Avro Ansons carrying out the magnetometer air surveys of Derby Aero Surveys Ltd. also returned periodically for checks and annual overhaul.

These varied and diverse tasks called for a completely equipped and comprehensively staffed engineering base, and to cater for this the Company had moved from the original Municipal Hangar to the main airport hangar, where, including attached workshops, over 75,000 square feet space was available. Of particular pride at that time was the aero engine workshop, where Pratt and Whitney R1830 and Gipsy Queen 70/3 engines were overhauled and also built up into power plants.

Main hangar interior at Burnaston, showing Dakotas, Marathon G-AMGW and The Miles Hawk Speed-Six G-ADGP belonging to Ron Paine, Technical Director. (W. W. Winter Ltd).

However, it was on the training side of the Company's activities that the chief claim to the Coming-of-Age Celebrations were made. Recently, and on the recommendation of Mr. E. W. Phillips (and who by now had been made an MBE in recognition of his services to aviation), the Company had acquired the

London School of Flying at Elstree, near London, and had centralised the training activities in that area. One of the then most comprehensively equipped flying schools in the country was operated at Elstree. A fleet of Chipmunks was used for ab-initio instruction, whilst full Link and class-room tuition, radio and signals training, messing facilities and so on were provided for the student who could, if he wished, take courses on to many types of aircraft up to and including heavy twin.

This aspect of activities, including the operation of several affiliated works flying clubs for well known aircraft manufacturers and other companies, came under the control of David Ogilvy, Chief Instructor and Manager of the Flying Training Division. David is now General Manager of the Shuttleworth Collection at Old Warden Aerodrome, Biggleswade, Herts., where he is carrying out magnificent work keeping vintage aircraft and vehicles in peak condition for posterity.

The fleet at the end of the year was:—

Dakotas	G-ANTD, G-AOGZ, G-APBC, G-AMSX, G-AMSW
Marathons	G-AMGW, G-AMHR, G-AMEW
Leopard Moth	G-ACLL

1960

The coming year was to be a time for consolidation. The Company's policy at this time remained one of continued expansion in the holiday inclusive tour market, the holiday scheduled service market, and, in a much more limited way, expansion in the year-round businessman's services.

Some of the routes obtained in 1959 had of course already had the inaugural flights completed for publicity purposes; nevertheless not all the routes had, at the beginning of 1960, had their inaugural services, but this would come. So short had been the previous years capacity that it will be remembered that the opportunity had been taken to ease the pressure a little by stopping the Oxford to Channel Islands service. With new routes to operate in 1960, obviously the aircraft strength would have to be increased and so it was that on 16th February 1960 a further Dakota joined the fleet, G-AOFZ purchased from Hunting Clan African Airways and promptly named "High Dale".

In addition to the aircraft fleet increase, it was decided to strengthen the sales organisation by dividing the country served by the company into regions as follows:

Midlands Region—	Derby, Birmingham and Northampton Airport
Eastern Region—	Luton Airport
Western Region—	Staverton Airport

Unfortunately, although it was not fully appreciated at the time, these regions were not more positively defined, with the result that many travel agents in the "fringe areas" of these ill-defined regions were not visited as the staff responsible were of the opinion that the neighbouring region was responsible. However, this fault would be rectified in time and at least a step in the right direction had been made.

In a successful attempt to bring air travel to the public's attention, in the Cheltenham/Gloucester region, an eight-day winter sports holiday in Switzerland was organised. The flight, commanded by the Chief Pilot Captain Ron Milsom, departed from Staverton on Saturday 9th January via Gatwick for Customs (Staverton did not have any customs facilities at this time), for Zurich. On the return flight members of the British Club in Zurich were carried so that the average cost of travel was well below the second-class rail fare. This was really intelligent use of air transport, at the same time giving much good publicity to both Derby Airways and Staverton Airport.

As mentioned above, the flight to Zurich had to land at Gatwick for Customs clearance. On Friday 19th February another charter flight from Staverton to Paris landed at Gatwick for the same reason but, much to the passengers' annoyance, there was no physical check at all, although on the return flight passengers were searched at Gatwick. The point made by the angry travellers was that an extra £80 had been paid by them to cover the extra flying involved in this officially decreed "detour", and as far as they could see it was a detour for no purpose at all. Letters to Members of Parliament resulted and only added further to the demand to provide Customs at Staverton.

Meanwhile, back at Burnaston, preparations were inevitably underway for the coming season, and of course charter work, which formed a large percentage of the company's activities in those days, was well under way. In 1957 the Football League had lifted the ban on football teams travelling by air, but it was not until 12th March 1960 that Derby County (The Rams), the Company's "local" football team, took advantage of air travel, when they flew from Derby to the Royal Air Force station at Leuchars near Dundee for their friendly match against Dundee United. Although the Company had flown other football teams before, notably the Show Biz team who regularly used Derby Airways for their Sunday charity match travel, and also the British Rugby League team, it was nice to think that The Rams would use their local airline for travel when the opportunity arose.

In March 1960 Aer Lingus had a prolonged strike of the pilots employed by them, the cause being the disciplining of some senior Captains resulting from an incident in the Shannon Shamrock during a nightstop at Shannon. As a result of this strike Derby Airways were approached with a request to operate the Dublin/Glasgow and Dublin/Liverpool services of Aer Lingus. In order to avoid any embarrassment to the Company's B.A.L.P.A. membership the Aer Lingus services were operated by senior management and non-BALPA Captains. The service given was a good one, and on more than one occasion the carriage of Decca on the aircraft (V.O.R. had not at this time been fitted) really proved its worth, so that the Irish were most impressed at some of the approaches made in appalling weather conditions on non-instrument aligned runways.

The new season's Channel Island services were begun earlier this year, mainly due to the Easter demand, and so it was that March 19th saw the commencement of these services. April 4th saw the first Derby to Dublin direct service, and additional Easter services were mounted. The first flight, with G-ANTD "Dove Dale" operating it, only had fourteen passengers on board, but the service was pioneered and in fact now runs at a twice daily frequency using Viscounts from the East Midlands Airport.

April 16th saw the commencement of the season's Staverton-Channel Islands services, and it was intended to operate a Derby connecting service at Whitsuntide. Already the Jersey/Guernsey bookings were double the 1959 figures, and all augered well for 1960.

March 24th saw the inauguration of the Cardiff and Bristol to Ostend services, scheduled for public service on the 28th May. The Lord Mayor of Cardiff, with the Lord Mayor of Bristol, and the Lady Mayoress, were aboard. Upon arrival (on schedule) in Ostend, the party, which included representatives of the press and travel trade, were met by the Burgomaster and Alderman of Tourist Affairs.

It was also announced on the 24th March, that a new Bristol to Amsterdam service licence had been acquired by the Company, although due to prior commitments it would not be operated until 1961. Bristol, however, was more enthusiastic over the possibility for it would then be possible to feed passengers into two major world airlines, K.L.M. and Candian Pacific, the latter only having two European termini, Amsterdam and Rome, for its Bristol Britannias en route to Edmonton, Calgary and Vancouver.

On the 28th April 1960 came the news that Luton Airport was to be granted Customs facilities on a "trial" basis. A new concrete runway had just been completed (much to the joy of Derby Airway crews who had suffered the grass field at Luton just as much as at Burnaston, particularly the Marathon crews who winced every time the nose-wheel hit a bump), and, in anticipation of many more passengers, the customs decision had been made. The Company of course fully endorsed the move. Having been the first airline to operate from Luton in the previous year, it really believed that Luton had a future. In fact, the local press referred to the Company as a "go-ahead airline" with big plans to extend its services from Luton to Palma, Costa Brava, Nice, Luxembourg and the previously mentioned car ferry to Le Touquet.

Sunday May 1st 1960 proved a disappointing day for the well-known "pop" singer Cliff Richard, for whilst giving a performance at the Derby Gaumont on that evening, his car was stolen. The following day Cliff had an engagement to keep in Carlisle, and what better and quicker way than to charter an aircraft from Derby Airport. Thus it was that Marathon G-AMGW, with Captain Cramp in command and Captains Assistant Roger Wise as his co-pilot flew from Burnaston to Silloth, an R.A.F. maintenance airfield near Carlisle, with Cliff and his manager, Mr. Charles King, on board. *Two* hostesses were provided (or did they volunteer), Jenny Dale and Joan Lester. Cramp invited Cliff up to the flight-deck for the flight which the star thoroughly enjoyed, particularly as "GW" had only just been fitted with the Decca Navigator Mark 8, which he found most fascinating.

In May a further improvement was made at Burnaston Airport when, with the completion in the Municipal Hangar of a bonded store for both bar stocks and bonded freight, Customs clearance of freight was commenced. In 1959 the granting of Customs facilities had not been extended to include freight clearance, and, welcome though passenger clearance facilities were, it was not the complete answer. May 1960 gave this answer.

On Friday May 20th 1960, the Show Biz XI football team were playing in Derby so what better way to arrive at Derby than fly by the local airline. The team arrived at Derby Airport with, among others, Billy Wright, the former England and Wolves skipper, referee Alf Bond and singer Toni Dalli. Quite a feather in the Company's hat in those days to fly such celebrities around.

With the smooth running of the Customs unit now at Burnaston, local firms were beginning to use the proximity of the airfield and the airline for air-freighting of commodities they would not otherwise have thought of shipping. One such enterprise commenced on Friday July 1st, when the Derby Co-operative Society's Peak Bakery sent 486lbs of Swiss Rolls to the Channel Islands. In the past the rolls had gone by sea, but now by using air the bakery would be able to send larger consignments to the islands. It may be of interest to note that 486lbs of Swiss Roll represents 1,000 feet in length. Each box in the consignment contained six 3-inch rolls, which makes a mile-and-a-half of Swiss Roll a week!

By now the holiday rush was in full swing, with more than 1,000 people leaving Derby's grass airport each weekend, to the Channel Islands, Isle of Man, Ostend and Luxembourg. Similar pictures were being painted at Sywell where the Jersey flights had been fully booked up since Christmas. At Staverton the traffic had risen by three hundred per cent since 1959, and bookings were still coming in thick and fast for the coming September! One item which helped this booking situation was a strike by seamen and dockers.

There now occurred two incidents within one month of each other which were to have a considerable effect upon the Company. On 28th July Marathon G-AMEW was inbound to Burnaston when the Captain reported that he was uncertain as to the position of the undercarriage. Fortunately the aircraft was empty so that no undue nervousness was caused, and in any event a successful landing was made when it was discovered that the undercarriage was in fact securely locked down, and that it was purely an indicator fault. The aircraft was properly checked and returned to service. On Sunday 21st August, however, inbound to Bristol and Cardiff from Ostend with Captain "Andy" Oates in command the nosewheel collapsed on landing. Fortunately nobody was hurt. Wing Commander Roxburgh, the joint Managing Director, flew to Bristol and immediately refuted suggestions that the mishap had been caused by a heavy landing. "To suggest this is to belittle Captain Oate's ability" he said. The mishap occurred at the end of the landing run, when the nose-wheel started to "shimmy" and the collapse occurred. Later it was found that a casting had fractured in the nose wheel.

As a result of these two incidents the Marathons were finally withdrawn from service, although this decision was not based on the two incidents alone. In fact

G-AMHR was withdrawn on 18th July, G-AMGW on 25th July and G-AMEW on 27th September. It fell to Captain Cramp to make the last operational flight in the Marathon, being a Derby-Dublin-Derby-Luton-Derby service on 26th September. This was a fitting end as it had been Cramp who delivered "EW" on 28th August 1957, and who similarly carried out the first commercial flight on "EW" 7th July 1958. Having also flown the type in the Royal Air Force, Cramp had the "honour" of having more hours on the type than any other pilot in the world, with just over 1,600 hours he could account for. Both "GW" and "HR" were broken up in December 1960, whilst "EW", stripped of engines and then sitting back on her tail, lay forlorn at Burnaston until she too was scrapped in 1962.

At the end of September, a move was made by Gloucester and Cheltenham Joint Airport Committee towards the provision of Customs facilities at Staverton in time for the 1961 season. An informal meeting between the Committee Chairman Alderman W. J. Smith, with Mr. C. M. Colbeck, Divisional Controller of the Ministry of Aviation, indicated that a "very necessary" first move was a survey to ascertain true estimates for passenger potential and accurate assessments of freight potential. This development, backed by the Ministry of Aviation and Derby Airways would, it was hoped, get the much-needed Customs installed at Staverton. The Company were by now absolutely convinced that the airport could leap ahead if Customs were granted. Looking back on a very good season, plans were really forging ahead for 1961. In addition the number of charter flights from Staverton had increased; already 400 passengers had been flown out of the airport in 1960. Once again the Company had been in the forefront of causing an airport to develop rapidly. Derby, Luton and now Staverton.

Whilst talking of development at Derby, the project at Castle Donington was still well under way at the negotiation stage. It was announced during 1960 that four other local authorities had decided to join Derby Corporation in backing the scheme, the four being Derbyshire County Council, Nottingham City Council, Nottinghamshire County Council, and Leicestershire County Council.

To support the argument for a need for an alternative airport to Derby (Burnaston), figures were issued covering the 1960 summer season (Easter to mid October) carried by the Company. Compared with 1959, passenger figures had doubled. The number of passengers who had "flown Derby" in the fleet of aircraft named after the Derbyshire Dales had risen from 16,200 in 1959, to 32,105 in the same period in 1960. Taking into account the all-year-round scheduled services to Dublin, and Glasgow, the number of passengers passing through Derby's Municipal Airport (operated, it must be emphasized by Derby Aviation on behalf of the Corporation) was now running at the rate of over 45,000 per year.

The biggest increase of the season was of course the traffic to the Channel Islands, to which the Company operated from Derby, Northampton, Cambridge, Luton and Gloucester/Cheltenham. New routes from Wales and the West Country all inaugurated in 1960 were Cardiff and Bristol to Majorca, the Costa Brava, Ostend and Luxembourg. These routes made a notable contribution not only to the overall traffic of the Company, but also to the facilities offered to the general public.

One of the notable achievements of 1960 had been the amount of freight carried from Derby. Considerable impetus to this type of traffic was given when earlier in the year Customs freight clearance facilities had been granted to Derby Airport, thereby opening up all the scheduled passenger services to supplementary freight. Over 100 freight flights with Rolls Royce Avon and Dart engines had left Derby for the Continent. Eventually 254 Avon engines were to be airlifted to Toulouse.

For the carriage of the Avon engines, which arrived almost literally hot from the engine test cells at Rolls Royce Derby for onward transmission to Toulouse and installation in the Sud Aviation Caravelle, special engine cradles were devised, fitted with twin-roller units at each corner. In the aircraft (the Dakota), two false floors were installed, one to act as a load-spreader, the other to take the "compression" load of the twin-roller units, whilst on the forward bulkhead a special block and tackle complete with a ratchet was fitted. The correct positions of the four roller units was marked on the top false floor, so that as soon as the engine arrived at the aircraft side the engine could be rolled into the aircraft, turned to align with the fuselage, and then be winched into position using the ratchet attachment. Using this method, an engine could be loaded in under thirty minutes. As the position of the engine in the aircraft was pre-computed, it was possible for the load/trim sheet to be completed before the crew arrived at the aircraft. It was normal practice for Rolls-Royce to inform the Company that an engine would be ready on the day in question, at which time a crew would be warned at home. When the engine was accepted off the test-bed a further phone call to the airport would result in the crew being called in, to arrive, usually, at the same time as the engine. Rolls-Royce were particularly pleased with the way the service operated.

To summarise, the year 1960 had been one of big expansion in the passenger and freight fields, and already plans were being made for an increase in activity for the next year. Capacity was going to be a problem, particularly now with the withdrawal from service of the Marathons. Another problem created as a result of all the increased activity was the gradual break-up of the grass surface at Burnaston, but at least remedial plans for this problem were underway with the Castle Donington project. All in all 1961 promised to be another exciting year.

The fleet as at the close of the year comprised:—

Dakotas   G-ANTD, G-AOGZ, G-APBC, G-AMSW, G-AMSX,
                    G-AOFZ.
Leopard Moth   G-ACLL.

1961

As will be remembered from the previous year, capacity for 1961 was going to be a big problem for the Company. To cope with the desired rate of expansion, both in terms of frequency and in number of points of origin and point of destination served, two more Dakotas were added to the fleet, G-AGJV and G-AKJH, "JV" actually going into service on 9th March and "JH" in May. Acquired from B.E.A., they arrived at Burnaston in the early part of the year as Pionair aircraft (Pionair being the B.E.A. class name for the Dakota) and were immediately taken into the hangar for overhaul and conversion into normal Dakota VI aircraft.

It might be prudent to point out at this stage that the Company's engineering standards were still as high as the original standards insisted upon by Roy Harben. An example of this lay in the Pratt & Whitney engine overhaul, where, upon the expiry of the current T.B.O. (Time Between Overhaul), the engine was removed from the aircraft, and parts due for replacement were done so with American manufactured parts and not British manufactured parts, it being an American engine. Some other operators returned major components to the engine if they were still within tolerance, and even when such parts did need replacing they were done so with British-manufactured parts.

However, to return to the capacity problem, although the arrival of "JV" and "JH" were of obvious help, due to the overhaul requirement there was still going to be a lack of capacity at the beginning of the year and in particular around Easter. To help out in this situation another Dakota, G-ANEG, was dry-leased, (i.e. leased but Derby providing its own crews) from Executive Air Transport Ltd., of Birmingham.

In August 1960, new legislation had been introduced governing the licencing and certification of public transport aviation. Generally this new innovation was welcomed by the airlines who had felt for some time that a much tighter control of such operations was needed, particularly in the Independent Airline sector, as there were still some sharp operators whose activities had cast grave doubts on the integrity and safety of all Independent carriers, most of whose efficiency was equal to, and in some cases better than, the nationalised airlines. Although not comparable with B.E.A. in size, the company considered its maintenance and operating integrity to be as high as the Corporation's, and so was one of the large majority who welcomed the new legislation.

A Flight Operations Inspector was appointed by the Ministry to monitor the performance of each carrier, and the first Flight Ops. Inspector appointed to Derby Airways was Captain "Dicky" Talbot who, by a,strange turn of the roundabout, was again the Company's Inspector in 1975.

Needless to say the application for the A.O.C. (Air Operator's Certificate) for the Company was successful, and the certificate was granted at the end of February 1961.

At the beginning of 1961, B.E.A. found themselves lacking in freight capacity and so the Company found themselves signing a contract with the Corporation to operate a nightly London Heathrow-Amsterdam freight service. The first flight,in this series was on the evening of 2nd February, when G-AMSX with Captain Milsom in command, and Captain Cramp as his co-pilot, departed Heathrow at 2320 to Amsterdam, returning to London at 0355. The contract lasted until well into the summer months.

On Friday 24th March, a major reorganisation took place in the Commercial

45

Department, with the promotion of Captain Terry Mayo to the appointment of Commercial Manager, based at Derby Airport. With his new appointment his responsibilities enlarged to cover traffic promotion of all of the Company network, including scheduled services passenger and freight charters.

One of the first of Terry Mayo's innovations was the opening of a Company office in Manchester. As office space, at Manchester Airport, was hard to come by, this new Company branch was in one of Manchester's leading stores, Marshall & Snelgrove, St. Anns Place, in the heart of the city. Yet another step in the right direction and another indication of the policy of expansion.

On the morning of Wednesday 22nd March a public enquiry opened into the proposed development of Castle Donington. The enquiry lasted some few days and of course the outcome was of tremendous importance to the Company for, having demonstrated most ably that the need for such an airport was a fact, the outcome of the enquiry would dictate the whole future. A significant statement was made by Councillor Tom Earnshaw, chairman of Derby Corporations Estates and Development Committee, in that "My council have agreed to join a consortium if it is formed, but have decided to develop Castle Donington on their own if the consortium does not come into existence." In so far as the company was concerned, this statement did not come as a surprise, being closely associated with Derby Corporation as the Burnaston airport operators on behalf of the Corporation, but nevertheless it was a most reassuring statement coming as it did at a public enquiry.

It was suggested by counsel for the objectors that there was no demand in the vicinity for the sort of air transport which it was hoped would be established at Castle Donington. Wing Commander Roxburgh retorted immediately by saying "We (the Company) obviously know there is a demand by the build-up in traffic over recent years." That statement has of course been borne out by facts.

The enquiry lasted, as mentioned, some days, at the end of which every employee of the Company waited with baited breath for the outcome which of course we now all know, but at the time there was a considerable amount of tension around the place.

On Saturday 15th April the Company achieved yet a further little piece of history insofar as it was the first carrier, civil or military, to use the new Royal Air Force Operations Block and Passenger Lounge at Royal Air Force Lyneham. G-ANEG was en route from Staverton to Jersey with thirty-six passengers and a crew of four, when the starboard engine began to falter, so the engine was shut down, and the propellor feathered. Now that very morning the new facilities at Lyneham had just been officially opened and the ceremony completed with all concerned dispersed, when "EG" arrived on the scene to complete a single-engine landing, and thus became the first user of these new facilities. An engineering team flew down from Burnaston in Executive Air Transport Dove G-AMDD, but in spite of intensive searching and engine running could not fault the engine and eventually "EG" completed the day's flying. Some few weeks later the same engine stopped as the aircraft was taxying out, and this time the trouble was traced to a pin-hole in the torque tube connecting the fuel tank selector cock to the fuel cock, causing air to enter the system and the engine to malfunction.

On Whit Sunday, May 21st, a Dakota departed Derby Airport with Captain T. Pike in command, and First Officer J. Vernon as his co-pilot, bound for Luxembourg on the inaugural scheduled service flight for that service. On board were civic parties from both Derby and Nottingham.

In those now seemingly far-off days of 1961, before legislation came into force governing crew duty hours, the crews worked very long hours and in sometimes appalling weather. One typical day for a Dakota crew was Saturday 27th May, when duty was commenced at 0615 and finished at 2025 having flown from Derby to Luton-Derby-Dublin-Derby-Luton-Cambridge-Jersey-Luton-Cambridge-Derby, that is 10 sectors in 15 hours 25 minutes. It was of course not only the crews who worked hard, for the engineers were hard at it clearing snags, re-fuelling, doing routine maintenance, continuing even when the last crew had arrived back. Similarly, the traffic staff worked just as long hours. However, engineers and traffic staff could get away for a few minutes for a hot meal and a small break, but the crews were hard at it all the time and there were only cold salad boxes available for them in those days. Still, everyone was needed to make up the team that had put the Company where it was, and the hard work and long hours were put up with almost willingly. If it had not been for the spirit of all concerned in those days, British Midland would not be in existence today. The same spirit still exists even now.

Another achievement was made at the beginning of June when the first Swansea to Ostend service was operated, stopping at Cardiff (Rhoose) Airport both ways in order to clear Customs. Although the good citizens of Swansea liked the new service immensely, the same could not be said of the crews for the airfield at Swansea was a particularly short one, the threshold of the main runway being crossed by a wooden fence upon which excited spectators would sit to watch the aircraft touching down, sometimes passing literally just a few feet over their heads. In addition, the airfield had a huge hump in the middle of it, so that, at the touch-down point, the end of the runway could not be seen until the "crown" of the hump was reached whereupon it would be seen that the runway end was almost on top of the crew. Many an ulcer was born at Swansea.

On Friday 14th July the Company carried its one millionth passenger, the lucky person, a passenger on the Dublin service, being presented with a bottle of Champagne. When one considers that in only a very few short years one million passengers had been carried, it really shows itself up as a remarkable achievement, even more so when it is realised that the largest single unit was a 36 seater Dakota.

It had become more apparent with the increasing traffic being carried, particularly on the Inclusive Tour flights, that in order to be more competitive the Company would have to expand into the larger four-engined market. This would give a better seat-mile cost to attract the tour operator, as well as giving a much more attractive aircraft in which the passenger would travel, thus making it easier to sell from that point of view. As a result of this line of thinking the Company began to look around for suitable equipment. At this point in time there were plenty of four-engined D.C4's around, but in order to be more attractive as well as competitive it was thought, and quite rightly too, that the aircraft chosen should be a pressurised type. Thus it came about that the choice fell on the Douglas DC6B, complete with large cargo doors, two of which were available from American Airlines in the States. After counsultation with the licencing authorities it was agreed that Captain Pike as Chief Pilot and Captain Cramp as Chief Training Captain would fly over to the U.S.A. to carry out the Ground technical instruction with American Airlines, and carry out their type conversion before flying the first aircraft across the Atlantic in order not only to do the actual ferrying, but to build up their hours in order to convert other crews onto the type at a later stage. The necessary licencing authority was to be given upon satisfactory passing of an examination and the issue of a certificate by American Airlines. The British authorities would accept the certificates for the ferry flight provided the British examination for the DC6 was passed upon return to the U.K. Having sat the British examination Pike and Cramp would return to the U.S.A. to ferry the second aircraft to the U.K., by which time sufficient experience would have been accumulated to allow the pair to commence training of the rest of the Company's crews who were to convert. Such was the plan, but at this time something of a disaster struck.

At the end of September, Overseas Aviation (C.I.) Ltd., a Gatwick-based operator, went into liquidation and most, if not all, of their aircraft were repossessed by the controlling bank, Lombard Ltd., and were of course put up for sale at a very low price indeed. The net result to Derby Airways was that five Argonaut aircraft previously operated by British Overseas Airways Corporation became available and were puchased from Lombards, part of the financial deal being that the bank took a large interest in the Company. Although not appreciated at the time, the decision was a disastrous one insofar as the aircraft were concerned for, cheap as they were, they were very expensive to operate and did not have either the range, capacity or the cargo doors of the DC6B. To clarify the remark about the Argonaut being more expensive to operate than the DC6B, let it be known that the T.B.O. (Time Between Overhaul) on the Argonaut's Rolls Royce Merlin 724/1C engines was 1450 hours provided a cylinder block change had been made at 650 hours, whereas the T.B.O. on the DC6B's Pratt and Whitney R2800 engines was 3000 hours with no work required at half life. In addition, the overhaul,cost of the Merlin was £5,000 compared with £3,000 for the R2800. From the engine handling point of view the Merlin required a great deal of attention with critical operating parameters. The R2800, on the other hand, did not require nearly as much crew attention and was an engine with which one could almost take liberties (but not literally so of course).

The range of the Argonaut was very low compared with the DC6B, and even the DC4 from which it was developed.

Because of the high operating costs of the Argonaut, it proved difficult to sell the aircraft in commercial sense to tour operators due to the high seat cost, so that the increase in I.T. traffic expected with the advent of the new venture did not come about to the anticipated degree. It would not be true to assume that no increased I.T. traffic came about, for it did, but even so it was soon realised that the buying of these aircraft, cheap though the unit cost was, was a bad decision, and was to cost the Company dear in the long term.

So it was, then, that on Thursday 5th October 1961 the first really big aircraft to land at Burnaston was Argonaut G-ALHS with Captain Van den Elst in command, and First Officer "Bluey" Wilson as his co-pilot. As Burnaston was acknowledged to be a small field, it was with bated breath that most of the Company staff turned out to watch "HS" land, wondering if the aircraft was going to stop in time or would end up by arguing with the hedge and lane at the far end of runway 27. What Van den Elst's thoughts were as he saw the pocket-sized grass airfield for the first time can be left to the imagination. Suffice to say that a beautiful landing was achieved, and, with reverse thrust selected a remarkably short landing run resulted. One way or another Derby Airways had taken a big step forward, and all in all the staff were glad to see the arrival of the Argonauts, in spite of the disappointment surrounding the DC6B.

Pocket-sized Derby-Burnaston Airport. (Aero Pictorial Ltd).

On Friday 6th October, Dakota G-ANTD departed from Derby bound for Hamburg, with Company staff on board for their annual weekend on the Continent to mark the end of the summer season. It had been decided this year that a change would be made from the usual trip to Amsterdam, hence the destination, Hamburg. It was intended that the trip should be a memorable one, and that it was.

As members of the party were strolling along the Reeperbahn in Hamburg on the Saturday evening enjoying themselves, they suddenly found themselves confronted with German placards displaying the photograph of a Dakota in familiar colours and with a familiar registration, that of the Company's own Dakota G-AMSW. Hurriedly buying papers and trying to translate the German text, it became all too apparent that "SW" had crashed in the Pyrennees in the south of France whilst en route from Gatwick to Perpignan, killing all thirty-four passengers and crew of three on board. The aircraft had been commanded by Captain Mike Higgins, with First Officer Rex Hailstone and Air Hostess Carol Bentley as his crew. The crash occurred on Mount Canigou on the night of the 6th/7th October.

The staff outing in Hamburg turned out to be a sour one indeed.

Early in November, a start was made on the first proper training school to be set up within the Company. With the advent of the Argonauts it was obvious that the problem had now to be tackled in a big way. Previously, although the standard of instruction had been high, there had not been any proper and permanent classroom available, all instruction being given in borrowed accommodation belonging to the flying school. In November, however, the ANT8 Link Trainer, which had been the pride of the Air Schools set-up during the war years, was dismantled, to be re-assembled at a later date in the flying school. The now bare Link room was then given a coat of paint, a blackboard was installed, and several cut-away parts of the Argonaut's Merlin engines obtained from Rolls Royce were put on display, together with items from the air conditioning system and oleo legs—all for instructional purposes. Similar items from the Dakota were obtained and displayed, whilst numerous system diagrams were drawn up, framed, and hung, all ready for the next years training session to begin. At long last, a school to match the standards of instruction was being formed.

On Friday 10th November the long awaited results of the public inquiry into Castle Donington were announced, in that it had been agreed that planning permission should be granted for the development of the old R.A.F. airfield, but it was to be over two years yet before work was to commence. However, the announcement was a most welcome one both for the Company and the staff.

Friday 22nd December saw the introduction of the first Derby-Birmingham-Cork service. This flight was initially put on just for the Christmas and New Year period after which it was withdrawn temporarily, being re-instated in the summer of 1962. Also over the Christmas period the usual rush of flights to Dublin took place; most of them at or near midnight, much to the chagrin of the crews who had to operate them, but nevertheless it was work.

The year ended with the fleet as follows:—

G-ANTD, G-AOGZ, G-APBC, G-AMSX, G-AOFZ, G-AGJV and G-AKJH—all Dakotas in service.

G-ALHY, G-ALHS and G-ALHG were all Argonauts being converted for service.

G-ALHN and G-ALHP—both Argonauts for spares and scrapping.

G-ACLL—Leopard Moth as Company hack.

1962

The year started with a tragedy both for the Company, and for many of the staff as well as the Directors, for on Sunday 14th January, the Chairman, Group Captain Wilcock, O.B.E., A.F.C., M.P., died suddenly in Westminster Hospital. He expressed a wish, in writing, that Mary Agar, Company Secretary should join the Board of Directors upon his death, and so it was that Miss M. M. Agar became the first (and only) woman to become a working member of the Board of the Company. Shortly after the Group Captain's death the Board of Directors voted Wing Commander Roxburgh as Chairman.

It will be remembered from the previous chapter that the Company were becoming well entrenched in the Cardiff and Bristol areas, and with the coming into service of the Argonauts, planned for the spring, it was necessary to appoint a reputable agency to represent the Company in these areas. The first step towards this was the announcement, on the 16th February, that Stewart and Esplen Limited, of 38 High Street, Bristol, had been appointed as sales and booking agents for the Bristol and West Country area. The association with this old established shipping agency was to be a firm and happy one.

In addition, a Company office was opened in Cardiff at 3 Park Place. Unlike the agency of Stewart and Esplen at Bristol, the Cardiff office was manned by the Company's own staff and was an indication of how Wales and the West were viewed as the generator of much air traffic.

On the 27th February, Arognaut crew training commenced when with Captain Van den Elst in command, G-ALHS flew from Birmingham to Jersey and return with Captain Pike, Chief Pilot and Captain Cramp, Chief Training Captain, carrying out the upper air work of their type conversions en route.

One interesting Argonaut exercise took place during part of the training in that on the night of 1st March, certification checks of DC4 flap jacks, as now fitted to the Argonaut, were undertaken. Owing to the shortage of spares for the type, it had been thought that the DC4 jacks would make a suitable substitute and the A.R.B. were approached with the result that the jacks were fitted. The flying tests made required the flaps to be extended and remain so well in excess of the normal limiting speeds. Needless to say they worked perfectly, and so one area of acute spares shortage was eliminated.

Wednesday 14th March, saw the inaugural Carlisle-Jersey service. Operated by G-AOGZ "Darley Dale", with Captain Pike in command and First Officer (now Captain) H. I. S. Clarke as his co-pilot, the aircraft departed from Carlisle Municipal Airport at 0845. The party were welcomed to Jersey by the President of the Jersey Tourism Committee, Deputy Clarence Dupre, who congratulated Carlisle on their initiative in promoting air services from their city, and added, "As for Derby Airways, they have once again shown great enterprise in establishing a new service to Jersey and they deserve every success".

Three days after the inaugural, Captain Pike, together with Captain Cramp, was on his way to Aden via Cairo with Argonaut G-ALHS which had been dry-leased to Aden Airways. Under the command of Captain Vic Spencer of Aden Airways, the ferry flight was being used to give line training to Pike and Cramp.

On the return flight from Aden, VR-AAT, an Argonaut belonging to Aden Airways, was operated, commanded by Captain Pete Williamson, Aden Airways.

Wednesday 18th April saw yet another new scheduled service being inaugurated, this time the Derby-Belfast route. Although in 1962 the service operated only on Wednesdays and Fridays (the Wednesday service operating via Carlisle in both directions), the service was to prove a popular one and indeed is now operated twice daily in each direction, Monday through to Friday, although of course Carlisle is no longer retained in the Company's route pattern.

On the 3rd May the Company put out its first policy statement associated with the proposed new airport at Castle Donington. Insofar as Derby Airways was concerned, the immediate effect of the move to Castle Donington would be to increase traffic on then existing routes.

The statement went on to say that the policy of Derby Airways would be first to consolidate the existing network, achieving greater traffic density on the established routes and to promote freight, and then to expand with the selectiveness that has typified the gradual but steady expansion of the airline's sphere of influence over recent years.

As if to further emphasise the foregoing statement on future policy and particularly with regard to the future move to Castle Donington, it was announced on the 7th May that Derby Airport, Burnaston had been designated as a full Customs Airport, which now meant that Customs would be available on-call at any hour. These facilities would be transferred to the proposed new airport at Castle Donington which would, therefore, start operation as a full Customs Airport of the same category.

Commensurate with all this activity, the Company were also in a position to negotiate their own freight rates on a distance and commodity basis. No all-freight routes were, at that time, operated, but certain licences for that purpose were held and no doubt, when the move to Castle Donington took place, that aspect of Derby Airways activities would be one of the first to see further development. Events were to show that this move, desirable as it no doubt was both to the Company and the community, was not so easily come by, but more of that later.

On the 9th May 1962, it was announced that by arrangement with Executive Air Transport Ltd., of Birmingham, Derby Airways was to take over that Company's routes from Birmingham to the Isle of Wight and to Newcastle. Preliminary arrangements had already been made for the transfer of the appropriate licences, and operations would commence at the latter end of May on the route Derby-Birmingham-Isle of Wight, weekly in each direction, using four-engined Heron aircraft. On the Newcastle service application had been made to include Derby on the route, operating Birmingham-Derby-Newcastle every Tuesday at a single fare of £3.15.0d.

In addition to the foregoing, it was also announced that Derby Airways had taken another Executive Air Transport activity, Midland Airport Services Ltd., together with their airport office and staff for handling passengers, freight and aircraft at Birmingham Airport. In addition to handling Derby Airways traffic, passengers, freight and aircraft of other airlines would also be processed. Commenting on the.transfer of these activities, Wing Commander Roxburgh said: "We are please that we are able to strengthen our organisation by adding these activities at Birmingham to our Midlands coverage. We already link Leeds, Glasgow, Belfast, Dublin, Cork and the Channel Islands with our network and Birmingham is a valuable addition. We look forward with confidence to this extension of the Group's activities to Birmingham Airport, as we are certain that we shall receive the full support of the Birmingham Airport Authorities".

There can be no doubt that the Chairman was "pleased", for behind this very astute move was a piece of negotiation that was well carried out and accompanied with some phenomenal luck. In addition, in order to provide the Isle of Wight service it had been necessary to lease Heron aircraft from Mercury Airlines Ltd. of Manchester, and this alone was to pay off in later years as will be seen. Both Midland Airport Services and Executive Air Transport had been the brainchild of Captain Alan Firmin, who up to that point had been the Birmingham/Midlands area manager for Air Safaris Ltd., operating Viking and Hermes aircraft. A local financier, Mr Neville, had provided capital backing, and the Chief Pilot was Captain Eric (Tubby) Ashton, D.F.C., who had spent many years flying for Sabena in the Belgian Congo. The aircraft used by E.A.T. were a Dove (G-AMDD) and a Dakota (G-ANEG). However, the undertaking was not a succesful one and Neville decided to pull out and recoup what money he could. Knowing of Derby Airways interest in E.A.T's activities (in March 1961 Derby Airways had air-tested G-ANEG at Southend and accepted it for E.A.T.), Neville telephoned Wing Commander Roxburgh and asked him if he wanted to purchase M.A.S. including the accommodation at Birmingham. With a tongue-in-cheek attitude, the Chairman replied that he would offer £100 for the undertaking. Probably much to the Wing Commander's surprise, the offer was accepted, and became effective on 1st May 1962, when Midland Airport Services Ltd., became a wholly-owned subsidiary company of the Derby Aviation Group of Companies.

Today M.A.S. (now part of British Midland proper) is very much a going concern and its Manager, Mr. "Viv" Woodhams remained with it until his retirement in 1974. Only British Airways and British Midland are allowed to handle traffic at Birmingham Airport, so the importance of the acqustion can be readily seen. During the first four weeks under the new management, 167 single movements were handled including those of Derby Airways, Euravia (now Britannia Airways), Lloyd International (now defunct) Dan Air, Autair (subsequently Court Line), Silver City (now part of British Caledonian), Starways, E.A.T. and Morton Air Services (all three now defunct).

Now that the Argonauts were entering service with the Company in a big way, and with the difficulties of operating these aircraft from Burnaston (they could not operate commercially in or out due to the short field length), it was obviously desirable to virtually base these aircraft at Birmingham, being the nearest large airfield to the Company's main base. So it was then that on 27th June it was announced that hangarage had been obtained at Birmingham, and it was here that a fair proportion of maintenance on these aircraft was carried out, even though most of the heavy engineering still took place at Burnaston. At the same time as the announcement was made, and in view of the strengthening of the Birmingham base by the acquisition of M.A.S., it was announced that apart from operating from Birmingham to Ostend, Luxembourg, Cork, Jersey, Newcastle and the Isle of Wight, an application had been submitted for a Birmingham-Amsterdam licence, a route which the Company thought could be operated with success (a remark which was to be remembered with a bitter taste later on). In addition, "A" licences for Birmingham to Barcelona, Palma and Perpignan (for the Costa Brava) had just been obtained ready for the 1963 season.

Argonaut G-ALHY in the original colour scheme just after its delivery in 1962.

Derby Airways had been operating to Majorca and the Costa Brava from Cardiff and Bristol for the previous three years, and the route had shown a traffic increase of more than 100 percent in 1962.

On 27th September, the new 1962/63 winter scheduled services were announced, this proving to be the Company's most comprehensive winter service programme yet. Regular services throughout the winter would be operated from Derby to Carlisle and Belfast, to Glasgow via Leeds/Bradford, to the Channel Islands and from Birmingham to Newcastle and the Channel Islands. The Channel Islands service via Birmingham would be continued throughout the winter with the exception of certain flights during late November and early December, whilst the Birmingham-Newcastle service would operate on Tuesdays only.

A new Cardiff/Bristol to Ostend service would operate every weekend from 22nd December, mainly for use by Winter Sports enthusiasts who would take coach connections to popular winter resorts. In announcing the new services, the Chairman stated that it was "the most comprehensive winter service the Company had yet offered. The fact that it was possible to continue so many of the summer services on an all-year-round basis reflects the gratifying measure of support we have received from the travelling public. We are particularly pleased that the Belfast service, inaugurated earlier in 1962, had been so successful that it was felt fully justifiable to continue the service on a 3—day-a-week basis throughout the winter". Thus began the glimmerings of a network of scheduled services based on the all-year-round requirements of the business community, instead of relying on the summer holiday traffic as the source of income. There was still a long way to go yet on this theme, but at last there was some positive thinking in this direction.

On Friday 28th September, Dakota G-AKJH took to the air at Burnaston with Captain Cramp in command to carry out the air test of the new V.O.R. (V.H.F. Omni-directional Range) equipment which had just been installed on the Company's aircraft for the first time. The test was successful, and the aircraft operated that night to Belfast using the new equipment. This new addition to the navigation equipment made Derby Airways Dakotas the best-equipped Dakotas in the country at the time, bar none. Apart from the V.O.R., the equipment included Decca Mk 8, I.L.S. and A.D.F. The aircrews certainly welcomed this new addition.

It was announced on the 1st December that Midland Airport Services would be undertaking the handling of Aer Lingus—Irish International Airlines at Birmingham Airport, M.A.S. having won the contract away from B.E.A. The fact that Aer Lingus had entrusted their handling to M.A.S. was a measure of the growing importance of the handling. The M.A.S. facilities by now included a complete cargo unit capable of handling any kind of freight, housed in one of the Derby Airways hangars at Birmingham and in the capable hands of the Cargo Manager, Jim Lenehan. The frieght shed had been erected by the Company as part of the Aer Lingus handling deal. It was certainly a feather in the cap of M.A.S.

During the first season of Argonaut operations, it had been obvious that the trim of the aircraft left a lot to be desired as they were definitely tail-heavy. In a successful endeavour to overcome this problem, the third Argonaut to be put into Derby Airways service, G-ALHG, had been completely re-worked by the Company's Engineering Division. The work included removing the horse-shoe shaped lounge at the rear pressure bulkhead and locating the toilets in this position (which incidentally, is where the toilets were in the original design until re-positioned forward whilst in BOAC service). In addition two more windows were cut in the pressure hull to enable an extra row of seats to be installed. Thus, not only was the trim of the aircraft improved but the capacity was raised from 70 to 75 passengers. At the same time, advantage was taken to introduce a new livery for the aircraft and thus it was that the basic Air Schools two superimposed blue triangles (one dark blue, one light blue) became the basic livery for Derby Airways. At the same time a large D and a large A appeared on the fin and rudder. Today's Company livery stems from this scheme.

Cabin Services aboard an Argonaut of Derby Airways.

Thus ended a very eventful year.
The fleet consisted of:—

Agonauts:	G-ALHG, G-ALHS, G-ALHY plus G-ALHN, G-ALHP for spares only.
Dakotas:	G-ANTD, G-AOGZ, G-APBC, G-AMSX, G-AOFZ, G-AGJV, G-AKJH.
Leopard Moth:	G-ACLL.

1963

As the New Year dawned, the flood-gates were opened to allow the reservations to come pouring through for the forthcoming summer season.

To ease the load and share the burden, it was announced on 28th January that the Company had granted a General Sales Agency to Mercury Airlines Limited of Manchester, for the Manchester area. In making the announcement the Chairman said: "Mercury Airlines have co-operated with us in the past and will continue to co-operate with us in the operation of certain of our scheduled services, in particular Derby-Birmingham-Isle of Wight and Derby-Birmingham-Newcastle, and we are very happy to strengthen our association with this Company. The public response to our services from Manchester to Ostend, Perpignan, Barcelona, Majorca, Klagenfurt and Genoa has been so gratifying that it is essential we have the best possible arrangements for processing the great many passengers we shall be flying from the area". At the same time a new scheduled service route was announced, Manchester-Ostend, with unlimited frequency, which would commence on 25th May.

Once again the Company were showing a picture of growth.

On Thursday 31st January, it was announced that each Monday and Wednesday from 1st April a new service from Carlisle to London (Gatwick) would operate. There had been a great demand for this service in the Carlisle area, and it commanded the general approval and whole-hearted support of the Carlisle Borough Council, owners of the airport.

The new 1963 Summer Timetable, now in the hands of all Derby Airways agents, showed several new services apart from Carlisle-London, including London-Belfast (using the new service and the Carlisle-Belfast service), Derby-Basle, Luton-Ostend, Manchester-Ostend, Derby-Rotterdam, and Cardiff/Bristol-Amsterdam. The Company Directors described it as "the most comprehensive time-table we have yet produced". It showed a wide network of services extending from Glasgow and Belfast in the North to Barcelona and Majorca in the South.

It was also publicly announced on 31st January that the new livery would be light and dark blue on a white fuselage with the large "DA" on the tail, as had been first seen on "HG" before Christmas. All the Company aircraft were eventually to have this livery.

In the United Kingdom in 1963 the only Argonaut operators were Air Links, a Gatwick-based carrier, and Derby Airways; and it was to the Company that the Ministry of Aviation (as it then was) turned for the training of its own Argonaut examiners. Captain Roy Westgate attended the Derby Airways Training School at Burnaston and underwent a two-week technical training course following which he commenced his flying conversion onto the type, his first flight being on the 13th February. He made several flying visits with the Company in the years to come and the Company Training Staff were to forge a useful liaison with the Civil Aviation Flying Unit which lasts to this day.

To introduce the new Carlisle-Gatwick service to the public, an inaugural flight was operated on Thursday 28th March, 1963. The City and County Borough of Carlisle were represented as were representatives of Carlisle Airport, the Travel Trade in the Carlisle area, Press, Radio and Television.

It was stated at the time that the air link between Carlisle and London was one for which there had long been an insistent demand. The new service would supplement the services from Carlisle to Jersey and Belfast inaugurated by the Company in 1962, and would materially assist in the development of the Carlisle Municipal Airport. It offered a non-stop flight of $2\frac{1}{4}$ hours to Gatwick, serving not only London and the Southern Home Counties but the Brighton and South Coast areas as well. In the reverse direction, it opened up a speedy link with the Carlisle area, the industrial region of West Cumberland, the Lake District, and perhaps more light-heartedly provided the swiftest access to the anvil of Gretna Green from London. In addition, an attempt was made to generate traffic through to Belfast from the South Coast by extolling the virtues of being able to fly from Gatwick instead of experiencing the tiresome journey of travelling to London Heathrow before being able to catch a plane to Northern Ireland. The aircraft to be used on the service was announced as the Derby Airways Pullman Douglas version of the DC-3, a phrase often used in the Company's advertising in those days. Where the connection was made between the interior of a Pullman railway coach and the interior of a 36-seater Dakota (in any event strictly speaking a C-47) is hard to imagine.

Speaking to the guests on board during the inaugural flight, Wing Commander Roxburgh said that he was very apprehensive about the new service. At that point in time, with only four days to go to the first public service, there were not any bookings, and unless there were any passengers for Monday 1st April, the service would not depart. It would means a loss of £1,000 per month to run a flight which did not justify its existence. If after a month more interest is not shown the service would be withdrawn. Mr. Michael Kidd, Carlisle Airport manager, was quite confident that the services would make good once the public realised its convenience.

April 1st, "April Fools Day" came, but no passengers arrived with it, and neither were there any for the only other flight scheduled during the week. During the second week of operation only 20 passengers used the service. On the first flight to arrive from London on 8th April was a London businessman, Mr. Peter Ryder, but upon arrival at the airport he found himself stranded until eventually he managed to obtain a lift from an aero club engineer who was going into Carlisle in his bubble car. He thought there ought to be some facilities for getting into the city once one had arrived at the airport. He was of course quite right; however it was not up to the Company to provide surface transport but for the Airport Authorities to make such arrangements.

Mr. Gordon Hepburn, Managing Director of Edenvale Travel Bureau in Carlisle, the Company's General Sales Agents in Cumbria, tried desperately to drum up traffic and interest in the service, but to no avail. He stated that due to certain Press and Television announcements a large proportion of the general public were under the misunderstanding that the new service had been withdrawn, and tried to impress upon people that the Company had not cancelled the services and were indeed giving it a very fair trial as they had the Carlisle-Belfast service. That was 5th April. On the 8th May the service was finally withdrawn. The Company had no alternative under the circumstances but to withdraw it. Perhaps it was a case of being over-publicised, but in the wrong sense. There can be little doubt that too much adverse publicity over the no-bookings for the first two flights did considerable harm, but similarly perhaps the Company did not do enough advertising in the first place, or perhaps not even the right kind of advertising.

The service has never been reinstated even to this day.

As with most airlines, Derby Airways issued its summer timetable effective 1st April each year, and so it was in 1963, but this particular April the Company issued its very first "Business Services Timetable" thus following an agreed policy of creating businessman's routes. The routes contained within this new document were:—

London (Gatwick)-Carlisle
Carlisle-Belfast
Derby-Leeds-Glasgow
Derby-Belfast
Derby-Birmingham-Newcastle
Manchester-Newcastle (actually a Mercury Airlines route)

Although, as has just been seen, the Gatwick-Carlisle service was a non-runner (perhaps even a non-starter), nevertheless the remaining programme was a beginning to a policy which was to reap great benefits, and also formed the framework for today's businessman's network stretching right into the Continent.

On 2nd April, it was announced that bookings from Welsh holidaymakers for Continental resorts had led the Company to mount the earliest-ever flight to Barcelona and Majorca from Cardiff (Rhoose) Airport. It was reported that staff at the airport had never known anything like it. Even enquiries for 1964 were coming in. From 1962 the services had had to be doubled to cope with the demand, and it was expected that a record 8,600 passengers would be flown to Barcelona and Palma, compared with 3,400 in 1962. There were to be four flights per week to Majorca, with five flights a week to Barcelona from April to October or November, all operated with Argonauts. However, as will be seen the whole operation, through no fault of the Company's, was to turn sour.

On Wednesday 3rd April, Derby Corporation announced officially that it would be joining the consortium to develop Castle Donington into an East Midlands Airport. It may be seen out of place in a history of British Midland Airways to delve into the origins and development of Castle Donington Airport, but when the reader reflects on the need for the airport being created by the generation of traffic brought about by the Company, no doubt this slight side-tracking will be accepted. It must also be remembered that the Company was still operating the Derby Municipal Airport at Burnaston; after all the main purpose now for the continued existence of the Company was to be an airline and not an airport operator. The coming into operation of Castle Donington could not come soon enough for Derby Airways.

The other authorities in the consortium were now insisting on the breaking up of the old R.A.F. runway and the laying of a completely new one. The capital cost of the whole project was by now budgeted at £1,000,000. It was agreed that Derby Town Council would in the meantime, prior to the transfer to Castle Donington, spend £6,852 to provide "adequate customs facilities" at Burnaston.

Expressing optimism for the Castle Donington scheme, Councillor Earnshaw Chairman of Derby Town Council Estates Committee announced that engineering work could start at a fairly early date. Negotiations so far had taken place with the other members of the consortium in a friendly atmosphere. Derbyshire County Council had been the first authority to announce that it would go into the consortium, whilst Nottinghamshire County Council were the first with a monetary motion.

Keeping within the £1 million target would mean deleting a number of items from the architect's report, but it would be possible to provide a "truly worthy airport" capable of serving the East Midlands for a considerable number of years. The members of the consortium were of the opinion that the old runway would have to be replaced, and the increased cost per consortium member over and above the original budget was nearly all accounted for by the breaking up of the old runway and its use as a base for the new one.

To maintain the £1 million, the length of the runway would have to be reduced from the planned 6,000 feet to 5,300 feet, but there would of course remain potential to expand. It was stated, however, that modern aircraft were tending to require less take-off length and it may be that the runway would never have to be extended What pious hopes. The need for a runway almost double the new planned length was to be clearly demonstrated on more than one occasion in the future.

Returning to the airline's story again, an event occurred on the 6th April that turned out to be the beginning of a long series of undesirable developments which were to culminate in the eventual withdrawal of the Company's interests in the Welsh and South West areas. An Argonaut, commanded by Captain S. D. Fenton, Operations Superintendent, was en route from Cardiff to Barcelona with 59 passengers on board, mostly schoolchildren, when first one, then another engine failed, one on each side. Both propellors were feathered, and the aircraft diverted to and made a safe landing at Bournemouth (Hurn) Airport. The passengers were ultimately transferred to two Dakotas and flown rather more slowly to Barcelona. The fault on the two engines was quickly diagnosed and the aircraft returned to service quite quickly, but it was to be some considerable time before the cause of the fault was to be diagnosed, and more of that later. Suffice it to say that the event was in reality a turning-point in the airline's history.

The Company's Joint Managing Director, Mr. "Ron" Paine, journeyed to London on 20th April to receive the Royal Aero Club Silver Medal for 1962 in recognition of his contribution to air racing. In 1962, Ron's cream Miles Speed

Six came in second in the King's Cup Air Race for the third year in succession. Unfortunately the King's Cup itself was to elude him forever.

On the 1st May Argonaut G-ALHS, with Captain Fenton in command, became the largest aircraft ever to land at Staverton when it flew in to take a party of industrialists, union officials and factory staff to Amsterdam for a two-day tour of Dutch industry. The visit had been arranged by the Gloucestershire and South Worcestershire Productivity Association as a contribution to National Productivity Year, and special customs facilities had been laid on so that, for the first time at Staverton, aircraft and passengers were able to clear direct for a foreign country. Although there were only twenty passengers in the party, the Argonaut was used by the Company in order to evaluate the aircraft's use in and out of Staverton. To see the public's reaction to the aircraft, the public were "cordially invited to come and have a look". In the event the aircraft was never used again through Staverton (other than the return flight) for either scheduled or charter flights as the Ministry of Aviation decided that the use of reverse thrust on landing could not be taken into account when calculating landing distance required, with the result that only 56 passengers could be on board, making the whole proposition uneconomical. Still, at least the effort had been made.

Argonaut G-ALHS on the apron at Staverton Airport.

On 3rd June, the Air Transport Licensing Board announced the granting to the Company of a scheduled service licence between Bristol and Cardiff to Valencia on a weekly basis, together with an I.T. licence for up to 16 flights a week with Argonauts between Cardiff, Bristol and Barcelona, Palma and Valencia, plus fortnightly I.T. flights from Cardiff, Bristol to Nice and Genoa, all licences for commencement of flights in May 1964. It now meant that the Company found themselves in a position of being able to cater for traffic demands and developments on these routes for some time to come, and the granting of scheduled service licences to Spain in particular was a great triumph for the Company, even though Spanish ratification of the licences on a bi-lateral basis had yet to come. However, as events were later to prove, the optimism was ill-founded.

Also on 3rd June the first direct service from Swansea to Ostend, with full Customs facilities at Swansea, was introduced. Although only 14 passengers were on board, it was a new route so no undue alarm was felt.

Another innovation, negotiated by the Company after discussions with the Continental railway authorities, was an air/rail (2nd class) ticket from Cardiff to Basle, via Luxembourg. Ordinarily a passenger to Basle would travel to London by rail, then fly to Basle, arriving in the very early hours of the morning, long before any connecting rail services operated to Switzerland and Austria, and at a combined fare of £30. By using the new facility, a passenger would leave Cardiff airport on Friday night at 2100, be served with supper en route, arriving at Luxembourg 0045 with a connecting coach to Luxembourg stations. From there he would take a train to arrive in Basle at 0638, connecting with most Continental rail departues, and all at a cost of £20.14.0d. ordinary fare or £18.10.0d. inclusive tour fare, both including coach transfers between Luxembourg airport and the station. The Company really introduced mass cheap travel facilities to Wales. What a pity events were to dictate that the fruits of all these seeds were not to be harvested.

Thursday 6th June saw the official formation of a joint committee "forthwith" to develop and administer Castle Donington. Not unnaturally the Company were delighted. The consortium now finally consisted of the County Councils of Derbyshire, Nottinghamshire and Leicestershire, the City of Nottingham and the County Borough of Derby.

A few days later, on 12th June, it was announced that architects and engineers had been instructed to go all out for an early start on the work. Schemes were now in course of preparation, and it was possible that specifications could be ready for tenders to be invited by the end of the year, although it was unlikely that work would commence until early in 1964. One matter still to be settled was whether to install pre-fabricated buildings, as a temporary measure or go ahead with more permanent structures. If temporary buildings were erected it meant that the airfield would become operational that much more quickly, and this would certainly be welcomed by Derby Aviation who were most anxious to use the Argonaut commercially from the area, a "luxury" the Company were denied at Burnaston.

With most airfields within the Company's network now having the use of

Customs facilities, it came as a further bitter blow at Staverton when it was announced in June that the facilities would not be granted for a party of Army Cadets travelling to Germany to train with the Rhine Army. The Company stated that they "looked upon this as another blow to the endeavours to secure improved facilities at the airport: the Custom authorities continue to adopt an unco-operative attitude; they just are not interested and seem to take the view that Bristol is near enough if concessions are wanted".

The cadet incident precipitated a violent row over the whole attitude of the Customs who were prepared, "as a concession", to clear parties of businessmen at Staverton but would not clear holidaymakers leaving on normal scheduled services. The Company were told that if sufficient traffic could be generated to prove the need then facilities would be provided, but not until this happened. As was pointed out, how could proper services be scheduled in order to prove the need when the facilities were not there in order for the need to be proved—a complete chicken—and egg situation. It was pointed out that the local customs officials were most helpful, but that it was the cold "blank wall" in London which was causing all the trouble. The only concession granted to holidaymakers were those passengers going to the Channel Islands when no out-going clearance was required, but return flights had to clear customs inbound at Bournemouth (Hurn).

The row went on for some two weeks or more until the afternoon of 19th July when the Town Clerk of Gloucester, received a telephone call from H.M. Customs in London to inform him that provided Derby Aviation forecasts for 1964 were equivalent in increase to the forecast for 1963 over 1962, H.M. Customs would, as an experiment for 1964, set up an "on call" customs facility at Staverton.

Thus was concluded a long and arduous series of applications and supporting evidence. Naturally all concerned were delighted at the turn of events. The Mayor of Cheltenham (Councillor A. E. Trigg), Chairman of the Cheltenham and Gloucester Joint Airport Committee, commented: "This is wonderful news. Our efforts have succeeded at last. Mr. Boggon, the Clerk to the Committee, has worked untiringly to achieve this. He has been up against obstacles all the way along".

During 1963, up to and including 19th July, Derby Airways moved 6,026 passengers on flights to and from Staverton where customs facilities were used. It was upon these figures that the latest plea to H.M. Customs had been made, and now, at long last, the battle was almost over.

The first airline office to open in Derby was at 24 St. Peters Churchyard on 1st July, when the Company opened its office there.

The fitting out of the new office was carried out entirely by Company staff, in co-operation with Midland Sign Services of Brick Street, Derby. The operation further strengthened a long-standing connection between the Company and Midland Signs, who for many years had been responsible for the lettering on the Company's aircraft familiar at all the major airports on the Continent. One wall of the new office was completely covered by a panoramic photograph of passengers boarding an Argonaut.

Later on in July, the 18th to be exact, it was announced that the Company had applied for a Class A (Scheduled Services) Licence from Derby and Staverton to Beauvais. It was stated that the application was in response to public demand from both areas for a service to Paris. It was hoped that the licence if granted would be for seven years from 1st March 1964. Why Beauvais was chosen and not Le Bourget is not known. The 40 km ride from Beauvais to Paris was not really appealing to a businessman travelling to Paris, as events with other carriers were to prove. However, with the move to the East Midlands Airport at Castle Donington now visible on the horizon, the application was at least a move in the right direction.

The first 3-engine Argonaut night landing to be carried out at Burnaston took place on the night of 28th July 1963. G-ALHY, commanded by Captain Cramp with First Officer (now Captain) H. I. S. Clarke and Engineer Officer T. Dethick as his crew, landed at Valencia from Birmingham, and during the turn-round check it was found that the exhaust system on No. 4 engine including the cross-over (which directed the exhaust gases to the side of the engine, away from the fuselage, thus cutting down considerably the noise level in the cabin), had disintegrated, and the hot exhaust was not very far from playing on an induction fuel line. There was no alternative but to leave the returning passengers at Valencia and three-engine ferry the aircraft back to Derby.

Upon landing at Burnaston (which under these conditions was a very short grass field), Cramp called for reverse thrust. To the initial surprise of both pilots the reverse guard could not be raised, and the end of the landing path was coming up at an alarming rate of knots. Simultaneously both of them realised that it was the No. 4 throttle lever in the wide open position that was causing the trouble, and both reached for it at the same time and closed it, wherepon Clarke raised the reverse guard and put the two inboard engines into maximum reverse. The aircraft stopped within fifty yards of the far airfield hedge, but all was well.

The cause of the exhaust disintegration was a further manifestation of the same trouble that had caused Captain Fenton to land on two engines at Bournemouth earlier in the year, but the cause had not yet been traced. This will be dealt with later on.

The Company had participated for many years now in school exchanges, particularly with France, where school children from both countries visited each other in their home towns. On Thursday 8th August, 150 school children were flown in two Argonauts, G-ALHY and G-ALHG, from Birmingham to Poitiers as part of an exchange organised by the Central Bureau for Educational Visits and Exchanges. Half of the children were French school children returning with their hosts of the previous fortnight. The cost to each child for the two weeks' holiday was only £15. The authority co-operating in France was the Union Regionale des Associations d'Eleves de l'Academie de Poitiers, who were responsible for the similar exchanges which had met with great success in 1960 and 1962.

The first pilot redundancy in the Company's history came to the public's notice on 9th August. There was, in spite of what had at first appeared to be a very good year indeed, a general decline in growth not only in Derby Airways but also in aviation generally throughout the world. British United had in fact given notice to 53 out of a total of 400 pilots, and the British Air Line Pilots Association had 150 pilots out of a membership of 3,000 out of work.

Once again the need for an all-year-round policy of work was being demonstrated, not only for the pilots but the Company as a whole. The whole work pattern was too summer-holiday oriented, giving a very high peak in the summer and a very low trough in the winter. The solution would eventually be found, but in 1963 it was still a very long way off.

During a training flight in a Dakota on 16th August, Captains Van den Elst and Fleming touched down at Burnaston but the brakes failed to slow the aircraft down (it was afterwards suspected that the wheels locked on the wet and greasy grass surface of the field). The end of the runway came up very fast, together with a lane and cars travelling along it. Partly in desperation and partly in instinct, the control column was pulled back. Much to everybody's amazement (both the crew and anxious on-lookers) the aircraft took to the air again—just—cleared the lane and ended up in a cornfield, undamaged and with a shaken but unhurt crew. A tractor was hitched up to the aircraft, two lorry-loads of gravel put into ditches running between the airfield and the aircraft, part of the hedge cut down, and one hour later the aircraft was back in the hangar being checked. That evening, it was back in service again.

A body-blow was delivered to the Company on 30th August when the Cardiff-based Inclusive Tour operator Hourmont Travel announced that it was transferring all of its requirements to Cambrian Airways. Ostensibly the reason was that Cambrian now had turboprop Viscount aircraft with the inference that they were more modern than the Company's Argonauts. The real reason was the fact that Hourmont passengers had borne the brunt of all the delays and diversions occurring to the Argonaut fleet, and this in itself was understandable; but the real cause of the trouble was not of the Company's making and was only just about to be diagnosed. These troubles have been referred to throughout this chapter, so perhaps now is the point within these narratives to explain the position fully.

The Rolls Royce Merlin 724/1C engines which powered the Argonaut began to lose power, the indication of the trouble being when listening to the engine as it shut down at the end of a flight. Engineers and crews would hear a noise similar to an old steam engine going chuff-chuff-chuff, and in fact crews would remark that they had another "chuffer" on their hands. The noise was caused by individual cylinders on the compression stroke, when the exhaust valves in that cylinder had had part of the valve head burnt away by the hot gases escaping during the exhaust stroke. During the compression stroke the mixture, instead of being compressed, was simply being pushed out of the cylinder through the sometimes quite large hole in the exhaust valve. This not only caused a severe loss in power, but the unburnt mixture would now ignite in the exhaust manifold when it came in contact with the exhaust gases from the other cylinders causing the disintegration of the exhaust system as was experienced by Captain Cramp's Argonaut at Valencia in July.

Not unnnaturally, a very great deal of concern was shown not only by the delayed passengers and the tour operators, but the Company and Rolls-Royce as the manufacturers. The problem had been tackled earlier on in the year in a two-pronged attack, one by the Company to see if the operating and engine handling technique was at fault, or the maintenance programme was at fault, and also by Rolls-Royce to see if the reason lay in either the manufacture or overhaul systems used by them.

To deal with the Company's efforts on the problem first, hundreds of instrument reading sheets were analysed to see if the crews were operating the engines within the parameters laid down by Rolls-Royce and the Company, whilst at the same time the operating techniques themselves were thoroughly scrutinised. Captain Cramp, as the Chief Training Captain, made many trips to the Rolls-Royce factory to discuss with the manufacturers all the pertinent details. Now it had been apparent for sometime that the power control charts acquired by the Company when the Argonauts arrived were far from adequate, and so during the discussions Cramp asked Rolls-Royce for some better charts. At that time a Danish operator of Argonauts was engrossed in conjunction with Rolls in producing such a chart, and the Company were promised copies of this when it was completed. In the event the Danes did not complete the charts, so Rolls-Royce gave Cramp some blueprint charts, containing all the necessary parameters and suggested that they be issued to the crews for power setting compilation. As the two charts were each approximately 18in wide by 2ft 9in long, it was considered that on a dark and stormy night the crews would find it impossible to use these charts and Rolls-Royce were told this. Rolls-Royce refused to be involved in this particular effort any more, but did say that if anything were produced based on these two blueprints they would want to approve it before it was issued. Captain Cramp took it upon himself to solve the problem, and some three months later produced the chart which was approved by Rolls-Royce and was in fact issued and used for as long as the Argonauts remained in service. This at least was one good side-effect that arose from the "chuffer" investigation.

BRITISH MIDLAND AIRWAYS LTD.
R.R. MERLIN 724/1C POWER CHART 950 B.H.P.
Capt. CRAMP

Press Alt.	R.P.M.	50°		60°		CHARGE TEMPERATURE 70°		80°	
		Max. M.P.	Av. F.F.	Max. M.P.	Av. F.F.	Max. M.P.	Av. F.F.	Max. M.P.	Av. F.F.
19000	2425	44.0	454	44.5	456	45.5	458	46.5	460
	2450	43.5	457	44.5	459	45.5	461	46.5	463
18000	2400	44.0	451	45.0	453	46.0	455	46.5	457
	2425	44.0	454	45.0	456	45.5	458	46.5	460
	2450	44.0	457	44.5	459	45.5	461	46.5	463
17000	2375	43.5	449	45.5	451	46.0	452	47.0	454
	2400	44.0	451	45.0	453	46.0	455	47.0	457
	2425	44.0	454	45.0	456	46.0	458	46.5	460
16000	2325	45.0	446	46.0	448	47.0	450	47.0	452
	2350	45.0	448	45.5	450	46.5	452	47.0	454
	2375	44.5	449	45.5	451	46.5	452	47.0	454

Alt	R.P.M.	M.P.	F.F.	M.P.	F.F.	M.P.	F.F.	M.P.	F.F.
15000	2300	45.5	443	46.5	445	47.0	447	47.0	447
	2325	45.0	446	46.0	448	47.0	450	47.0	452
	2350	45.0	448	46.0	450	47.0	452	47.0	454
14000	2250	46.0	439	47.0	441	47.0	443	47.0	443
	2275	46.0	441	46.5	443	47.0	446	47.0	446
	2300	45.5	443	46.5	445	47.0	447	47.0	447
13000	2225	46.5	437	47.0	439	47.0	441	47.0	441
	2250	46.0	439	47.0	441	47.0	443	47.0	443
	2275	46.0	441	47.0	443	47.0	446	47.0	446

F. S. GEAR

Alt	R.P.M.	M.P.	F.F.	M.P.	F.F.	M.P.	F.F.	M.P.	F.F.
12000	2400	42.5	429	43.5	430	44.5	432	45.0	433
	2425	42.5	431	43.5	432	44.0	434	45.0	435
	2430	42.0	432	43.0	433	44.0	435	44.5	437
1100	2375	43.0	427	44.0	429	45.0	430	45.5	432
	2400	43.0	429	43.5	430	44.5	432	45.5	433
	2425	42.5	431	43.5	432	44.0	434	45.0	435
10000	2350	43.5	425	44.0	427	45.0	428	46.0	430
	2375	43.0	427	44.0	429	45.0	430	46.0	432
	2400	43.0	429	44.0	430	44.5	432	45.5	433
	2425	42.5	431	43.5	432	44.5	435	45.0	435
9000	2300	44.0	422	45.0	424	46.0	426	46.5	428
	2325	44.0	424	44.5	425	45.5	427	46.5	428
	2350	43.5	425	44.5	427	45.5	428	46.0	430
	2375	43.5	427	44.0	429	45.0	430	46.0	432
8000	2275	44.5	420	45.5	422	46.0	424	47.0	426
	2300	44.0	422	45.0	424	46.0	426	47.0	428
	2325	44.0	424	45.0	425	45.5	427	46.5	428
	2350	43.5	425	44.5	427	45.5	428	46.0	430
7000	2250	45.0	418	45.5	420	46.5	422	47.0	424
	2275	44.5	420	45.5	422	46.5	424	47.0	42.6
	2300	44.5	422	45.0	424	46.0	427	47.0	428
	2325	44.0	424	45.0	425	46.0	427	47.0	428
6000	2225	45.5	416	46.0	418	47.0	420	47.0	422
	2250	45.0	418	46.0	420	47.0	422	47.0	424
	2275	45.0	420	45.5	422	46.5	424	47.0	426
5000	2200	46.0	414	46.5	416	47.0	418	47.0	420
	2225	45.5	416	46.5	418	47.0	420	47.0	422
	2250	45.0	418	46.0	420	47.0	422	47.0	424

Below 5,000 ft pressure altitude, use 2200 r.p.m. and 400lbs fuel flow.
Maximum manifold pressure for cruise—47.0 ins. hg.

This table is for 950 b.h.p. only. To obtain lower powers than this, a 25 b.h.p. reduction may be effected by a reduction of 50 r.p.m. in low gear, or by 1000 r.p.m. in high gear. These reductions are a working approximation only and the chart on the reverse should be used as a check.

On reaching desired altitude:—
1. Initially set the R.P.M. (in bold print).
2. Throttle to give the fuel flow consistent with the set R.P.M. and charge temperature.
3. Ensure that resultant manifold pressure does not exceed that stated, should it do so, throttle to give that M.P. and accept the resultant fuel flow.
4. When charge temp. has settled down, re-check engine settings.

N.P. Throttles should be fully open after engines have settled down, if not, decrease R.P.M. in steps of 25 as indicated, and re-set engine settings.
If the (bold print) R.P.M. will not allow the tabulated F.F. and M.P. to be obtained, increase R.P.M. in 25 steps as indicated.

In the meantime, Rolls-Royce were undertaking their own investigation. Their normal production monitoring technique was to "sample" engine components by taking them at random from the production line and subjecting them to exhaustive laboratory tests. The position had by now been reached where virtually complete engines were made up of components which had nearly all been laboratory checked before being released, and yet some of these engines were only lasting as little as 35 hours. Clearly something was drastically wrong and the answer had to be found, and found quickly, or else Derby Airways was going to be out of business through apparently faulty Rolls-Royce engines, which could never be allowed to happen. Rolls-Royce as an engine manufacturer had probably more to lose than the Company if the answer was not found.

Although it is jumping ahead in the story, it was not until the near-end of September that a Rolls-Royce "boffin" in Glasgow came up with the possible answer. He proffered the hypothesis that an additive used in oil used by the Company (and approved by Rolls-Royce) was forming a shellac on the valve stem which, when the valve became hot during engine operation, became sticky thus preventing the valves, the exhaust valves in particular, from rotating due to "valve bounce". The problem now was that it would take at least two months of laboratory tests to prove this hypothesis, and could the two companies wait this long? Frank Marshall, Derby Airways Chief Engineer, considered not and immediately telephoned Derby from Glasgow giving instructions for all of the Company's aircraft, Dakotas as well as Argonauts, to be drained of the detergent oil used forthwith, and for this to be replaced by the well-tried non-detergent previously used by the Company. The results were dramatic. Almost overnight the trouble ceased, not only with the Merlin engines but with the Pratt & Whitney engines also. In these latter engines on the Dakota, broken valve-heads had been a problem, and this now ceased. In all some 42 engines had had to be prematurely changed due to the oil problems.

As a result of the above, a joint action by Derby Airways and Rolls-Royce against the oil company was settled satisfactorily out of court. However, the damage to the Company's reliability and reputation had been done, and it was beyond repair. No amount of money out of court could restore the bad name the Company had acquired in South Wales and the West Country as a result of this problem. As a consequence Hourmont transferred his business and Cambrian Airways, who up to this time were really hard put to find sufficient good work, were handed all of the results of the Company's hard pioneering work almost on a plate; forcing Derby Airways ultimately to cease virtually all operations in that area.

Not all flights with the Argonaut in 1963 were dramatic, of course, and one flight ended amusingly as Captain Cramp and his crew found out in Jersey on 22nd September. Flying northbound from Palma to Birmingham, Cramp had just crossed the French coast at Dinard when he heard another Company Argonaut, commanded by Captain Eric Lines, flying southbound. Knowing that a large part of the U.K. was becoming fog-bound he asked Captain Lines, who was en route from Birmingham, what the weather was like there, to receive the reply that the best thing to do was to divert right now into Jersey. Thanking Eric Lines for his advice, Cramp immediately called Jersey, to discover to his horror that they had just ceased operation for the day, and in fact it was only by chance that Cramp's call had just been received. However, when hearing of the circumstances, Jersey immediately opened up an Air Traffic Control watch and allowed the Argonaut to land.

Having taxied up to the apron and shut down all four engines, the crew were told to stay on board with all passengers, as all the Customs and Immigration officials at Jersey had quite naturally gone home, and although requests had gone out for them to return it was at that precise moment too early. After waiting ten minutes or so and having explained the situation to the passengers, the crew began to get anxious about the aircraft's battery power as all the lights in the aircraft were still on ships batteries only, there being no airport staff around to connect a ground power unit to the aircraft. In the end Captain Cramp and the Engineering Officer, Roy Dethick opened the crew door, threw out an escape rope and slithered down it; they walked across the apron and found some passenger steps which the then proceeded to push, covered in confusion and gold braid, to the aircraft to enable the passengers to disembark.

At this point some customs officers arrived and the air traffic control officers, having now officially shut the airfield down, came down to see if they could help. The aircraft cabin staff retrieved some dry stores (coffee, biscuits, sugar, etc.) from the aircraft, together with an urn of hot water and some blankets, thus enabling the children to be kept warm with the blankets (it was midnight by now and quite cold) and all to have a hot drink. Having cleared the passengers in, the customs officials now set to with the A.T.C. officers, the crew and Derby Airways staff (who had heard the Argonaut making its approach whilst on their way home and, realising what had happened, had about-turned and returned to the airport), to arrange accommodation for the passengers. After some 1½ hours all but four had been accommodated. At that time of the night transport to hotels and guest houses was a problem, but it was overcome by the co-operation of all concerned, not least the passengers themselves, some of whom went in police cars and even a Black Maria to their accommodation. An exercise in good-humoured co-operation had ended what could have been a tiresome day all round. The passengers eventually arrived in Birmingham at 1325 the following day, quite content.

On 15th October it was announced that the Company's Commercial Manager, Captain "Terry" Mayo, was leaving the airline and returning to the Army where he would be rejoining the Royal Engineers movement control and transportation branch in his old rank of Captain. Terry had not been too happy in recent months and in particular had had many confrontations with Hourmont Travel over the continual delays with the Argonauts; and in reality he felt he had had enough. His successor was not announced at the time and in fact the Company had been caught unawares by his resignation and so were unable yet to name a successor.

On 26th October, Mr. R. R. Paine, until now Joint Managing Director with

Wing Commander H. A. Roxburgh, became sole Managing Director, with the Wing Commander remaining as Chairman.

November saw the announcement in Cardiff of the Company's plans for 1964. All services were to be scheduled services, for both holiday-makers and businessmen. The services mentioned were Cardiff-Valencia, Palma, Barcelona, Ostend, Amsterdam and Genoa, of which the Valencia and Genoa routes were new, the Genoa route being the first ever scheduled service from Wales to Italy. The Company stated that they were highly delighted with the public response to the 1963 services, when the traffic from Cardiff had increased by more than 100 percent. By providing its own handling unit at Cardiff under the Station Manager Mr. R. A. Lisney, an improved service to the public had resulted and in 1964 both the staff and the facilities would be augmented. The midweek night tourist fares had proved very popular, and 1964 would see them offered on all routes except Ostend. A further innovation would be a "Fly Now—Pay Later" scheme underwritten by Lombard Banking Ltd. who by now had a large stake in the Company, mainly due to the Argonaut purchase deal. The same routes and facilities out of Cardiff would of course apply to Bristol, but the handling at Bristol Airport would be carried out by Dan-Air Ltd.

The new Commercial Manager, to replace Terry Mayo, was announced on 11th November. It was Captain B. G. Cramp, until now the Company's Chief Training Captain. The appointment came as a complete surprise to Cramp as he had not been involved in any commercial business whatsoever, but the Board of Directors considered that his ability and application to work were what they required. Having accepted the appointment, he immediately sat down and read through every enclosure in every file in the Commercial Manager's office.

Whilst involved in the task of reading through all the Commercial Manager's files, Cramp was amazed to find that an application for the Company to become signatory to the IATA Multilateral Interline Agreement on Traffic, Baggage, Cargo and Cargo Claims Agreements had been commenced but had been allowed to "hang in mid-air". As the emphasis was to be on more and more businessmen's routes, with associated interline carriage on other carriers, the cessation of the application was more than amazing, and Cramp soon had this rectified with the result that the Company became a signatory in April 1964, and the Agreement took effect on 1st May 1964.

On 27th November the Company Chairman, Wing Commander Roxburgh, succeeded Mr. Harold Bamberg, Chairman of British Eagle International Airlines, as President of the British Independent Air Transport Association (BIATA). On 3rd December, "Roxy" gave some straight-from-the-shoulder talking about the Company's past and future operations at a cocktail party given to the Press and Travel Agents in Cardiff. He admitted that the operations in and out of Rhoose were not up to the standard the Company required, and part of the blame was put on too-tight scheduling. However, for 1964 larger buffers between flights were being allowed and a much better job for that year was promised. (The trouble caused by the engine oil was not mentioned, and it is only now that the real truth can be told). The Chairman went on to say that the cabin service, already acknowledged to be of a high standard, was to be further improved.

Almost as a belated Christmas present (or maybe it was a New Year's present), it was announced on 28th December that the new Joint Airport Committee for the East Midlands Airport at,Castle Donington was to provide £137,000 for accommodation for the Company at the new airport. The money was to be spent on a new hangar, workshops and administrative premises, and the Company would pay an undisclosed rental to cover debt charges, maintenance and other charges. In addition a further £7,000 was to be spent on the renovation of an existing T2 type hangar only half of which would be (and still is) used by the Company.

So ended another year, one full of event and promise but also tinted with sorrow in some respects. A lot remained to be done if the transfer to the new airport, when it finally came, was to be carried out smoothly, and the loss of the Welsh traffic from Hourmont had to be made up. In spite of everything, 1963 had in reality been a good year.

The fleet as at 31st December was:

Dakotas: G-ANTD, G-AOGZ, G-APBC, G-AMSX, G-AOFZ,
               G-AGJV, G-AGJH
Argonauts: G-ALHS, G-ALHY, G-ALHG
Leopard Moth: G-ACLL

1964

As yet another New Year dawned, Derby Airways began to do battle with the coming season's requirements. Even now, and although the policy of businessmen's service was beginning to become more effective, it was still the summer holiday traffic that took pride of place in the Company's thinking. For the New Year, and in keeping with the so-far-kept tradition (it could not really be looked upon as a policy) of introducing at least one new service each year, it was announced that a new service from Luton to Belfast would be inaugurated in the coming year. In addition it was the intention to introduce the Argonaut on the Luton-Jersey service to cope with demand. With the granting of Customs facilities at Staverton, increased frequencies from there to both the Channel Islands and Ostend were announced in view of the upsurge in bookings arising from the fact that en route stops for customs clearance were now abolished. A new freight service from Cardiff and Bristol to Amsterdam was announced as was a Derby and Birmingham to Rotterdam freight service (although neither of them was in fact ever operated).

In order to cope with the sales demand, and also to ensure that the future would be catered for properly, Captain Cramp laid down, for the first time in the Company's history, proper boundaries of sales responsibility for the various regions. As was mentioned in an earlier chapter, although geographical boundaries had been allocated previously, the definition and delineation of the areas was far too loose with the result that salesmen left some areas completely alone, thinking that their neighbour colleague would be covering that particular area, whilst the colleague was thinking exactly the same. That hole had now been plugged.

Unfortunately, as the above announcements were being made, the Air Transport Licensing Board announced its decision to refuse the licence applied for from Derby and Staverton to Beauvais. In the event this was to prove non-embarrassing, as will be seen later.

As possibly a counter to the morale-effect of the ATLB's announcement, the Company announced publicly on 6th January that Wales would see the Cardiff/Bristol to Valencia and Cardiff/Bristol to Genoa services start in the year. The battle was on.

Some years previously, the Company had bought as a "Company Hack" a beautifully preserved De Havilland Leopard Moth, G-ACLL, and this the reader will have noted in the aircraft list appearing at the end of each chapter. Now up until this time "LL" had only been used spasmodically by the Directors and a little more frequently for positioning aircrews and spare parts arund. Now the new Commercial Manager found the aircraft of increasing value in the making of business calls which were outside the Company's own service network. He could often be seen flying the Leopard Moth to Staverton, Bristol, Cardiff, Birmingham and even to London where he would land at Elstree (remember the Flying Training Division of the Company was based there), and then cadge a lift or a taxi to the nearest Underground Station and so in to the City.

The Leopard Moth concerned was in fact the oldest of three such aircraft surviving. It had been "modernised" in a number of respects, being equipped with a self-starter, a Fairey-Reed metal propeller, a Chipmunk tail-wheel in place of the normal tail-skid, and a Standard Radio and Telephones STR12D V.H.F. radio. The wings could be folded back for easier stowing in limited hangar space, but the delight of all who flew it was the lever on the starboard side of the cockpit which, when pushed down, would turn the wheel-strut fairings at 90° to the airflow to act as airbrakes! Very effective they were as well. No navigation aids were fitted, but the aircraft cruised very slowly, and the M1 was being extended northwards so who wanted nav. aids? Cramp's main problem when he first flew the aircraft was to accept 40 mph as a landing speed. After flying Argonauts he found that speed far too low for comfort. He still acknowledged, however, that "LL" was a delight to fly.

Early on in January Mr. Dennis Aldridge, Charter Manager, approached Captain Cramp and informed him that the committee set up to run Enniskillen airfield in County Fermanagh, N. Ireland, had written to ask whether Derby Airways would be interested in running a service to the area. Aldridge himself had seen the airfield during a visit to the area in the previous year, and he thought there might be some potential there. After some deliberation, Cramp agreed to visit the area and take Aldridge with him. So it was that in mid-January the pair flew to Belfast and then hired a car for the three hour drive to Enniskillen.

The country in the area of the town, situated between Upper and Lower Lough Erne, is beautiful and attracts thousands of tourists a year, in addition to the pilgrims who made their annual pilgrimage to the shrine on a small island in Lough Derg in County Donegal. These facts, coupled with the decision to stop the steamer service from Glasgow to Londonderry on which many Irish and Scots had relied for their annual trek to Donegal, Sligo and Bundoran, attracted Aldridge and Cramp to the idea. Mr. Ian Cooper, who owned the Imperial Hotel in Enniskillen entertained them both to dinner, and explained the situation to Cramp. The following morning Cramp saw the airfield for himself for the first time. His heart fell, for only one runway of the wartime airfield was in use, and to use this the sheep would have to be driven off first. At the north end of the runway someone had decided to rip up one complete section of concrete, but at the south end the ground rose sharply and sitting right in the middle of the take-off path, on top of the hill, was a church. There was no doubt that the Argonaut would not be visiting the airfield of St. Angelo, but the Dakota would just, but only just, be able to.

Whilst in the area Cramp and Aldridge carried out a proper survey of the region, assessing its remoteness, and therefore the desirability of a service to the area, together with a look at the light industry which could take advantage of the service should it be mounted. Upon their return to Derby, Cramp put in his recommendation to the Board that the service should be mounted and the licence applied for immediately. In the meantime the airport committee were informed of the recommendation, and the fact that a tower radio and a radio beacon for navigational aid would have to be installed before a public transport service could be authorised by the Ministry of Aviation.

By the end of January it was obvious that once again the bookings were going very well indeed. In fact the Channel Islands bookings from Staverton were 75% up on 1963, and the Ostend service bookings from the same airport were well ahead of anticipated bookings. 29th January also saw the Derby/Birmingham-Newcastle service increased to three a week; on Tuesday, Wednesdays and Thursdays.

On 7th February, and in spite of the initial optimism shown for these services, the routes from Cardiff/Bristol to Valencia and Genoa had to be cancelled owing to lack of support. The licences had been applied for and obtained mainly to meet the requirements of Hourmont Travel in Cardiff, but it will be remembered that, owing to the repetitive engine troubles with the Argonaut, Hourmont had transferred his business to Cambrian at the end of 1963. Hourmont's requirements remained high for 1964, but Cambrian remained on the Valencia and Genoa routes, whilst the Company withdrew. It was not appreciated at the time, but the beginning of the rot had arrived.

The recommendation to the Derby Airways Board to operate the Enniskillen service was taken up and the licence applied for, and 17th February saw the public announcement on all this. The initial intention was for the existing Luton-Derby-Belfast service to be extended to Enniskillen, and also that the Derby-Leeds Bradford-Glasgow service should also be extended to Enniskillen with one aircraft routing Derby-Leeds/Bradford-Glasgow-Enniskillen-

Belfast-Derby-Luton and the other aircraft commencing at Luton and operating the opposite way round, terminating at Derby from Glasgow and Leeds/Bradford.

The promised and long-awaited on-call Customs facilities at Staverton came into effect on 21st February, when a customs official travelled up from Avonmouth to clear a charter flight to Paris. The aircraft carried a party of pupils from Whitefriars School, Cheltenham, and their parents, in the charge of the Headmaster Father J.E. Maguire, to see the England v France Rugby match.

For some time now Frank Marshall, Operations Engineer, and Captain Cramp Commercial Manager, had been concerned at the number of rumours which always fly around any organisation, but which within the Company seemed to be getting more and more out of hand. Having discussed the problem in some depth, they decided that its root lay in a lack of communications between Company and staff, and to effect a cure the pair started a staff news sheet, known in the first instance as the Derby Airways News Letter. To be published monthly, it was hoped that the Newsletter would be both informative and at the same time entertaining.

The first edition, noted that the Engineering Division were currently engaged in a major repair to Dakota G-AOGZ. This aircraft suffered a serious fire in the fuselage during major overhaul. At first this appeared to be a big set-back to prospects of the aircraft being ready for the 1964 season, but with determined effort by all concerned a plan of action was immediately instigated. The aircraft had been undergoing a Check IV overhaul when a flash-fire occured in its belly, the fire originating in the area of the centre-section and travelling back towards the tailplane, flashing upwards into the toilet compartment (fortunately the toilet had been removed) and continuing forwards. Two men working in the fuselage jumped out with clothes on fire and these were extinguished by their colleagues. In the process the aircraft's rear fuselage had been badly damaged and in parts the stressed-skin had actually melted.

After a careful survey of the damage, it was apparent that the quickest method of affecting a repair was to replace the damaged portion of the fuselage, the problem being where to locate either a fuselage or a complete aircraft at the right price. Fuselages were located in Hong Kong, Switzerland, and the U.S.A, but after some remarkable negotiations by Mr. R. R. Paine a complete Dakota G-AMZE was purchased from Smith's Instruments and flown to Derby by Captain Fenton. The rear fuselage of this aircraft was removed and fitted to the fuselage of G-AOGZ, thus replacing the damaged area.

Engineering's motto of "miracles in five minutes, the impossible takes a little longer" appeared to be true in this case.

Friday the 13th, an ominous combination of day and date in most people's minds. Such a combination occured in March 1964, and it was on this date that the Company made yet another tiny piece of aviation history by operating the first commercial service ever into St. Angelo, Enniskillen. Laid on primarily as a proving flight, a party of keen anglers who were members of the Slack and Parr Sports Club were going to taste the delights of uninhibited fishing in Ulster where there is no coarse fishing season at all. The Company had approached Slack and Parr Ltd., of Kegworth, very near to the new East Midlands Airport, with a proposition to fly the angling section of the Sports Club into County Fermanagh at cost price to the Company. It is of interest to note that as a direct result of this particular visit Slack and Parr ultimately built a factory at Enniskillen. However, back to Friday 13th.

Dakota G-AOFZ, commanded by Capt. "Andy" Oates, and with Captain Cramp as his co-pilot, departed Derby at 1615 on the 13th bound for Enniskillen direct. The weather situation was not good, due to fog. All of the airfields in the Republic of Ireland were out in fog, as were Prestwick, Glasgow and Edinburgh. The only airfields which were in fact open were Enniskillen, Belfast, and the Isle of Man, and even as the flight progressed Belfast went out in fog. Now for this particular operation a temporary radio link had been set up at Enniskillen, manned by an air traffic controller loaned for the occasion from Belfast. Unfortunately this radio link did not function, so all instructions to the aircraft were passed by telephone from Enniskillen to Belfast and thence by radio to the aircraft. By the time "FZ" arrived overhead Enniskillen the weather situation over the rest of the country was decidedly nasty.

Those anxiously waiting on the ground for the first flight heard the aircraft pass overhead, indeed heard it turn away towards the northwest until the sound slowly disappeared and silence reigned. The air traffic controller appeared on the war-time control tower balcony and pistol in his hand, pointed it to the sky. He pulled the trigger and there was—a click. He re-entered the control tower, appeared again and pointed his pistol again at the sky. Again a click, but no flash. Angrily he dashed back again into the control tower and reappeared a third time on the balcony with his Verey pistol pointing skywards. It was not needed; "FZ" was on the point of touching down.

As they touched down, the aircraft crew were relieved to see that some thoughtful person had removed all the sheep from the runway, but it was not until the landing run was almost complete that the biggest surprise was revealed to them. The crowds that had gathered to see the arrival must have been in their thousands. As someone later remarked, it was as if the whole of County Fermanagh had turned out to witness the event.

In mid-March it was announced that Mr. E. C. Dyer, Southampton Airport Commandant, was to be appointed East Midlands Airport Director with effect from 1st May 1964. The work on the airport construction had already begun in mid-March, and a target date for the opening of the new airport had been set as 1st April, 1965. What fool chose April Fool's Day as an opening date? A farce involving the Company was to occur on the opening day, as will be seen.

By mid-March 1964, the volume of freight traffic was increasing by leaps and bounds, and bearing in mind the intention to operate the Derby-Birmingham Amsterdam night freighter in the coming winter, it was obvious that a collection and delivery service would have to be instituted. At first, all such collection and delivery was given to the local road hauliers, in fairness to their livelihood. However, it soon became obvious that this method was far from satisfactory as the trucks would arrive late if at all, and very often when the Cargo Manager,

Keith Lawton tried to arrange collection and delivery he would meet with the reply that no capacity was available and would he try again next week. As a result of all this an application was made to the Traffic Commissioners in Nottingham for a Road Haulage 'B' licence restricted to a radius of 50 miles centred from the airfield, the centre to be transferred to East Midlands Airport upon transfer of the operation to that field. The application was successful, and the collection and delivery service was immediately put into operation. It has proved both necessary and successful ever since.

A publicity meeting was held at Burnaston on Thursday 9th April, when it was disclosed that the overall booking situation at that point in the year was not as good as it had been in the previous year. Mrs. Everett, the Reservations Manageress, stated that the Company was 1213 bookings down on the Jersey service over the same time last year, and after a lot of discussion it was agreed that the most likely reason for this downfall was that Dakotas were being used in competition with B.E.A's Viscounts leaving Birmingham. At the same meeting, Cramp, as Commercial Manager, had tried to push home his philosophy of the businessman services first during the week, and the holiday makers' services at the weekends, on the assumption that the holiday maker, with time to spare, could fit in with a businessman's service midweek, and that on the other hand the businessman wanting to travel at weekends would of necessity fit in with the holidaymakers' traffic.

One interesting comparison with the present day is the amount of money allocated to advertising. The total amount allocated to the Commercial Manager for advertising in 1964 was £9,500, later raised to £11,500 to promote the introduction into service of the Handley Page Herald. Eric Sample stated at the meeting on 9th April that in the previous six months £809 had been spent in the Birmingham area.

Avro Anson 1A G-AMDA (Aviation Photo News/B. Stainer).

In April, David Ogilvy of the Flying Training Division announced that the Anson I G-AMDA which it will be remembered was employed by the now defunct Derby Aero Surveys, had been restored into its original Royal Air Force colour scheme as N4877 VX-F, and was operating at the Skyfame Museum at Staverton. (In passing it may be of interest to note that another Anson I was operated by Derby Aero Surveys, G-AIPA, and this aircraft carried out surveys in both Italy and Turkey; however, as this history is basically that of the parent Company, the Aero Surveys story has not been dealt with in much detail, but the note is made above for the enthusiast).

Also in April the Company completed, some eighteen months before the mandatory requirement date, the major modification programme to the Dakota wing structures. This modification introduced heavy wing attachment angles and doublers to the outer wings and centre section. Although carried out early it was considered desirable to complete the embodiment at the soonest possible moment, to ensure that the Company's aircraft were always at the highest possible structural standard. The same standard applies equally well today and is a tribute to both the Company's policies in this respect and to the Engineering Division's approach to their responsibilities.

The work in hand at Castle Donington was progressing nicely in April of 1964, with the old wartime runways almost completely ripped up, to be used as hard-core for the new runway about to be laid down. In the meantime, the Company were still managing and operating the airport at Burnaston and were longing for the day when they would become airline operators only.

The old war-time runways at Castle Donington being ripped up. The North-South runway is in the foreground with the present main runway visible.

With the forthcoming transfer from Burnaston to East Midlands Airport drawing nearer to reality at a gathering pace, it became more and more obvious that the time had come for re-equipment with a modern turbo-prop aircraft, and so the evaluation exercises began. On Wednesday 27th May, Hawker Siddeley sent their demonstration HS748, G-ARAY to Burnaston for all to see and, where appropriate, to fly. Certainly the single-engine performance was most impressive. In the afternoon it was hoped that the engineers (other than the management engineers who had inspected the aircraft in the morning) would have had the opportunity to really inspect the aircraft, but unfortunately G-ARAY had to fly to London to be ready for H.R.H. The Duke of Edinburgh, who was to fly in it to Yeovilton to open the new Fleet Air Arm museum and be present for the 50th anniversary review of that Service's foundation in Yeovilton, on the following day.

Now obviously the 748 was not the only turbo-prop to be looked at, and following the 748 demonstration a cost and operational evaluation and comparison between the 748 and the Viscount 798 was made. The committee who carried out the exercise was Captain Cramp for the operational and commercial aspects, Frank Marshall who covered the engineering requirements, and Allen Clay, cost accountant (Allen had joined the Company earlier in the year in the Company's first serious attempt at cost analysis).

It will be noted that, in all of the deliberations, the Handley Page Herald had not even been considered, in spite of that type's appeal to the Company in earlier years, and yet it was to be the Herald that was finally chosen. It is also interesting to note that the committee's recommendations to the Board in 1964 was the Viscount, but it was not until 1967 that the type was finally acquired and operated.

Late in May, the A.T.L.B. awarded the Enniskillen licence for a period of two years in the first instance, and it was hoped to extend the existing Belfast services to Enniskillen in mid-June, but the Glasgow to Enniskillen service would have to await the outcome of a new application at that time before the Licencing Board, although it was anticipated that the licence would be issued without a further hearing.

Midland Airport Services at Birmingham had a justifiable complaint (to a certain extent) in June when they were presented with a set of aircraft steps for passengers which had become surplus to requirements at Staverton. The R.A.C. were asked to supply a route for the lorry making the delivery, which added 70 miles on to the normal route as low bridges had to be avoided.

However, in the process of delivery three bridges were scraped and at a fourth the steps actually got stuck under the bridge on the motorway, and the hand rails had to be "removed". Upon final delivery at Birmingham it was reported that "Viv" Woodhams the Station Manager, and some of his staff shed tears at the sight. Having waited ages for some much needed passenger steps, just when everything seemed to be in sight, here they were being presented with what was almost a ruin. However, true to type, Viv and his colleagues set to work and repaired the steps, which eventually did go into service.

A bone of contention among airlines for many years had been the fact that bonded stores, i.e. whisky, brandy, gin, cigarettes, tobacco and so forth, could only be uplifted in limited quantities, the actual amount being based on the seating capacity of the aircraft, including crew. Today, the income from bar sales to passengers makes a sizeable proportion to any airline's profit, and to restrict bar sales in any form was a dampener on all carriers, not to mention the irate passenger reaction when he or she could not be provided with what was required. During his term of office as President of the British Independent Air Transport Association, therefore, the Company Chairman tackled this problem with gusto and was finally rewarded with a capitulation by H.M. Customs, so that on Monday, 1st June, 1964 all restrictions on the uplift of stores for sale on board aircraft were removed. It is not recorded as to whether or not the State-owned Corporations acknowledged that the Indpendents had helped to raise their income.

Monday, 15th June saw the Leopard Moth airborne from Derby to Newtownards in Northern Ireland, en route to Enniskillen, with the Commercial Manager at the controls. Now Capt. Cramp was the first to admit to more than a slight degree of apprehension at flying across the Irish Sea (or any other sea for that matter) on one tiny engine (after all, he was used to flying a multi-engined airliner with all modern aids). This particular Monday was also the subject of a particularly nasty depression, so Cramp elected to fly around the south west corner of Manchester Control Zone, thence up to Blackpool and along the coast line to Stranraer, thus reducing the sea-crossing to a 22-mile stretch between Stranraer and Newtownards. Dennis Aldridge accompanied Cramp on this trip, and sat in the passenger seat behind Cramp quite contentedly until some forty minutes after becoming airborne, when in the teeth of the gale, he realised that the first turning point had not even been reached, and that it was going to be a long trip. At this point Dennis decided that a cigarette was long overdue and proceeded to "light up", much to the alarm and horror of Cramp. Pointing very energetically in the direction of the two fuel tanks in the wing roots just above their heads, and to the fabric covering of the aircraft, Cramp made Dennis extinguish the offending cigarette immediately. Three hours and thirty minutes after take-off, the Leopard Moth landed at Newtownards, and after refuelling departed for Enniskillen, arriving one hour and twenty minutes later.

Leopard Moth G-ACLL landing at Newtownards, Co. Antrim.

79

On the return trip the following day, Cramp was checking the oil contents of the Leopard Moth when in transit through Newtownards when to his horror an elephant's trunk appeared at his right side. Turning round he saw the owner, a baby elephant being used in a publicity film by Short Bros. & Harland Ltd., for their Skyvan project. A keen photographer snapped this incident and subsequently the photograph was published, with suitable comment, in Roger Bacon's "Straight and Level" in Flight International.

At a meeting in Manchester early in July Colin Jones, Company Representative, in a group discussion with staff from other airlines operating out of Manchester, heard with pride the comments on the marvellous service given on a recent charter to Hanover, both by the flight deck and cabin staff. The hostess in particular had helped the Company much more than any other medium of advertising and, as far as Manchester was concerned, all present at the meeting agreed that Derby Airways was a First Class airline. Praise indeed coming from airline staff at Manchester.

Thursday 2nd July, saw Dakota G-AOGZ depart Glasgow for Enniskillen, for the inaugural service on that route. The crew were Captain J. Shaw, First Officer R. Wheatley and Air Hostess L. Robson.

A consignment of freight from Enniskillen to Nottingham was uplifted on this the first scheduled air service from St. Angelo airport. It was announced during the trip that the first Belfast-Enniskillen service would operate on Monday, 13th July, operating every Monday and Wednesday, whilst each Thursday the Glasgow-Enniskillen service would operate, commencing Thursday, 16th July. The first Glasgow service finally operated as a tremendous success, with 32 passengers on a 36 seat aircraft and all the time the Enniskillen services were operated, the Glasgow one was a success, but Belfast-Enniskillen proved to be a non-starter.

The I.A.T.A. Multi-lateral Interline Agreement which came into effect as far as the Company were concerned on 1st May was, in early July going reasonably well, with the following carriers having concurred in the application:—Aer Lingus, B.E.A., B.O.A.C., British United, Canadian Pacific Airways (cargo only), Cathay Pacific, Central African, Iberia, Lufthansa, El Al (not cargo), K.L.M., M.E.A., P.A.A., Sea-Board World, Sabena, Trans Australian, U.T.A., and United Airlines of America. The Agreement would allow the Company to, sell, by prior agreement, its own tickets on those routes operated by concurring carriers, thus allowing the standard I.A.T.A. discounts to be applied. These "Interline" contributions are a considerable source of income to any carrier.

The Company also issued a statement at this time outlining its policy insofar as Castle Donington was concerned, and that was to provide facilities for both passengers and cargo whereby any destination in the world could be reached without the necessity of travelling to London or Manchester. This aim would be achieved by using Interline Agreements, particularly with transfers taking place at Amsterdam, Dublin, and Glasgow. At Castle Donington itself work was going on at a cracking pace, and in mid-July the Terminal Building foundations were laid and half of the Company's administrative block was already completed.

At this time Capt. Cramp used to take the P. R. O., Eric Sample, over to Castle Donington in the Leopard Moth once a month in order for him to take photographs of the construction work in progress, as will be seen from the photographs in the book.

With the imminence of the transfer to the new airport, it was necessary to make application to I.A.T.A. for a 3-letter designator for the airport, and in view of the public authorities involved, and in order of the contribution towards the airport, the Company requested that the designator be "DNL" (Derby, Nottingham, Leicester). Unfortunately the American military objected to this English civil airport designator so I.A.T.A. suggested "LDN", but this was too close to being misinterpreted as London, so the Company rejected this, as they did "LND" for the same reason. Now, without any further discussion I.A.T.A. allocated "CDD" (Castle Donington, Derby). The fact that Castle Donington is factually situated in Leicestershire escaped everyone's notice in I.A.T.A., but the designator was accepted.

An amusing story is associated with the use by the Company of 3-letter designators in those days when, before CDD was finally allocated, all concerned were using at the time, quite wrongly EMA (East Midlands Airport) and in writing out future timetables referred to EMA—IOW service (for the Isle of Wight). One very quick-witted travel agency wrote in to congratulate the Company on being the first British Independent carrier to break into the American domestic market by operating on the route Ellamar Alaska to Iowa City (EMA to IOW).

Consideration had been going on for some time regarding a change of name for the Company in time for the move to the East Midlands Airport, it being felt that the existing name was too parochial. It was therefore announced in mid-July that, with effect from 1st October, the name would be changed to BRITISH MIDLAND AIRWAYS LTD.

In mid-August, the new accommodation at Staverton came into use. It consisted of three rooms, one being utilised as a general office, one (separated from the first by a cedar wood counter) was converted into a reception room for people making enquiries, and the third became the Station Manager's (Mr. Sullivan) office. A fourth room, shared with the Airport Corporation, housed the teleprinter. Staverton had now become a very pleasant little station indeed.

Some time previously, the Commercial Manager had proposed to the Board of Directors that a new all-cargo scheduled service should be operated from Derby-Birmingham-Amsterdam in the coming winter. Cargo figures as a whole were on the up and up and the new service, if operated, would be nicely settled in by the time the move to Castle Donington came about. Tacit approval to this new venture was given by the Board, and Cramp had many discussions with K.L.M.-Royal Dutch Airlines about the service, which would rely on Interline connections with K.L.M. at Amsterdam for world-wide connections. In August, K.L.M. agreed to carry out and share the cost with the Company of publicising both the Derby/Birmingham and the Cardiff/Bristol to

Amsterdam cargo services, which had been scheduled to operate on Tuesdays, Wednesdays, Thursday and Friday evenings commencing Tuesday, 6th October. The Belfast to Derby service would be retimed slightly for the winter to allow cargo on that service to connect with the Amsterdam service.

In mid-August the construction work at the East Midlands Airport was still going ahead very fast indeed. The Terminal Building framework was completed, both upper and lower floors, with the roof also installed. The Company's admin. block framework was completed, as was the roof, and the sides of the building were well under way. The new hangar being erected on behalf of the Company (the existing main hangar) had half of the girder work completed. The new runway had two thirds of its length now laid with its first layer of bitumastic.

The Main Terminal Building under construction at East Midland Airport.

In the past, all of the Company's printing had been done by outside jobbing printers, and of course all letters and memorandum with a large circulation had been carried out using stencils and a duplicator. Now, in late August, and after exhausting sessions with the Directors, the Commercial Manager had persuaded the Company to install its own "in-house" printing department, and had purchased for this purpose a new Rotaprint 40/80 off-set Litho printing machine, capable of working with up to four colours, backed up by a "Copycat" plate-making machine. In addition a commercial artist, Mr. Rod Stevens, was to take up an appointment to form the nucleus of the first Commercial Art/Publicity within the Company. The accommodation earmarked for the new equipment was the old Pilot/Hostess Training School so patiently built up by Captain Cramp some few years before, but as the move to the East Midlands would shortly be taking place it was only a temporary arrangement. The equipment arrived one afternoon before anybody really expected it to, and also whilst Cramp was away. Not knowing exactly where the proper place was for the printing machine, a junior clerk told the lorry men to place the machine "in

Capt. Cramp's Office", which they promptly did. Upon arriving in his office later that evening Cramp saw, to his horror, that the machine was so heavy that the floor of the wooden hut used as administrative offices at Burnaston was visibly giving way under the strain. An urgent call to Engineering brought forth some hands and a fork lift truck and soon the Rotaprint was safely in its proper resting place—and on a solid floor too.

On 17th August, Argonaut G-ALHS was flown to Royal Air Force Northolt, where it was used in the filming of "The High Bright Sun", starring Dirk Bogarde and Denholm Elliot. On Thursday 20th Capt. Cramp, with First Officer Neil Fagg and Engineer Officer "Jed" Bowker flew "HS", by now painted in BOAC livery, around the circuit at Northolt whilst the cameras recorded the take-offs and landings. The control tower at Northolt received many telephone calls saying that a BOAC airliner was approaching Northolt and that it should be warned to land at London Heathrow instead. Now "HS" had been sprayed with a thin rubber solution over its "Derby Airways" livery, and the old-style BOAC livery was then put on top. In the evening, after the shooting was completed, the film crew began stripping the rubber off the aircraft. At least, that is what should have happened, but unfortunately it didn't work out that way. In desperation the film company called in some off-duty R.A.F. and U.S.A.F. personnel to assist them in stripping the rubber off. At 1900 Cramp, realising that the aircraft was due for a minor check that night apart from being required for service the following day at 0630, told the film crew to leave it as he would have to take the aircraft back to Derby. Reluctantly the film company agreed (they wanted to complete the job as agreed but understood the urgency), but said the Company were to bill them for the cost of removal (it came to £630 in the end), and Cramp departed Northolt for Derby. In spite of it being a beautiful still and cloudless evening, for the crew it sounded as though they were flying through a perpetual hail storm as the rubber, in strips, together with the loose masking tape, kept on flapping all over the aircraft. Nevertheless the aircraft was cleaned in time (many of the engineers bringing their wives in to the hangar to help in stripping the rubber off) and was out on service the following day on schedule.

On Wednesday 9th September, at the Farnborough Air Show the Company Chairman signed a contract worth £600,000 for two Handley Page Heralds, Series 200, the first to be delivered in six months. This announcement came out of the blue, for as mentioned before, the Herald had not figured to date in any of the negotiations. Thus the 748 and the Viscount went "out of the window", at least for the time being.

Mr. Sullivan, Station Manager, Staverton, whilst on holiday in Palma, said that he had come into contact with many people who had travelled to Majorca on the Company's aircraft. Without anyone knowing had had any connection at all with the Company, he heard nothing but praise for the aircraft and especially the Cabin Staff. It was also interesting to hear couriers of the Tour Operators who used the Company's services make a special point of informing their clients of our good timekeeping and reliability. What a change from 1963 with all those engine failures.

By mid-September, Rod Stevens, the new commercial artist for the newly formed publicity department, had joined the Company, and one of the first tasks set for him was design a new Company motif. After some hard thought on the subject and several dummy runs, Rod produced a small selection of motifs for the consideration of the Board, and the one chosen was a stylised Boeing 707 fin and rudder with the B above and infront of the "fin", and the M below, the letters being completely encompassed by an ellipse. When the new motif first appeared in public (which in fact was on Company letter-headed notepaper and information bulletins), most staff immediately referred to it as the "flying egg". The motif did in fact appear on the Herald engine nacelles when it was first delivered, and it was used by the Company for some eighteen months, before being superseded by the present motif, but more of that later.

Thursday 1st October 1964 saw the much-announced Company name change from Derby Airways to British Midland Airways. Many of the long-serving staff were, not unnaturally, sad at seeing the change implemented, but agreed that in toto the change was for the better. There was no doubt that the name "Derby" was too parochial, after all, the Company claimed to be "The Airline of the Midlands", and it was British, so what better title than "British Midland"? When the new aircraft livery came out into the open there were many wisecracks like "Here come the quacks" (being a reference to BMA and the British Medical Association), but in reality the airline and travel industries accepted the change of name very readily, and of course it remains to this day and with a remarkably good reputation too.

Tuesday 6th October arrived, and with it the commencement of the Derby-Birmingham-Amsterdam freight service. It will be remembered that joint advertising with KLM had been undertaken, and all possible local advertising had been carried out. Departures from Derby at 2045, Birmingham at 2200, with arrival in Amsterdam, at 0115, together with a return from Amsterdam at 0700 arriving Birmingham at 0815 and Derby at 0930, had been carefully worked out to ensure that exporting cargo arrived in Amsterdam to connect with most of KLM's outgoing freight services all over the world. Similarly, importing cargo could be picked up during the night when all of KLM's inbound freighters arrived, together with those of such other carriers as Sabena etc., and delivered to the Midlands first thing the following day. Departures from Derby were on Tuesdays, Wednesdays, Thursdays and Fridays, once again purposefully planned that way so that any manufacturers' output during the week right up until 1800 Friday evening could be on its way. Monday was deliberately omitted on the grounds that a factory emptied on Friday evening, would possibly not have enough output for the Monday.

The first service, on October 6th, departed Derby on schedule, without a landing at Birmingham, direct to Amsterdam—a disastrous inaugural flight. Only 1½ kilos were on board from Derby, bound for Johannesburg, and nothing from Birmingham, hence the direct flight to Amsterdam. The next few flights suffered similarly. The reasons for this non-interest in what appeared to be a good and much-needed service baffled those concerned within the Company. After all, a consignment leaving a Derby or Nottingham factory as late as 1800 could be in New York the following day at 0900 New York time, at 0500 in Brussels or 0610 in Copenhagen. A space-booking system enabled a shipper to telephone through to Derby Airport and obtain immediate confirmation that was available through to anywhere in the world.

At the end of October things started to improve for the new service, when yet another blow fell. The British Motor Corporation were introducing the new 1100cc range of cars and wanted publicity material rushing through to Continental destinations urgently. The Corporations forwarding agent used the BMA service one Friday evening and the consignment arrived in Amsterdam on schedule. Now KLM had just introduced into their cargo warehouse at Schipol Airport a new computer-controlled cargo system and this particular evening it suffered the first of its teething troubles, with the result that the BMC consignment did not depart Amsterdam until the Monday morning. Naturally, BMC were very irate, and the blame fell on BMA, with instructions to the forwarding agent that the service was never to be used again.

At the beginning, one point against the service was the rate structure which common-rated Derby with Birmingham, and that rate was calculated using the London rate with an add-on. This practice stemmed from the days when no freight service originated in either Birmingham or Derby and when consignments were shipped to London Heathrow on a lorry and then flown on from here. Now however, the situation was different and it was wrong, for example, for cargo destined for Copenhagen to be calculated on a London rate plus an add-on, when Copenhagen was nearer Derby/Birmingham than London. As a result of this situation the Company applied to IATA, through British Eagle International Airlines (it will be remembered that the Company was not, and is not, an IATA carrier, but only a signatory to the Multilateral Agreements) for a Derby/Birmingham commodity rate. The application did not get very far however, as it was not accepted.

Dakota G-AKJH as an all-freighter aircraft.

85

In preparation for the 1965 season, the licence covering the Cardiff/Bristol to Barcelona/Palma route, being an "A" scheduled service licence, required ratification by the Spanish authorities. In the past the Spanish would not accept the licence in its "A" form and therefore the British had allowed the service to operate as a "B" (I.T. service) licence, with the acquiescence of the Spanish. For 1965 however, BMA wanted the full status, of the "A" licence being recognised, mainly in order to recover the traffic lost to Cambrian Airways through the Argonaut engine debacle. With this in mind therefore, Capt. Cramp flew to Madrid on Friday 9th October, for talks with both Iberia and the Spanish Civil Aviation authorities.

Senor Delgado, Commercial Director, Iberia, stated that although Iberia were not happy about the proposal, no objection would be raised. However, should BMA agree to pooling the services with Iberia, the latter would infact endorse the proposal.

The Spanish Civil Aviation Authorities however, were not willing to grant recognition immediately but stated that, if the Ministry of Aviation (British) were to make application immediately, i.e., not wait for the next bi-lateral discussions between the two countries, that the proposals would be considered. The application should state, said the Spanish, that BMA would be the only British carrier authorised on the route. Iberia and the Spanish authorities would not tolerate a repetition of the B.E.A./B.U.A. position whereby BUA became the second British carrier on the route to Malaga, with only one Spanish carrier. In the event the October 1964 application never succeeded and the licence was eventually converted to a "B" licence without a hearing. BMA might just have been the first British Independent to have a pooling agreement with a foreign flag carrier.

For some time now the Commercial Manager had been negotiating with B.K.S. Air Transport Ltd., to take over the handling of BMA at Leeds/Bradford, Newcastle, Teeside, Belfast and Dublin. In addition a General Sales Agency agreement was concluded between the two carriers, and an announcement to this effect was made on the 24th November. The agreement did in fact emphasise that the services of the two airlines were complementary rather than competitive, and further co-operation of a similar nature could be expected in the future. In fact both carriers printed each others connecting services in their respective timetables for 1965.

It was with some fair measures of sincere regret that on 2nd November, it was learned that Mercury Airlines Ltd., of Manchester Airport, were to go into voluntary liquidation. To save the situation to a certain extent, and also to enlarge the Company's sphere of activities, Wing Commander Roxburgh called an urgent Board meeting to discuss a possible take-over, and so it was that the accouncement was finally made on 12th December that BMA had acquired Mercury. Mercury was formed in 1960 by Lord Peter Calthorpe, and had operated scheduled servics from Manchester to Newcastle and Teeside, Isle of Wight and Exeter. BMA announced that it intended to preserve the continuity of the services to Newcastle and Teeside, and in fact would be operating a new service from Birmingham-Manchester-Teeside-Newcastle every Tuesday,

Wednesday and Thursday. Lord Calthorpe said that Mercury had co-operated with BMA in the past and he was very pleased that it was the Company who would be continuing the services Mercury had inaugurated.

Apart from the routes acquired from Mercury, the Company had also now acquired offices and check-in bays at Manchester, something that had been unobtainable hitherto, and also (although nobody knew it at the time of course) a future Managing Director and Chairman, in the shape of the then Mercury Station Manager, Mr. Michael Bishop. At the same time Mercury's Director of Operations, Captain Ian Wallace, transferred to BMA (he was later killed in a Viscount crash at Manchester) and Capt. T. Holliday (now retired).

The November issue of the Company newsletter came out with a new title the "Midland Herald", designed to reflect the new Company name, and the coming into service soon of the Handley Page Herald.

Also in November, it was announced that the Company had arranged a connecting bus service to connect with the Barcelona and Palma scheduled service arrivals. The time-table was published in a new Sales and Traffic Manual that the Commercial Manager had written (the first the Company had ever had), and the service was available both to tour operators and individual members of the public—another first for the Company, way before any other carrier had inaugurated any such facility. Another feature of the Sales/Traffic Manual was the ability to book hotel rooms in Spain and Majorca through the Company. All details were published in the Manual together with prices. Although the Company have never owned hotels, it was one of the first Independent Companies to offer this facility.

In the aviation industry in 1964, it was the practice to commence selling the next year's services on new Years Day. Captain Cramp however thought that this "tradition" should be broken and had persuaded the Board that it was the correct thing to do by commencing the sales on 1st December, one month before all the other carriers.

Just in time for Christmas, it was announced that the Technical Manager, Mr. Frank Marshall, was to be appointed to the Board of Directors with effect from 1st January, 1975. Frank had joined the Company in 1940 as an apprentice engineer, but had joined the Royal Air Force in 1943 as a Flight Engineer on Stirlings with 299 Squadron, rejoining the Company in 1947.

So ended a very hectic year.

The fleet was still as 1963.

1965

The year started with, not unnaturally, a fair degree of optimism. After all, the long-awaited turbo-prop equipment was on its way, and the move to the East Midlands Airport was almost at hand. Having had a bright start to the New Year, all staff concerned were sadly disappointed when on the 7th January, senior staff were called into Burnaston House to be told that, the Chairman would be retiring "because of ill health". It was ironical that one of the men who had worked hardest to bring into being the East Midlands Airport should now be denied the fruits of his efforts just on the eve of the move.

Monday, 1st February came and with it the first Herald, G-ASKK, a Series 211, originally leased by Handley Page to Sadia. The Company Directors and Senior Management attended the handing-over ceremony at the Handley Page

Handing-over ceremony at Radlett of Herald G-ASKK. From left to right are Mr. E.W. Phillips M.B.E., Miss Mary Agar, Sir Frederick Handley Page, Mr. R.R. Paine, Mr. D.W. Sullivan, Mr. F. Marshall.

factory at Radlett. It seemed a strange production line for a civil airliner, if the term production line applies, for the Heralds under construction were being built in between Handley Page Victor V-Bombers which themselves were either being built or were being modified or overhauled. One's mental picture of lines of Heralds in various states of production was completely knocked for six. After all the speeches were over, guests boarded KK for the flight up to Burnaston, with Capt. Lines in command. A pass was made over the nearly completed East Midlands Airport, and formating on the Herald was the aircraft belonging to "Flight" magazine, which journal subsequently printed the story of BMA and the delivery flight.

As the aircraft made its approach into Burnaston, everyone on the airfield held their breath, knowing full well that at the end of the landing run the new livery would be covered in mud from the water-logged airfield, which proved correct. All around gave three cheers to the engineers, who, in those days, stood by with a hose to wash not only the Herald but all of the Company's aircraft down.

Herald G-ASKK over the almost completed runway at the East Midlands Aiport during its delivery flight. (Flight International).

The next few days saw demonstration flights with the new acquisition from Staverton, Cardiff, Luton, Manchester and Birmingham. This was followed by route flying in order that the crews could be line trained, a total of 180 crew training hours having to be flown by 1st April. All of this route flying was carried out on the Glasgow service, to the delight of the regular customers on this route, mainly Rolls Royce staff.

On Monday, 8th February the new (again) Reservations Manager, Mr. V. S. J. "Micky" Finn started with the Company. Ex-BOAC, it was hoped that Mr. Finn would be really stream-lining the reservations system to bring it up to the standard required, although there was no doubt that he was going to have his work cut out to keep on top of the system that he had inherited and would have to work for most of 1965. In the meantime Cramp and Walden had been hard at it bringing the Agency side of the Company's organisation up to date. Previously no proper Agency Agreements had been in force and neither had any proper Agency Certificates been issued. However this was now rectified, the in-house print facility working hard at producing these documents. In addition, all BMA Appointed Agents were informed of the BMA office through which they should conduct their business. A lot of business had been lost in the past because Agents had to phone through to Derby for reservations and for Agents in the Newcastle and other distant areas this was costly, with the result that the Agent would rather send his client via another carrier with whom he, the Agent, could book more easily and cheaply.

To augment the Nottingham bookings, a new Reservations Office was opened in mid-February at 99 Carrington Street, Nottingham, some fifty yards from Nottingham's Midland Station. At the same time, Cramp arranged for a telephone answering unit to be installed in the Reservations Department at the East Midland's Airport, this to cater for all the many complaints that after 1800 nobody could make a reservation on the Company's network.

February 11th saw a statement to the effect that the Company were considering buying Britannia aircraft, possibly one or more of the 100 Series which BOAC were still trying to dispose of. So deep was the thought on this, that the Company's main hangar, at that time nearing completion at the East Midland's Airport, was designed to take a Britannia and was referred to in those early days at the Airport as the "Britannia Hangar". In fact the project never did get beyond the thinking stage. With the acquisition of the Heralds, plus the move away from Burnaston, any further re-equipment could not be contemplated in 1965.

When the company first went into the scheduled service market and particularly with the introduction of the Dakota in 1955, in order to ensure that passengers were able to arrive at the airport at all (remember, bus services to Burnaston were in the order of two per day past the airfield), the Company had to contract-hire buses from outlying towns and cities like Nottingham and Derby, and charge the passengers for this service. Now that Castle Donington was about to open, the Company felt that the time had come when it should no longer have to worry about surface transportation. After all, the Company would no longer be an airfield operator but at long last would be purely an airline operator, so why should the airport authorities not have the surface transport responsibilities?

All of the foregoing was put to Eric Dyer, Airport Director, and he agreed, as a result of which a joint approach was made to the two major bus operators in the district. Trent and Barton provided services, which still run to this day.

On 4th March a meeting took place at Derby Airport with BKS to consider, amongst other things, the proposed Newcastle-Glasgow service. Various organisations in both Newcastle and Glasgow had approached the Company with suggestions that there was a need for an air service between these two very important ship-building centres. Surface transport was difficult, a change of train at Edinburgh having to be made in both directions if using the rail services, whilst the road journey was tedious to say the least, particularly in winter. Both the Commercial Manager and the Scheduled Services Manager had investigated the need and the potential for the service, and both were convinced that it should be operated. The licence was applied for and obtained and eventually the service, which was an extension of the Birmingham, Manchester, Newcastle service, began operation on Monday 5th April. After three weeks the service was pulled off as being uneconomical, which it was, the traffic loads being very poor indeed. However, as the Commercial Manager pointed out, what else could be expected when no proper publicity had been given to the service? Only £250 extra had been given to advertise the route. Needless to say another carrier picked up the licence and today the route is a profitable one.

On the 15th March, Dakota G-AMSX with Capt. Rothwell in command and First Officer Wise (now the DC9 Fleet Captain) departed from Derby for Copenhagen and Helsinki with a power station generator weighing two tons on board, accompanied by instrumentation weighing half a ton. Eight hours and forty-five minutes flying time later the aircraft landed at Helsinki, and there it nightstopped. The following day, but with the crew now augmented by a Russian navigator and a Russian radio operator, "SX" departed Helsinki for Moscow's Sheremetevo Airport, where the load was taken off to be installed by John Browns in the power station. Having refuelled, "SX" departed Moscow immediately and arrived in Copenhagen six hours and twenty-five minutes later. After a further night stop the aircraft (minus the two Russians) flew back to Derby, clocking up a total of twenty three hours and twenty minutes for the whole trip. It was the Company's first trip to Russia, although of course several further trips behind the Iron Curtain have since taken place.

The February and March issues of the "Midland Herald" contained some interesting staff news, some of which is shown below.

Mr. M. D. Bishop appointed Northern Region Manager based at Manchester Airport (now Managing Director and Chairman).

Mr. A. J. Smith joined the Inspection Department from Autair (later Technical Director)

Mr. Graham Norman joined the Reservations Department (now Commercial Manager).

At the same time, and commensurate with the move from Burnaston, the following Senior Staff appointments were made.

Captain T. H. Pike (formerly Chief Pilot) became General Manager (Flying).

Captain S. D. Fenton (formerly Operations Superintendent) became Chief Pilot.

Captain I. D. Wallace, D.F.M., became Deputy Chief Pilot.

Captain E. W. A. Lines relinquished the post of Deputy Chief Pilot for personal reasons.

Captain B. G. Cramp (formerly Commercial Manager) became Operations Manager.

Mr. L. W. Hopkins joined as Commercial Manager.

On 19th March prior to the departure from Burnaston, a small get-together was held in Burnaston House when, on behalf of all Staff, Mr. Dennis Aldridge presented Wing Commander Roxburgh with an engraved silver tray.

As a final gesture, the Company Dance held on 26th March 1965 was termed the "Farewell Burnaston" dance.

The Great Day came at last, 1st April (All Fool's Day) 1965, and the early morning departure to Glasgow saw the Herald "KK" operating the service with Capt. Lines in command. On board was the Mayor of Derby, the idea being that as the Mayor of Derby at the time had been on board the first scheduled service from Derby to Glasgow way back in 1956, the aircraft being commanded by Capt. Lines, it would be nice if the present Mayor departed on the last Glasgow service to leave Burnaston and the first to arrive at the East

Midlands Airport. Alas it was not to be. The blame must surely lay at the feet of whoever chose 1st April as the opening date of the new airfield. Before the airfield licence could be issued, the Ministry of Aviation Inspector had to be satisfied that all the facilities such as runway lighting, navigational aids, safety equipment and vehicles etc., were up to the standard required. All went well until the evening, by which time "KK" was southbound out of Glasgow, and in fact was waiting at Leeds/Bradford for the signal to say that the East Midlands Airport operating licence had been granted. The Civil Aviation Flying Unit Dove was making its final run-in on the approach lighting check when a bull-dozer being used to fill-in some ditches near the runway sank in the soft mud. In trying to extricate itself, it ripped through the cables feeding the lead-in lights and blacked them out. By now it was dusk and of course, with no full night flying facilities, no licence could be issued for night operation although it was issued for daylight operation. Very reluctantly a signal was sent to Leeds/Bradford and "KK" departed only to land back again at Burnaston. There were some very red faces about that night. In fact the lead-in cable was repaired the following morning and the full operating licence granted in the afternoon allowing "KK" to land ex-Glasgow at the East Midlands Airport, for the first time, on 2nd April, 1965.

The move from Burnaston, so far as the office equipment, engineering equipment, reservations boards and so forth were concerned, was carried out without a hitch over March 31st, April 1st and 2nd, using a fleet of lorries and private cars.

1st April also saw the departure of the Company's first Dakota to be sold. G-AKJH was sold to Gregory Air Services Ltd.

Finally, on this very hectic All Fool's Day, the third Reservations Shop was opened in Jersey. The installation of a teleprinter in this shop would, it was hoped, iron out all the many complaints from passengers received in the previous years when the Company were not carrying out their own reservations.

During the planning stage of the 1965 summer programme, both Eric Sample and Capt. Cramp had decided that the 1965 summer timetable should be a pocket edition, and some careful thought had gone into the design, which measured $5\frac{1}{2}''$ x $3\frac{7}{8}''$. During the summer the journal "Aeroplane and Commercial News" ran a feature on timetables of the world's airlines, and the British Midland timetable achieved fourth in order of merit of those featured and first out of the United Kingdom operators' timetables. Not bad for a small company.

Some six weeks after the move to East Midlands, a very sharp-eyed engineer was carrying out an inspection on the Herald when he noticed some corrosion appearing on the underside of the fuselage in line with the "chine" that was a feature of the Herald. As a direct result of this find, the maximum cabin pressure differential allowed on any Herald anywhere in the world was reduced from 4 lbs/sq.in. to 2.5 lbs/sq.in.

As if the foregoing was not enough, another Herald operator discovered during a routine inspection that where an ice guard in the plane of rotation of

92

the propellers had been fitted, an over-zealous member of the manufacturing team had, in cutting away the sheet of rubber which formed part of the guard, dug his cutting-tool in so deeply, that the main aircraft skin in the vicinity of the guard had been half cut through. This discovery was made not two weeks after the corrosion find, with the result that the ARB instructed that all Heralds must be flown unpressurized.

As a result of this instruction, Handley Page put into being a modification programme, and G-ASKK was delivered to the factory at Radlett for this purpose on 17th August, another Herald, G-ATHE, being loaned in exchange. It was almost a month later when Capt. S. D. Fenton delivered "HE" back to Radlett on 15th September, returning with the modified "KK".

At the S.B.A.C. Farnborough Show in September, and after much thought, a contract was signed with the British Aircraft Corporation for two BAC 1-11 Series 300 aircraft, for delivery early in 1967. The real brains behind this project was Frank Marshall, the Technical Director, who for some time had been of the opinion that the Company should go forth into the jet age. Having had arguments galore with his co-Directors, the Board finally agreed and the contract was signed.

On Wednesday 10th November, a press announcement was made about the proposed purchase of the 1-11's. It was stated that the aircraft would be used on services from the East Midlands to Barcelona, Palma, Jersey, Glasgow and Ostend, from Manchester to Barcelona, Palma, and Valencia, and from Liverpool to Barcelona and Perpignan. It was also stated that it was the Company's intention to steadily phase out the Dakota and the Argonaut.

Once again a statement had been made that was not to be fulfilled, for, as will be seen the 1-11 Series 300 aircraft did not materialise.

One method of using purposefully the by-now ageing Dakotas was to convert them to pure freighters and use them only in this role. This the Company did with G-AGJV, and it was this aircraft which inaugurated the Company's first all-freight service to the Channel Islands on 1st December 1965. Mainly carrying fresh flowers and produce from Jersey and Guernsey, the service was timed to arrive back at the East Midlands Airport at 2120, allowing the produce to be at the markets the following day.

The second of the Company's Dakotas to be sold was G-AMSX, which, as VP-GCF, was delivered to Guyana Airways, being flown out by that company's Chief Pilot on 22nd December. When the aircraft departed he flew down to Dakar, filled right up and flew directed to Natal, not even routing via the Ascension Islands where the Americans were in full force. Furthermore, the aircraft did not carry a navigator, and the only navigational aid they had on board besides the compass was a radio compass. The aircraft was not even fitted with a drift-sight. Brave men indeed—or may be foolish ones? The ferry flight was in fact completed safely and without incident.

The Fleet at the end of 1965 comprised:—
Herald 211   G-ASKK
Argonauts   G-ALHG, G-ALHS, G-ALHY

Dakotas   G-ANTD, G-AOGZ, G-APBC, G-AOFZ, G-AGJV
Leopard Moth G-ACLL
Just before Christmas 1965 E. W. Phillips, M.B.E., retired at the age of 67,
but he continued to have a shareholding in the Company.

1966

WITH the prospects of new jet type on the horizon, morale at the beginning of
the year was high. Not only was the new type a pure jet, but it was also to be the
first brand-new aircraft the Company had ever operated. On 7th January a
team consisting of Frank Marshall, Technical Director, Captain S. D. Fenton,
Chief Pilot, and Capt. B. G. Cramp, Operations Manager, departed East
Midlands Airport en route for the British Aircraft Corportion's factory at
Weybridge. Travelling in the Chief Pilot's car they arrived late, having made a
diversion en route to pick up Mary Agar, Financial Director. The team were
introduced to members of the B.A.C. Sales and Customer Support teams, and
then the first tentative attempts at the contents of the Operations Manual for the
type were begun, beginning with the requirements that must be fed into the
computer programme run by BAC as part of the customer support programme.

It was then arranged that the Operations Manager would return on 17th
January to BAC accompanied by Mr John Crisp, Deputy Operations Manager
for at least two days, taking with them copies of the Dakota, Argonaut and
Herald Operations Manuals. At this meeting the following would be
discussed:—
i)   A complete run through of the 1-11 Flight Manual.
ii)   Talk on the BMA format for the 1-11 Operations Manual.
iii) Talk on the method BMA required for depicting the weight and balance
      of the aircraft.
The agenda of the meeting on the 7th January has been put down in some
detail, so that the reader may gather that the intention to operate 1-11 was
definitely there on that date. However, the meeting arranged for the 17th
January never did take place. Some few days after returning from Weybridge,
the Managing Director informed the Operations Manager that there was some
doubt as to whether the purchase of the 1-11's would now go through. In fact it
never did, and BMA never operated the 300 series.

On the 31st January the Operations Manager resigned and emigrated to
Canada where he went bush flying, so Capt. Fenton once again took control of
Operations.

22nd March saw the next Dakota to be sold (the third) depart from, East
Midlands for the Persian Gulf, where it was to serve with Gulf Aviation. G-
AOFZ did in fact end its days with Gulf, finally coming to grief whilst landing at
Bait near Muscat in the Trucial Oman.

The summer timetable for 1966 was a very lavishly-produced affair indeed.
Designed by Peter Beddoe, MSIA (who incidentally designed the swept-wing

BMA motif which appeared on the Company's aircraft publicity and stationary from the Spring of 1965 onwards) it was a very informative and well-illustrated timetable, most of the photographs in it being printed in four colours. The destinations listed in the booklet (for that is what it really was) were:— Barcelona, Basle, Belfast, Bergen, Birmingham, Bristol, Cambridge, Cardiff, Dublin, East Midlands, Glasgow, Gloucester/Cheltenham, Guernsey, Isle-of-Wight, Isle-of-Man, Jersey, Leeds/Bradford, Luton, Manchester, Newquay, Ostend and Palma, not counting another carrier's Paris service.

2nd May, and the "Scottish Herald", as the Company's Glasgow service had come to be known, mainly due to the Herald aircraft being used on the service, departed East Midlands for a slightly new destination at Glasgow. The old airport, Renfrew, had finally been closed as it was incapable of further extension, a "must" if more modern aircraft were to be able to operate into Glasgow. As a result the old Royal Naval Air Station at Abbotsinch had been purchased from the Admiralty and was developed as the Civil Airport for Glasgow.

In April it was announced that a contract had that day been signed with British United Airways for a Viscount Series 831, G-ASED, and for a Viscount Series 736 G-AODG with seating capacities of 80 and 64 respectively. A third Viscount 831 purchase was also being negotiated for the Spring of 1967, G-APNE. Thus it will be seen that already there had been a reversal of the decision to standardize on the Herald. Part of the reasoning behind the policy change was the dramatic increase in passenger carryings, for which the Herald's seating capacity of 50 had become inadequate. The remaining life on the Argonauts was only in the region of one to two years, mainly due to the difficulties encountered in obtaining spares, for the Merlin engines in particular. In addition the overhaul costs of the Merlin, together with its relatively very low overhaul life, made the Argonaut not too much of an economic proposition. The B.A.C. 1-11 Series 300 contract had by now been cancelled, sot the only alternative really was the four-engined turbo-prop Viscount. As the Herald had in reality out-proved itself, there was not much point in retaining it, so British United accepted the aircraft in part-exchange for the Viscounts. Then, on the evening of Monday, 21st November, R. R. Paine and Joint Managing Director (Frank Marshall had been declared Joint Managing Director some months before) stated that the Company were once more negotiating with the British Aircraft Corporation for the 500 Series BAC 1-11, to seat 119 passengers each. The deal was expected to cost in the region of £4 million.

The Commercial Manager, Laurie Hopkins, discussing the Company's future plans said:— "We are developing our year-round services with the introduction of the Viscount, and this not only gives us twice daily operation on the Glasgow service but introduces twice daily services to Belfast and seven days a week services to Dublin. We have applied for a licence to operate to Amsterdam and Dusseldorf and we hope to introduce this service in October 1967, the destinations being Barcelona, and Palma. There will also be an increase in our Channel Islands services from Castle Donington of about 80 per cent because of the introduction of Viscounts to replace the Heralds, which seat substantially less than the Viscount's 70" (he was referring to the 700 Series Viscounts, the 810 Series seating 80).

"The next main development is a "vast" increase in inclusive tour work, amounting to nearly double the operations that were carried out in the first year of operation from Castle Donington. We have introduced at this airport a new concept with a group of bus companies carrying passengers from several points inside and outside our direct catchment area. The group includes Midland Red, Sheffield United Tours, Trent Motor Traction, Barton Transport, Northern and General, and Blue Cars. The new transport arrangements", Mr. Hopkins continued, referring still to the increase in inclusive tour proposals, "mean that wherever a passenger in the airport catchment area started from, direct coach services would be available to the terminal buildings of the airport. These services are expected to include a new limited-stop service operated by Midland Red from Birmingham to the East Midlands Airport".

He went on to say that the increase in freight carried since the move to the East Midlands Airport had seen the most dramatic increase, with 20 tons a week being moved, with a converted Dakota on the exclusive five days a week freight service to Belfast which connected two textile areas, Derbyshire and Northern Ireland.

The foregoing then amounted to a policy statement insofar as the Company was concerned. However, once again, and in spite of the careful thought that had been given, most of it was not to materialise, particularly the inclusive tour projects and the bus company tie-up. With hindsight, it is difficult to believe that Midland Red could provide a viable service from Birmingham to Castle Donington Airport, as most passengers in the Birmingham area would, naturally, wish to depart from Elmdon.

Monday 28th November saw substantial snow falls over the Midlands and the following morning the Glasgow and Belfast flights were delayed in departing. One of the problems was that during the night the snow began to thaw and then in the early hours of morning the freezing conditions began to return. The services eventually departed two hours late.

The fleet at 31st December was:

Dakotas	G-ANTD, G-AOGZ, G-APBC, G-AGJV
Argonauts	G-ALHS, G-ALHY, G-ALHG
Herald 211	G-ASKK
Leopard Moth	G-ACLL

1967

VISCOUNT 736 G-AODG with 64 seats, and reputedly purchased for the sum of £175,000 was handed over to Mr. R. Paine as Joint Managing Director at Jersey Airport on Tuesday 10th January. The price paid included the painting of the aircraft in the Company livery (which still included the large 'B' and 'M' on the fin), all checks complete on the aircraft and complete with seats to the Company's requirements. It was hoped that the Glasgow evening service the following day, 11th would be operated by the Viscount. Taking delivery of the aircraft, Ron Paine said part of the Company's immediate development depended on the result of the recent public inquiry into the runway extension at the East Midlands Airport. However, he was, he said, hoping to add Vanguards to the BMA fleet, purchasing them from BEA. He added that the 1-11 order announced in 1966 for the BAC 1-11 still existed and it was hoped that the position of the 500 Series would be finalised within the next few weeks.

The second Viscount to arrive at East Midlands landed on 15th February. This aircraft, G-ASED, was a 78 seater Viscount 831, and the same day saw the final departure of the Herald G-ASKK which was going in part exchange for the Viscounts.

The introduction of the Viscounts had allowed the frequency and capacity of the Glasgow and Belfast services to be doubled. In addition it was now possible to put increased capacity onto the Newquay service, and to improve the services to Spain. However, both the Herald and the Viscount lacked the short grass-field performance that the Dakota possessed, and so it came about that 1967 was the last year of the Isle of Wight services and also the last year that the Dakota was used by the Company on scheduled passenger service.

The Chief Pilot, Captain Fenton, had a rather embarrassing experience on 7th March when, on completion of a short air test in Argonaut G-ALHG, the nosewheel collapsed whilst still on the runway at East Midlands. Fortunately nobody was hurt and the aircraft, although damaged, was not long before it re-entered service.

Another old friend departed on 1st April, when Dakota G-AOGZ was delivered to Strathallan Air Services of Perth. It will be remembered that "GZ" was the second Dakota to join the Company in 1956, having previously been Field Marshall Montgomery's personal aircraft KN628. To offset this somewhat sad loss, the third Viscount, an 831, G-APNE, landed at mid-day on the 4th April, coinciding with a "wings parade" for the season's cabin staff graduates, amongst whom was Steward Stuart Wakefield who is now a Training and Check Steward with the Company on the Boeing 707 fleet.

There was now no doubt that the introduction of the Viscount onto the Glasgow service was sucesssful, for on 24th April it was announced that traffic on the route was up 50 per cent. On Monday 1st May the Company opened its own unit at Glasgow to replace the handling agents, Scotia Air Transport Ltd. The passengers would now be required to check-in at Desk No. 11 in the main concourse, the Company's own check-in desk. The Station Manager for the new unit was Mr. R. T. "Bob" Apps. Bob joined the Company in 1963 as Apron Supervisor at Cardiff (Rhoose) Airport, and had worked his way steadily through the Company, culminating in his last appointment prior to the Glasgow posting as Senior Duty Officer at the East Midlands Airport.

The fourth Viscount to join the Company's fleet arrived on the 2nd June. It was G-AVJA, an 815 Series, originally owned and operated by Pakistan International Airlines, and refurbished by Hawker Siddeley Aviation from which organisation it was purchased. A sister aircraft, G-AVJB also ex-Pakistan and Hawker Siddeley arrived on 5th July.

On the 4th June, the Company suffered its most tragic loss in all of its history, when Argonaut G-ALHG crashed at Stockport whilst en route from Palma to Manchester, with the loss of 69 passengers and three crew. Twelve people survived the crash, including commander Captain Harry Marlow. The aircraft was approaching Runway 24 at Manchester's Ringway Airport after the flight of some 4½ to 5 hours when first No. 4 engine failed followed by a failure to deliver power on No. 3 engine. The aircraft attempted to carry out a right hand 360° turn but when the turn was almost completed so much height had been lost that Captain Marlow had no alternative but to put the aircraft down in the only clear area he could find, which was a piece of waste-land in the middle of a built up area. In doing this Marlow managed to avoid a high-rise block of flats. Very exhaustive tests were carried out by the Board of Trade, and the Royal Aircraft Establishment with the full co-operation of the Company. One Argonaut, G-ALHY, went to Boscombe Down in December as part of the investigation. Although the results of all of these investigations completely cleared the Company of any responsibility, the two remaining Argonauts did not fly on public transport service again after the 1967 season. G-ALHS was withdrawn from service on 16th October, and G-ALHY on 6th November. Both were sold to Chartwell Aviation on 19th October, 1968.

There followed a statement issued on 12th September, that the Company would bring into operation in the summer of 1969 at least two jet aircraft, and that the Argonaut and Dakota would be phased out. However, the jets would have to operate under a handicap until the runway extensions at the East Midlands were completed in 1970. In addition the 67/68 winter timetable would show a direct East Midlands/Channel Islands service in winter for the first time, and a specially modified Viscount would operate on the Belfast service carrying supplementary freight. This modification, which could only be installed in the 831 type of Viscount as that model had a much larger forward entrance door than the other variants, consisted of a fibre-glass freight container which was bolted to the forward section of the fuselage floor, leaving a properly-conceived gangway down the starboard side of the fuselage to give access to and from the crew compartment. Moulded into the rear end of the container were the usual "No Smoking" and "Fasten Seat Belt" cabin signs, as were individual passenger fold-away table fixtures. The whole modification allowed twenty-two passengers to be accommodated, but it took two hours to install and to remove, a distinct disadvantage if the aircraft, on return to base, was required to go out again in full passenger configuration.

The inaugural service to Edinburgh from East Midlands was operated on Tuesday, 3rd October. The aircraft returned the same morning with a party of civic personalities and industrialists, who were to spend a day in the East Midlands area as guests of the Company.

On 4th November, it was announced that Minster Assets were increasing their participation in Invicta Airways. Invicta's original capital of £100,000 was held as to 60 per cent by Minster and the remainder by the airline's Managing

Director Wing Commander Hugh Kennard. The capital was now to be increased to £250,000 with Minster subscribing for £100,000. Although not really part of the British Midland history, the event was of subsequent importance to the Company as will be seen.

Thus ended the year 1967, with a dramatic change of fleet structure, and a major disaster. A major increase in both passenger and freight traffic had been realised and now all of the passenger services were, for the first time in the Company's history, turbine powered.

The Board structure at this time was:—

Mr. R. R. Paine   Joint Managing Directors
Mr. F. A. Marshall

Miss M. M. Agar   Financial Director & Company Secretary

The Fleet:—

Argonauts	G-ALHS, G-ALHY (both now withdrawn from service)
Viscount 831	G-ASED, G-APNE
Viscount 815	G-AVJA, G-AVJB
Viscount 736	G-AODG
Dakotas	G-ANTD, G-AGJV, G-APBC
Leopard Moth	G-ACLL

1968

THE year opened with all advertising announcing that British Midland would be all-turboprop (or prop-jet as it was advertised at the time) for 1968. This was not quite true as one Dakota, G-AGJV, was kept for freighting, "BC" and "TD" departing later on in the year. Freight was really on the up and up and so, on 5th February, a through service by air and road was introduced from Birmingham, Coventry and Wolverhampton to East Midlands Airport and vice versa for the Belfast service. On the flight the DC3 wo¾ld be utilised with the overspill taken up on the Viscount.

One result of the withdrawal of the Dakota from passenger service was the Isle-of-Wight could not now be served. In order to offset this to some extent, a licence application was made, and granted, for a Viscount Manchester-Southampton licence, but an endorsement on the licence stated that, in order to protect BUA on the same route, the Company could only move passengers originating in or travelling to the Isle of Wight. Naturally BUA objected, but they need not have worried as so few passengers were forthcoming that the service never operated. There were no more Isle of Wight services again by BMA.

At about this time the Company's attitude towards the State-owned airlines was that the role of the Independents was to provide feeder services into the major airports, enabling long distance passengers to fly from their local airport to their final destination without the need to travel by surface means to major airports first. Examples of this were the BKS services from Newcastle and Leeds/Bradford to London, the Company's own services to Glasgow for onward connections ex-Prestwick, and the East Midlands to Dublin service for

Trans-Atlantic connections with Aer Lingus. With this in mind therefore, a very cleverly-worded Aer Lingus advertisement was placed in the press in the Nottingham area at the beginning of February, which said, "A lot of people go out of their way to get from Nottingham to North America. Our way, you don't have to". The main point of the advertisement then went on, "Flying from Castle Donington, Nottingham's nearest airport, British Midland take you in the right direction from the start—right to Dublin—where you connect with the giant Aer Lingus—Irish Boeing heading for New York or Boston. Also services to Montreal or Chicago". This was a very nice piece of inspired advertising and certainly a fair number of Trans-Atlantic passengers used this facility.

Another Viscount joined the Company on 12th April, when G-AWCV, a Viscount 760, arrived. The aircraft was purchased from BOAC Associated Companies. Its previous registration was VR-AAN.

Now that this Viscount had arrived, a Dakota prepared to leave. On 30th April, G-APBC, third of the type to be acquired by the Company, was sold to Southwest Aviation Ltd., of Shoreham.

As if to accompany the new Viscount acquisition, a new cabin staff uniform was announced on the 19th April. Designed by Mary Agar, Financial Director, Mrs. Audrey Franklin, Chief Stewardess, and Miss Margo Dunlop, Training Stewardess, the new uniforms were worn when 19 new air stewardesses received their "wings" at a ceremonial parade, at what had by now become an annual event. The turquoise collarless two piece suit, beige blouse and navy accessories replaced the previous navy and black uniform which the stewardesses had worn for the past few years. The cloth for the new uniform had to be specially dyed to match the turquoise strip on all of the Company's aircraft and was made up by a Derby firm. The complete uniform, costing £50, comprised jacket, two skirts, four blouses, hat, two pairs of shoes, handbag, raincoat and gloves. Only the shape of the hat retained any semblance of the previous uniform. Regulation length of the new uniform was "on the knee", but many of the new recruits were sporting hemlines well above.

Laurie Hopkins, Commercial Manager, resigned at the beginning of May and returned to South Africa. As a result of this two new appointments were made on the 9th May. Mr. "Tim" Walden, up to that time Manager Scheduled Services, was promoted to Manager, Commercial Sales, responsible for all the selling activities of the Company; in addition he would remain as Company representative at the Air Transport Licencing Board.

The other appointment was that of Mr. John Wolfe, who joined the Company in its first year of operation at the East Midlands Airport in 1965, as Manager, Commercial Services, responsible for the overall control of the Company's Cargo, Charter and Traffic departments, as well as taking care of the commercial planning activities.

On 27th May yet another Viscount joined the fleet, this time a Series 785 G-AWGV, an ex-Alitalia aircraft I-LIRE (no wonder the Italians wanted to sell it, with that expensive registration).

In July 1968 British Rail, to the glee of airlines such as BMA, decided to go on a work-to-rule. As a direct result of this industrial action, the amount of cargo being pushed through the Company's cargo department went up by leaps and bounds, particularly on the Belfast service. By this time a DC3 freighter left every night except Thursdays at 1815 from East Midlands to Belfast, and on Fridays the DC3 was augmented with an additional all-freight Viscount. The rail go-slow now meant that the aircraft were filled to capacity. As Alex Low, the Company's Cargo Manager at the time explained, "If it fits we'll take it". The amount of cargo carried from 1st January to 3rd July, on the Belfast route had exceeded the one-million kilogramme mark. The total freight on the Belfast service from 1st January to 31st December 1967 was 1,271,000 kilos. Other routes too, were showing remarkably good freight returns, the Channel Islands in particular where the Dakota freighter G-AGJV was used every Thursday (hence there was no Belfast service on Thursdays).

In July, the highest-ever number of people to be carried by the Company to the Channel Islands in any one year was reached, with still 2½ months to go before the summer season came to an end, an indication of the fantastic success of mounting an all-Viscount fleet, as had been recommended to the Company in the Cramp/Marshall/Clay survey of 1965.

On the 22nd August the official inquiry report into the Argonaut crash at Stockport was published. Both the Company and Capt. Marlow, who survived, were exonerated. The cause of the crash was confirmed as the inadvertent transfer of fuel in flight from the main to the auxillary tanks, this being brought about by the design of the fuel system components which, although acceptable at the time the Argonaut was certified in 1949, would not have reached the standards required from a design viewpoint in 1967. In the meantime Capt. Marlow had been informed by the Board of Trade that he was permanently unfit for flying due to injuries he received to his back, legs and head in the crash, and he would never be able to fly again.

G-ANTD—"Tear Drop", the Company's first Dakota, finally left on 17th October, when she was sold to Cameroons Air Transport as TJ-ACF. "TD" had served continuously with the Company for thirteen years and had logged 13,600 hours with BMA alone, carrying during that time some 250,000 passengers, and had recently notched up her two millionth mile of passenger carrying. The only Dakota now left with the Company was G-AGJV, used exclusively as a freighter.

A wet-lease contract (that is aircraft with crews) was obtained from Ghana Airways in mid-October with another wet lease to Nigerian Airways commencing on 10th November. In both cases the aircraft were Viscounts and were accompanied by engineers. Both aircraft remained in Company livery. The aircraft to Ghana was commanded by Capt. Roger Wise who flew Viscount 831 G-APNE to Accra via Seville, Las Palmas, Dakar and Robertsfield. The routes operated during the period of the lease were from Accra to Lagos and return, and Accra to Abidjan, Robertsfield, Freetown, Bathurst, Dakar and return.

The 1st November was the day that the Company's first Jersey Station Manager, in the normally accepted sense of the term, was appointed. He was

101

Mr. George Giles, who had been Station Manager for Channel Airways at Jersey during the previous seven years. The appointment was made in view of the opening that week of the Company's own traffic unit at Jersey, but British United (Channel Islands) Airways were to continue to provide the engineering back-up. Mr. Giles' responsibilities were to be the overall handling of the passengers and aircraft (there were to be as many as 60 flights a week to Jersey in the peak summer weeks), the sales promotion of the Company's services from Jersey to East Midlands, Luton, Staverton, Cambridge and Coventry, and the continued development of freight traffic from Jersey to the mainland.

The former largest shareholders in the Company, Lombard Banking Ltd., had given up their interest in the Company some short time previously, and in order to strengthen the Company's finances another merchant bank, Minster Assets Ltd., were approached who immediately provided the Company with £150,000. There was of course more money in the bank in any event. Ron Paine explained that Minster would take a substantial stake in the Company, with £150,000 in convertible loan stock which on full conversion would give the bank control. The Company were very happy with the arrangements which ensured full continuation of the operation.

Two days before Christmas, it was announced that since 1st January, 2,000,000 kilos of cargo had been carried on the Belfast service.

To mark the occasion, the Company carried a consignment from Height Heels of Leicester Ltd., free of charge in a specially constructed crate painted "2,000,000 Kilos" on its side. The free transportation for Height Heels was made as a gesture of thanks by the Company to all the shippers in the East Midlands and Northern Ireland who used the service. The total lift for year ending in December 1967 had been 1,271,000 kilos, so that the record figure of 2,000,000 reached before Christmas 1968 showed an increase of nearly 60 per cent.

So ended yet another hectic year, one full of events. The fleet now stood at:—

Viscount 831	G-ASED, G-APNE	Viscount 785	G-AWGV
Viscount 815	G-AVJA, G-AVJB	Dakota	G-AGJV
Viscount 736	G-AODG	Leopard Moth	G-ACLL
Viscount 760	G-AWCV		

1969

THE New Year opened with an air of expectancy within the Company, even more so when on 3rd January, the following announcement was made:—

"The Board of British Midland Airways Limited, and Invicta Airways Ltd., announce that they have reached agreement in principle for the merger of the two Companies. The merger has the approval of the Minster Assets group of companies who are major shareholders of both companies. The Boards have retained Messrs. Peat, Marwick Mitchell and Company to recommend the financial terms for a merger, and it is hoped that the terms will be finally agreed by early February 1969.

"Pending a complete merger it is agreed that the two companies will immediately commence close co-operation in all facets of their operation".

At,the time, British Midland Airways had a capital of £175,500 of which Minster Assets held £150,000. Other principle shareholders were the Board of Directors, R. R. Paine, D. W. T. Sullivan, M. M. Ager and F. M. Marshall, together with E. W. Phillips, M.B.E., who had retired in 1965.

Invicta, based at Manston, operated two Viscount 755's, G-AOCB and G-AOCC, together with three C-54A Skymasters, G-ASEN, G-ASPM and G-ASPN.

On the 14th January the first visible signs of the Invicta merger were shown, when a Viscount from Invicta was flown into the East Midlands Airport to undergo a major check by British Midland Engineering Division.

20th January saw another ex-British United Airways Viscount 831, G-APND, delivered to the Company, making three of this series now in the fleet.

On the 8th February the details of the merger with Invicta were announced. All the Viscount aircraft would be operated under the name of British Midland, and the fleet of C.54A Skymasters under the name of British Midland-Invicta Cargo. The merger would cause about 50 redundancies (none at Castle Donington "at this stage"), but crew complement would be increased. Terms, which the Boards of both airlines would recommend their shareholders to accept, would technically require British Midland Airways making an offer for the share capital of Invicta. Minster Assets (who inspired the whole move in any event) agreed to the proposed terms.

On the merger becoming effective (on March 18th), the Board would be:—

Mr. Peter Cannon (head of Minster Assets) Chairman Designate

Mr. R. R. Paine—Joint Vice Chairman and Managing Director

Mr. H. C. Kennard—Joint Vice Chairman

The remaining Directors of both companies would remain as Directors. The issued share and loan capital was now £626,000, of which £600,000 was deposited by Minster, giving them the controlling interest. It was Minster's idea to project a Minster-controlled group, to be known as Air Britain, though retaining the name British Midland Airways. This idea was now well on the way to fruition.

During a snow-storm at the East Midlands Airport on 20th February Viscount G-AODG, the first Viscount to be delivered to the airline, was written off in a landing accident. As if this accident were not bad enough, at 1558 on Thursday, 20th March, Viscount G-AVJA, with Captain I. Wallace in command, First Officer R. A. Weeks as his co-pilot, and Stewardess S. Wallis and Stewardess J. Timson on board crashed whilst taking off from Manchester on a training flight to Edinburgh, the only survivor being Stewardess Jane Timson.

16th March saw another Viscount, a Series 814 G-AWXI, go into service. Previously owned by Condor Flugdienst as D-ANOL, the aircraft had been delivered to the Company on the 22nd January and had been overhauled and refurbished by the Company's Engineering Division. This aircraft was in fact the first to appear in the slightly altered livery commensurate with the merger with Invicta. The basic British Midland livery was retained, but the fin was now altered to be all white (a continuation of the roof line) and the Invicta symbol of a white rampant horse on a dark blue background, the background being a disc, replaced the usual British Midland sign.

On Tuesday 25th March, it was announced that fourteen staff were in fact to be made redundant. In addition it was announced that the Edinburgh service was to be discontinued.

The streamlining was aimed at increasing the profitability of the Company. In addition it would put British Midland Airways in a position where it could think about extending its scheduled service network. That could only be done if the existing routes were making a profit, which the Edinburgh service was not. A considerable amount of money had gone into promoting the route, but the passengers had not bee forthcoming, and although the Company did not like wielding the axe there was no other alternative. The Glasgow service was to continue and would in fact provide three services a day (two from East Midlands and one from Leeds/Bradford).

In addition, the Company's reservations offices in Derby, Nottingham, Leicester and Sheffield were closed immediately, and it was their staff which went to make up most of the fourteen redundancies.

Yet more was to come. Mr. Peter Cannon, Chairman-designate, had on 5th March stood down in favour of Mr. James Hodgson, another Minister Director. In fact, Mr. Cannon found that at the time he could not cope with being Chairman of Minster, B.M.A. and Invicta, and devote the proper amount of time necessary to all three, so for the time being he dropped out of the airline world. At this a spate of rumours began to circulate to the effect that disenchantment with the investment had set in at Minster. There was speculation that Minster were selling the Company, possibly to British Air Services. At a Board meeting on 20th March, two new Directors were appointed from within the Company, Mr. M. D. Bishop (General Manager) and Captain S. D. Fenton (Operations Director). The meeting also confirmed the appointment of an accountant, Mr. H. Free, to the Board.

Mr. Hodgson was expected to make some fairly sweeping changes within the Company. Of Michael Bishop he said "He has already proved himself and his appointment makes a significant step forward for the Company."

The question of the sale of the Company was definitely ruled out. The truth of the matter was that the presence of Minster Assets had suddenly hit the Company like a bomb. With over £600,000 invested, Minster was now applying pressure and wanted to protect its investment and to make sure that the Company realised the potential for success which Minster believed, quite strongly, that it had. The hard commercial impact of the Minster pressure proved a shock for those concerned, but at least it showed the industry that Minster not only saw an opportunity for the Company to get into the black, but it also saw every chance that its present approach would build a viable unit deserving of further investment and expansion.

As if to justify their new-found confidence in the Company, it was rumoured in City circles on 5th May that Minster had increased their investment in British Midland Airways to more than £800,000 this to finance the intended B.A.C. 1-11 purchase.

To make up for the loss of capacity due to the two Viscounts written-off in February and March, the Company leased a British United Viscount G-APTD on 20th April, this augmenting a further Viscount, type 702, G-APPX, acquired from BOAC Associated Companies (ex VP-BBV) on 4th April. The Viscount fleet now consisted of:—

Viscount 833 – 1 off
Viscount 831 – 3 off
Viscount 815 – 1 off
Viscount 814 – 1 off
Viscount 785 – 1 off
Viscount 760 – 1 off
Viscount 755 – 2 off
Viscount 702 – 1 off

All of the above variants were different one from the other, although the 833 and 831 could be considered as the one basic type, the main differences between them being the radio installation. However, there was a major difference between these two and the 815/814 which again could be considered as virtually compatible with each other.

The 810 series again were completely different from the 700 series which again within themselves differed immensely. As a result of all the above it was decided to "Fleet" the crews. Some of these flew all of the 833/831 and the 760 Series (known as Fleet 1) and the rest flew the 815/814 and the 785/755/702 Series (known as Fleet 2). All of this was necessary because of the complexity of flight deck layouts, Operations Manuals, check lists etc., and it imposed a tremendous strain on crewing, Engineering (and in particular the Stores because of the spare parts holding) and catering due to the variations in catering equipment stowages, not to mention Reservations and Operations because of the varying seating capacities of the different Series.

By this time the last remaining Dakota, G-AGJV, had been disposed of to Air Envoy of Birmingham, delivery being made after the aircraft had spent a short period on lease to Gibraltar Airways.

On 3rd June, five directors announced their resignation from the Company "for personal reasons". They were Mr. D. W. T. Sullivan, Mr. F. Marshall, Miss M. M. Agar, all of British Midland (Miss Agar also resigned as Company Secretary, being replaced by Stuart Balmforth) and Captain P. J. Bruce-Souster and Mr. D. Telford both of Invicta.

The same day as the resignations were announced it was revealed that the Company had ordered two B.A.C. 1-11 Series 523 for delivery in 1970, with an option on a third. The aircraft were to be fitted with 119 all-tourist seat configurations, with seat-back catering provided. The Company planned to use the jets to spearhead its rapidly expanding International I.T. operations to the Mediterranean, and also on certain domestic scheduled services.

Yet another Director resigned in early June, this time it being Mr. John Castle, a nominee of Minster Assets on the B.M.A. Board. Mr. Castle who was a main architect of the Invicta merger, resigned as a director of Minster Trust in March.

A further development in the Invicta merger came about on the 7th July, when a surprise announcement was made to the effect that Invicta were to set up on their own again as independent operators specialising in freight and trading under the name of Invicta Air Cargo. Hugh Kennard acquired the assets of Invicta, valued at £250,000. Subsequent to this move the Invicta motif of a white rampant horse on a blue disc background was removed from all of British Midland Airways Viscounts, and was replaced by an all blue fin with the B.M.A. flying flag motif right across the fin and rudder.

The original order for the two B.A.C. 1-11's placed on 3rd June was accompanied by an option on a third such aircraft, and this option was taken up on 16th July when the order was confirmed. Also in July, a licence variation was applied for that was to be of paramount importance in later years, and that was an extension of the existing East Midlands/Birmingham/Brussels licence to take it on to Frankfurt. It was proposed that the variation was to be effective from 1st October, 1969. In fact the route was inaugurated in 1972.

Early in August, Autair International (later known as Court Line) announced its intention of withdrawing from the Teesside to London (Heathrow) route. This service had had a chequered career, having been previously operated by BKS with Birtannia 100 Series aircraft, only to be eventually given up as non-viable, at which point, Autair applied for and obtained the licence, operating smaller 748's on the route.

With the announcement by Autair that they, too, were to withdraw, B.M.A. applied for the route, the announcement being made public on 20th August. Strangely enough, B.K.S. stated that they were intending to apply for the service again but in fact never did, the only objectors to British Midland's application being from Dan Air, and even their objection only came at the last moment accompanied by their own application to operate the route. In addition to the London services the Company also applied for Teesside to the Channel Island, also hitherto operated by Autair.

It was intended that, should the licences be granted, the London service would be picked up the first day of the Autair withdrawal, i.e., 1st October, and would be operated initially twice a day, the off-peak service calling in at East Midlands to provide a London service from the Midlands as well. The service would be a year-round operation but the Teesside-Channel Islands service would be a summer season only operation.

Package tours had long been established to the Mediterranean resorts and elsewhere, but so far as the Channel Island were concerned, the flights fell within the category of British domestic services, and package tours had always been taboo. Then early in August the Company became the first British airline to make an approach to the Air Transport Licensing Board to operate Inclusive

Tour flights to Jersey. It was proposed that during the period March 28th to May 8th Clarkson's Inclusive Tours to the island should operate for seventy eight flights, with a maximum of 3000 passengers for the experimental period. Should the initial venture prove a success it was hoped the scheme would be extended, with the Air Transport Licensing Board's permission, to include also the end of the season, i.e. the first week in September until the 1st weekend in November. The tours were to last for one or three days and would only operate from Luton. British United, British United Island, and B.E.A. all objected to the Company's proposition, but the Company were of the opinion that there was a need for the same type of growth that the Mediterranean had experienced. Jersey at that time, it was felt, was not ready for the "explosion" that had occured in the Mediterranean and therefore only the shoulder months of the season had been asked for. It was a bold move on the part of Michael Bishop, but then, foreign carriers had been operating package tours to Jersey as they were not picking up in the U.K. and therefore the flights were international and not domestic and therefore permissable. The Danes in particular had operated these flights. The application was granted and the tours operated successfully at a later date.

A further development in the by now much-contested Teesside-London route came when on 27th September it was announced that the Chairman of the Teesside Airport Joint Committee was to travel to London to talk to senior executives of B.K.S. about operating the route. Then, on 29th September, it was announced that the Air Transport Licensing Board had granted B.M.A. an exemption to fly the route, and British Midland added that it intended to commence operations from 3rd November.

The speculation was not yet over though, and it was obvious that the Airport Joint Committee were sceptical about B.M.A. taking over the Teesside-London route, the scepticism being based on the fact that the Company had held a Manchester-Teesside-Newcastle licence but did not operate the route very long, and the worry now was: would the Company in fact operate the Teesside-London route? This nervousness on the part of the Joint Committee showed itself when on 2nd October Teesside Airport officials travelled to the East Midlands Airport to meet Company representatives, to discuss whether or not the option to operate the route would be taken up. After the meeting, a statement was issued saying "A frank and constructive discussion has been held and both parties have adjourned to consult with their appropriate committee and Board of Directors with a view to British Midland Airways being able to make a decision by October 8th for the continuation of services after the termination of the present operator's licence".

All the speculation, came to an end on Monday, 13th October when, at a Press conference called at Teesside Airport, Michael Bishop announced that the Company would be starting operation on Monday, 3rd November with Viscount aircraft, twice daily in each direction, Monday to Friday, with a ten-minute stop at East Midlands. Mr. Bishop said that a very close watch on costs would be made, and the future continuation of the service would depend on these assessments. Asked about the introduction of BAC 1-11 jets on the service, the Managing Director said that although the Company was taking delivery of three of these aircraft, their introduction to the Teesside-London route would depend on support. It was also announced that Mr. Michael Finlay, Station Manager of Autair International, had been appointed Station Manager for the Company. Today the service operates four times daily Monday to Friday, and also operates twice a day at weekends.

On the 14th October, the Company announced that it intended withdrawing its operations in and out of Staverton at the end of the year. The runway there was not big enough for BAC 1-11's and even the Viscount found it hard going there. As the Airport Committee at Staverton could not see any way of lenhthening the runway (it would cost £1½m), the Company could see no option but to withdraw. It would be sad to be going, as services had been operated for 11 years and a lot of hard work had gone into the operation.

The Company's entry into the jet era, already announced through the acquisition of the BAC 1-11's, was further enhanced when on 23rd October it was hinted in the aeronautical press that a $50,000 deposit had been put down with Pan American for two Boeing 707's. The Company declined to comment on this; however one travel trade paper went so far as to say that both Boeings were to be delivered in the Spring of 1970 and would go to Aviation Traders to be fitted with a large freight door.

The first British Midland Airways Teesside-Heathrow service operated as promised on 3rd November, coupled with the first-ever East Midlands-Heathrow service. Five hundred advance bookings had been made for the Teesside service and the first flight left with 50 passengers, a 50% increase on the Autair inaugural flight on the same service in the previous year. Fifteen passengers were picked up at East Midlands, and there was in addition 200 kilos of freight on the flight. One month after the commencement, it was announced with pride that every flight had left Teesside Airport on schedule, and more than 2,000 passengers had been carried. For the month of November, it was a particularly good record bearing in mind the fog that normally persists at that time of the year. Not a bad start to the new service.

To close the year on a pleasant note, it was announced on 29th December that the Company's first B.A.C. 1-11 (523) G-AXLL would be handed over very early in the New Year.

The fleet on 31st December was as follows:—

Viscount 833 – G-APTD (on lease from B.U.A.)
Viscount 831 – G-ASED, G-APNE, G-APND
Viscount 815 – G-AVJB
Viscount 814 – G-AWXI
Viscount 785 – G-AMGV
Viscount 760 – G-AWCV
Viscount 755 – G-AOCB, G-AOCC
Viscount 702 – G-APPX
Leopard Moth – G-ACLL

1970

The New Year, and for that matter the '70's, were heralded by the delivery to the company at the East Midlands Aiport on Monday 5th January of G-AXLL, the first of the BAC 1-11 Series 523 to be required, and of course the first jet aircraft to be operated by British Midland. Officially handed over by the Vice-Chairman of the British Aircraft Corporation, Sir Geoffrey Tuttle, "LL" was accepted on behalf of the Company by Mr. J. H. Hodgson, Company Chairman. Mr. Hodgson said, "Delivery of our first BAC 1-11 jet is a significant and progressive development in our endeavour to provide continuing improvement in scheduled services by British Midland Airways. It will improve services in particular from the East Midlands Airport". He later went on to say that the Company intended to build an airline that the community would be proud of and all could benefit from. He praised the courage and foresight of those who had started the East Midlands Airport and hoped they would be encouraged by the £6 million investment that would bring the jets into service by April.

The aircraft was in one-class configuration with 119 seats upholstered in mustard and orange. A recessed space on seat backs was provided for clip-in pre-packed meals which were inserted before take-off, thus eliminating in-flight service.

Michael Bishop, Managing Director, announced that the Company's advertising copy would acclaim "B.M.A. now has a sting in its tail", a reference to the 1-11's tail-mounted Auxiliary Power Unit. He also stated that the aim of British Midland Airways was to dilute its scheduled service network by expansion of the Inclusive Tour market activity to a point where the rate was roughly 35% schedules, 55% I.T. and the remaining 10% as ad hoc charter. Three to four years later there was to be a complete reversal of this policy when no Inclusive Tour work would be done and 95% of all flying was devoted to scheduled services. However, that was in the future.

B.M.A. now has "A sting in the tail" BAC 1-11 G-AXLL undergoing a check 'A' prior to flight. (Hall)

109

The situation on that 5th January was that the three 700 Series Viscount were up for disposal, leaving just the 810 Series, much to the delight of the Viscount training Staff who would now at least have their total training work-load reduced, and to the delight of the Operations Planning Department, who now would have Viscount crews who could operate all of the Company's Viscount aircraft instead of just two variants, thus making for greater flexibility. For the 1-11's, contracts were already in being with Blue Sky, Global, Arrowsmiths, Lun-Poly and Vista with a commitment of more than 5,000 hours.

Finally, reference was made by the Chairman to the possible acquisition of Boeing 707's. At that time "feasibility studies" were being made to discover on what routes, if bought, the 707 would be most profitable. Talks had been held with Pan American World Airways, Qantas, Eastern Airlines and Boeing.

Guests at a luncheon in the Albany Hotel in Nottingham that day were privileged to see for the first time the Company's new cabin staff uniform for "jetting into the seventies". Due to production difficulties only one stewardess appeared in the new uniform in the person of Miss Diana Moore. The new uniform was in flame red, contrasting completely with the turquoise blue collarless style in use up until that time. The new style was designed by Teddy Tinling and represented a complete break from the traditional hostess uniform, comprising a short sleeved A-line dress well above the knee, a loose fitting jacket with mandarin collar and matching top coat, all in bonded jersey. The hat was to have been a wide-brimmed style but these were considered to be "too natty", so a style more in keeping with Robin Hood style was designed. In winter the girls wore knee-length black boots, and in bad weather a "wet-look" scarf was worn over the hat.

New Cabin Staff/ Ground Staff uniform introduced when the BAC 1-11 went into service. (British Aiports Authority)

It will be remembered that the Teesside-London service was being operated on a "permit-to-operate" pending a full A.T.L.B. hearing for the licence for the route, and that Dan-Air Services had lodged objections to the application. On Tuesday 20th January, the hearing took place with Tim Walden, Scheduled Services Manager, representing the Company. The Viscount being used on the route was a much more suitable type, in economic terms than the type used by Autair, the previous operators. During November and December a total of 3,642 passengers had used the service. Walden asked the Board for a quick decision in order that appropriate time-tables could be finalised and published and other arrangements finalised.

Three days after the hearing, i.e. on Friday 23rd January, the Licensing Board made known its decision in favour of the Company the licence proper to take effect from 1st February. At the same time licences from Teesside to the Channel Islands, Belfast, Dublin and the Isle-of-Man, effective on 1st April were granted.

On Thursday 22nd January, Viscount 814 G-AWXI arrived at London-Heathrow from Teesside via Castle Donington. After the 38 passengers had boarded, the aircraft commander, Captain Roger Wise, called for start-up clearance and the aircraft taxied out and commenced the take-off run. At about 1200-1500 feet a bang was heard and the aircraft was felt to shudder. The fire warning bell sounded, and No. 4 engine fire warning light came on. Captain Wise contact London Radar informing them that he had an engine on, fire, and received heading and height instructions to position on a right-hand downwind leg. (It should be mentioned here that the weather was right on minimum limits and was not good by any standards). Wise now asked F/O Guilbert for a visual check on the progress of the fire and was told it was burning badly. This information was passed to radar. Meanwhile the Cabin Staff, having seen the fire and heard the fire bell (which they took to be the crash bell) had ensured that the passengers were strapped in, instructed them to adopt the brace position and leave the cabin by the port exits when the aircraft stopped.

At this point, London Approach requested the aircraft type and number of souls on board (comforting thought), and then instructed "XI" to descend to 1500 feet and turn on to base leg. On completing the turn Captain Wise saw the approach lights and informed approach control. A normal landing was carried out and the aircraft was brought to rest on the runway.

Captain Wise ordered F/O Guilbert to shut all engines down and, using the Public Address system on the aircraft, ordered the passengers to evacuate. Wise then ordered Guilbert to carry out his evacuation drill, who then left his seat and pushed the flight deck door outwards, only to have it stuck against the escape rope access panel from the rope stowage above the crew entrace door, which Stewardess Crocker was attempting to remove. Guilbert pulled the panel clear, squeezed thrugh, found the cabin staff seat down, pushed it up and followed the first passenger down the escape rope. In the meantime Captain Wise left the flight deck, stood at the flight deck door, holding the cabin staff seat up and controlling the flow of passengers to the forward exit.

Onm passenger, Mr. R. Dawson of Bramcote, near Nottingham, slipped and fell off the port wing after leaving by an overwing exit, and also sprained an ankle. Mr. Dawson, a wartime airman said "Strangely enough I was not worried, and that goes for most of the passengers. There was no sort of panic. Captain Wise did a tremendous job and that goes for the cabin crew as well". Two other passengers had minor finger injuries, one had a minor foot injury, and one had to be treated for shock.

The primary cause of the fire was a cracked swirl chamber in No. 5 fuel burner of the engine, causing local torching, overheating part of the turbine disc which expanded so that the blades either came adrift or were torn out when they came in contact with the nozzlm box. The blades penetrated the nozzle box casing, and struck and disconnected the throttle and H.P. cock rods (thus preventing the feathering of the propeller). The fire started when the combusion chambers parted, burning holes in the inner cowling skin and an access panel. This now allowed external airflow inside the cowling. Fire destroyed the seal around the firewall, allowing the fire to progress into zone 3, where a hole was burnt in the wing leading edge undersurface. No. 4 fuel tank was charred and the fire had penetrated into the leading edge heating duct. All of the crew acted with coolness and courage and deserve all credit.

The British Aircraft Corporation calculated that the starboard wing, weakened by the fire, had approximately 20 seconds of life left when the aircraft came to rest. A very lucky crew and passenger list indeed. G-AWXI never flew again and was eventually broken up, the nose section being purchased by the Leicester Police Force for use in emergency training, so it is still, after all that, doing a useful job.

A statement appeared in the national press on 29th January to the effect that Minster Assets, who had just arranged a loan of £3m from the National Westminster Group, were to put £1.5m of that loan into the Company. Minster now owned 90% of British Midland Airways, and the Chairman of Minster, Mr. Peter Cannon reckoned that the Company could become a viable internal airline with proper management and the sort of sound financial backing Minster intended giving.

Another new innovation launched by the Company was announced on 5th February, when the Company entered the Inclusive Tour business again but with a difference, for this time it was a domestic route that was the object of the exercise—Newquay. Believed to be the first holidays of the kind in Britain, the scheme was the result of negotiations between the Company and Newquay Hotels Association. Holidaymakers from Glasgow, Manchester, Birmingham and East Midlands Airport would be able to fly to Newquay staying in hotels, guest houses and even caravan sites of their choice. Proprietors of several of these kind of establishments had applied to join in the scheme and already an encouraging number of bookings had been received.

The evening service to Belfast on 24th February was a notable one in that it was the first flight by the Company using a jet (the 1-11) with fare-paying passengers. Although not officially going into service until 1st April, the aircraft was being slotted into the route structure as required in order to carry out crew line training. In fact only that morning, after a proving flight to Jersey from the East Midlands in 46 minutes, (a route record) had the Air Operator's Certificates for the 1-11 been issued. Two days later "LL" operated the morning service to Glasgow via Leeds with 23 passengers on board from East Midlands and picked up a further 18 passengers at Leeds. Within minutes three telephone calls were received from local residents complaining of the noise. As the aircraft was operating at a light weight (the runway at Leeds/Bradford was a short one for the 1-11), one wonders how many complaints would have been received if it were at maximum take-off weight.

In mid-March, the third and final B.A.C. 1-11 was delivered, and at the same time the news was released that the financing of the three aircraft was through a lease arrangement for the first two (G-AXLL, G-AXLM) from British Aircraft Corporation, whilst the third aircraft (G-AXLN) was leased from Eastlease Limited, a leasing subsidiary of the Norwich Union Insurance Society. On 26th March it was stated that the Company were in fact considering buying two further 1-11 523's, but, these never did materialise.

In order to officially introduce the new jets to the travelling public, a 1-11 operated the morning Glasgow service on 20th March, returning with the Lord Provost of Glasgow, and the Lady Provost, together with key figures from the travel agency world, industrial transport and Scottish Press.

Speculation had been rife for some weeks about the purchase of long-haul 707 jets, after it was stated in the press that the Company were seeking U.S. Civil Aeronautics Board approval to operate trans-Atlantic charters, the flights being in six categories for group, single-entity, circle-tour and inclusive-tour charters between points in the U.K. and points in the U.S. Permission was also sought for charter flights between 20 European countries and points in the U.S. Then, on 26th March it was confirmed that the first 707, a Series 321, had been purchased from Pan American for a cash outlay of £1,600,000, and that an option had been taken on a second 707 for delivery in September. The first aircraft to be delivered, G-AYVE, was handed over to the Company on 1st April at Windsor Field, Nassau, in the Bahamas. The ceremony took place immediately after the aircraft arrived in Nassau, following a 4-hour delivery flight from the Boeing plant at Wichita, Kansas. Both Mr. Hodgson and Mr. Bishop were present, together with other senior executives of the Company. The 707 Fleet Captain, Captain "Billy" McCash, commanded the aircraft when it left with all of the party on board for Miami International Airport, Florida, where intensive crew training was carried out under the supervision of Pan American Airways training staff. After the training was completed, the Boeing, with 189 economy class seats, was ferried across the Atlantic on Sunday, 26th April via Gander and Keflavik, to become the first Boeing and the largest aircraft yet to have landed at the East Midlands Airport.

To step back in time a few weeks, on 28th March a 1-11 departed from Luton on Britain's first inclusive tour charter to Jersey, a four-day package holiday in St. Helier. Senator Clarence Dupre, President of the Jersey Tourism Committee, said "Tourist traffic to Jersey can be greatly improved by the use of charter tours. The island's hoteliers fully support my committee in encouraging this traffic". It had in fact taken years of work to arrange what could be thought of as the last frontier in the inclusive tour market to be broken, but all concerned will agree that it has paid off and should have been permitted before.

Teesside Airport was and is a favourite location for airlines to carry out their crew training, and British Midland Airways is no exception. Therefore in April it was decided to base a 1-11 there to carry out the training of crews transferring from the Viscount. At the same time it was realised that here was an ideal opportunity to assess passenger reaction to the jets if they were to be dovetailed in to the Teesside-London service, and so it was that on Monday 13th April, for a period of two weeks, the Viscount was withdrawn from Teesside and then replaced with a B.A.C. 1-11. Following this short period came the surprise announcement that the Company was to start on Monday, 4th May, a three-times-a-day jet service direct from Teesside to London. Announcing this on 20th April Michael Bishop said "The new service would cut the journey time down from one hour forty minutes (including the stop at East Midlands) on the Viscount, to 50 minutes. We are very much hoping our new service will be supported by business houses, industry, and the ordinary travelling public. It really could be a question of use it or lose it. We are doing this without any grants and clearly have to put a time limit on our investment".

Alderman Arthur Pearson, Chairman of the Airport Joint Committee said "This is a major breakthrough—one we've been waiting for for years. The development of Teesside has for long been hampered by lack of really good air services, not because of any shortcomings in the airport. British Midland are to be congratulated on their courage and foresight and on their faith in Teesside".

There was no doubt that the introduction of the non-stop service between Teesside and London was popular, for in the first week of the service over 1,000 passengers used the service and bookings were 50% up on the same period in 1969 when Autair operated the service (it will be remembered that Mike Finlay, Station Manager Teesside, had also been Station Manager for Autair the previous year, hence the known accuracy of the figures).

With the introduction of the new jet equipment, a major problem now beset the Engineering Division, and this was to organise a team of trained technicians to service the new aircraft. The bringing into service of two jet types at the same time complicated the task in any event. The intention at this point was to carry out complete maintenance on the B.A.C. 1-11, but with the 707 it was decided only to carry out line servicing in the first instance within the Company, with the major servicing being contracted out to Aviation Traders Limited at Stansted Airport, Essex, where the Company's 707 base was to be. It was the long-term intention however, to carry out all 707 servicing at the East Midlands Airport.

In May 1970 the strength of the Engineering staff at Castle Donington was 82 which, bearing in mind that there were four Viscount 810 series aircraft, plus the three new 1-11's, was not a team of any great size, and it was therefore incumbent on that team to be the best in the business and carrying on, it must be stressed, the tradition of high quality maintenance that had been set down by Roy Harben in the beginning and maintained throughout the Company's history.

Preparations for Gamma Radiography of transition ducts for crack detection. Boeing 707—
Pratt and Whitney JT4 engine

Now that the 707 engineering requirements were sorted out, and the required work for the type to be incorporated on the Air Operator's Certificate almost completed, it was necessary to obtain the operating permits required, particularly in the United States, where it was anticipated that a lot of the flying would be to and from. In March the Company had applied to the U.S. Civil Aeronautics Board for the permit, as had been previously stated, and the hearing was taken in mid-May. At the hearing it was stated to the C.A.B. that a profit of £70,000 was expected in the financial year ended 30th September, with assets of £500,000 and £2.4m in additional finances was available which Minster Assets would provide. No passenger-carrying U.S. airlines made any objection to the application being made, and a C.A.B. examiner recommended that a "Foreign Carrier Permit" to be granted. On 28th May President Nixon approved the granting of the permit, which was issued on 2nd June. The speed

115

with which the permit was obtained, altogether 12 weeks from start to finish, and the hearing only lasted one day, was at that time without precedent. Indeed the speed with which the type endorsement on the Air Operator's Certificate was achieved stands as something of a record in itself, it being barely five months from the time the decision was taken to enter the long-haul jet field to the A.O.C. endorsement being awarded in May. The first trans-Atlantic flight to be operated by the Company departed from Stansted early in June for New York, with 186 passengers from an international friendship club.

To keep the Boeing in the air requires of course not only engineers and aircrew, but also sales staff to "sell" the aircraft to the travel trade, and it was here that Mike Kemp, 707 Fleet Sales Manager, came into his own. Mike joined the Company from the by now defunct British Eagle International, with which company he had also been selling 707 space. He also confirmed what a lot of other people had been saying for a long time, and that was that Americans and Canadians like nothing better than to see the name "British" painted on the sides of aircraft. Most certainly they liked to feel that they were travelling with a British company, and there was undoubtably a need for another British carrier in those markets.

After Mike Bishop's warning to Teesside that "you use it or lose it" with reference to the London jet service, passengers began to return to the service. Some fairly aggressive marketing was used to promote the service, one aspect of which involved sending out free tickets to local businessmen for the service, the face value of which amounted to £30,000. No British airline had ever used this kind of promotion before and it was felt in some circles that reaction from other airlines could be critical. However, Mr. Julian Rogers, Publicity Officer for the Company stated, "It is an unusual promotion but the circumstances behind it are also very unusual. The service was just about justifying itself with two Viscount services a day—now we find ourselves more or less overnight with four times as many passengers to find for the jet service to justify itself. We are going to need every man-jack on Teesside to do this."

One of the free tickets was even being sent to Mr. N. R. A. Paton, British Rail's Eastern Region Divisional Manager, but Julian Rogers explained that the Company were not trying to cut out British Rail, but to overcome the inertia of businessmen with regard to air travel. The voucher system used for this "free sample" was a big success, with 800 tickets being used out of the 1500 being offered, and by the middle of June 1249 passengers used the service in one week (15th to 19th June). However, the most significant fact was that the service carried 488 more passengers that week than the same week in 1969. The Teesside service was just about established, but there was a fair way to go yet.

9th July saw the simultaneous opening of the Company's new sales offices in New York and London, using a trans-Atlantic telephone call. Bill Allen, in the office at 516 Fifth Avenue, New York, made the call to 33 Saville Row, London and officially declared both office open. At the Saville Row end, the Chairman Mr. Hodgson announced that a second Boeing 707 was being negotiated with Pan American. The original intention, he said had been to operate two, but it was later decided to adopt a more cautious approach and use only one 707 initially. Now the nature of the order book would seem to justify the taking of the second 707 in May 1971.

It was announced that a major Inclusive Tour programme was to be mounted in 1971 from the East Midlands Airport, using the 1-11's. Up to 11 flights a week commencing May and ending early October would be made to Alicante, Barcelona, Cagliari, Ibiza, Palma and Rimini. The main series was a co-operative venture for Hickey Borman and Millbanke Travel of the Forte Group, Blue Sky and Cosmos Tours. Sheffield United would also be operating flights from the East Midlands to Palma, and to connect with its European Coach holidays.

Mr. Hodgson made two related points. One was that he wanted to dispel the idea that British Midland Airways was growing too fast for its own good; the other that the new Boeing was justified by the volume of business the first aircraft had been able to attract.

Michael Bishop revealed some interesting scheduled service figures at the opening. 85,272 passengers were carried in the three months 1st April to 30th June compared with 54,391 during the same period in 1969. Biggest gain over the period was the Glasgow service 20,930 (13,720 in 1969), Isle-of-Man, Ostend and Newquay 4,843 (3,408), Channel Islands 35,562 (27,860), Dublin 4,203 (3,937) and Belfast 6,254 (5,916).

Also on the 1st September, Captain B. G. Cramp, who had been Operations Manager when he left the Company in January 1966 to emigrate to Canada where he flew float-planes for a time, rejoined the Company, this time as a Viscount Training Captain and Instrument Rating Examiner.

The long-awaited decision about the future of the Teesside-London service was made public when on 24th September the Company announced its intention to keep the route going. The announcement came as the 25,000th passenger boarded the 1-11 board for London. Mike Bishop making the announcement stressed however that if the service was not used to its full advantage then the Company would have no option but to pull out. Alderman A. Pearson, Chairman of the Airport Joint Committee, said the announcement was a real boost for Teesside. "We welcome it. This is indeed a step forward in the right direction". Another report stated that the decision came as a relief: "British Midland Airways put Teeside Airport on five months trial. In return for a daily jet service to London it asked for at least 1500 passengers to use the flights. The trial period is now up and the target has not been reached. But the passenger increase has been so encouraging that the airline has withdrawn its threat to pull out. The decision is a vote of confidence in our airport and it is now up to the Region to give the support". Yet another commentator said "Teesside has cause to be grateful". The Company's faith in Teesside has of course paid off, for by 1972 the service was operating four times a day from Monday to Friday plus a weekend service. Later on five services a day were to be operated, and in 1976 the DC9 entered service on the route.

Although in October 1969 it had been stated that the Company would not operate through Staverton in 1970, services were in fact operated to the Channel Islands through that airport during 1970. However, the last scheduled service to operate through Staverton was Flight BD 173, departing at 1505 on Saturday, 26th September 1970. Unfortunately the service did not operate "for operational reasons", so that in fact the last British Midlands Airways scheduled service from Staverton took place on Saturday 19th September.

Announcing the 1970/71 Winter Timetable at the end of September, Michael Bishop said that the 1-11 had helped to boost the scheduled service carryings by 52%, for in the five months ended 31st August, the number was 183,215 fare-paying passengers as against 120,425 during the equivalent period in 1969. The new timetable reflected the Company's desire to build further traffic on trunk routes, with Teesside retaining the 1-11 on a twice-daily service Monday to Friday, and Jersey, for the first time, was to have a jet service from East Midlands and Birmingham. Glasgow, Belfast, and Dublin were to retain the existing summer services throughout the winter.

At the same time the Luton via East Midlands to Glasgow service was to stop although it was planned to recommence it in the Spring of 1971 (in fact it has not operated since).

On Sunday 11th October, Mrs. A. Joyce, vice-President of a 2,000 strong branch of the Catholic Women's League based on Hebburn, Co. Durham, signed the Company's first Teesside-based trans-Atlantic charter contract. The agreement, signed on board a 707 which had flown to Teesside to take part in an air display, was to take 186 members of the League to Toronto on 14th August, 1971, returning on 5th September. After the signing ceremony the aircraft was put on view to members of the public.

So ended a most remarkable year. Three 1-11 523's plus a Boeing 707 had been introduced into service, and a major "bread and butter" route had been firmly established. Passenger carryings had shot up and all looked well for the future—or so it seemed. Unfortunately the immediate effects of all these developments on the finances was less heartening, and at the end of 1970 were only just being seen. The introduction of the 1-11 coincided with a period at which peak European Inclusive Tour traffic growth rate was more or less zero.

Rates were extremely poor and with the introductory costs to bear were hardly profitable. Most of the traffic growth was in fact on the "shoulder" and off-peak months, where time-charter rates tend to be geared to direct operating costs and not total operating costs. Additionally, although the 1-11 most definitely put the Teesside-London service on its feet, and the Glasgow service from the East Midlands, the 1-11 was simply not the right aircraft for the work, especially with the traffic potential available.

Similarly for the 707, both the aircraft and the Company's own related organistion met up to the demands made, but the marketing for this very different kind of travel proved to be more challenging than had been anticipated, and dividends were slow to be yielded. However most of this would be more than apparent in 1971.

At the end of 1970 it was decided that flying training no longer fitted into the Company's requirements and so it was that the Midland School of Flying ceased to be operated by the Company, although the Chief Flying Instructor, Frank Spencer, bought the School himself and continued to operate it under the same name, thus in a sense continuing the long line. It was 32 years previously when Air Schools came into operation and there had been an unbroken continuation of flying training ever since.

However, it was as an airline that the Company wished to continue, and so it was inevitable that the training side of the activities should ultimately cease and Air Schools as a company or as a group ceased to exist with it. 1970 was, in any event, a most remarkable year.

The operating fleet at 31st December, 1970 was:—
Viscount 831 – G-APNE, G-ASED, G-APND
Viscount 815 – G-AVJB
BAC 1-11 (523) – G-AXLL, G-AXLM, G-AXLN
Boeing 707-321 – G-AYVE
Leopard Moth – G-ACLL

1971

The year started with bad weather, fog and ice playing havoc with all forms of transport. A charter flight using one of the Company's 1-11's diverted from Luton to East Midlands, and the party of Swiss businessmen were most unimpressed with having to wait for an immigration official to travel 80 miles or so from Hull to the Airport, and made their feelings on this point well and truly known. This incident was in fact the first of several such occurrences and was to culminate in the cancellation of a trans-Atlantic series into the East Midlands. This, it might be added, was sufficient to make officialdom stop creaking at the seams, and the problem was finally solved, and not before time.

As if the foregoing were not enough to herald in the New Year, the Boeing (GAYVE) was in-bound from Seattle to Stansted but had to divert owing to bad weather, to Manchester, whereupon a full alert was mounted when an undercarriage unlocked warning was given. Fortunately it was only an electrical fault and the aircraft landed safely.

January saw the birth of "B.M.A. News" the Company house magazine, Sales orientated, the magazine was also distributed to all staff, and was published on behalf of the Company by I.P.R. Consultants, the Company's P.R. contractors, with Nigel Cleavely (at that time Sales and Reservations Manager) as Editor. It is interesting to note that I.P.R. opened their London office at 69 Fleet Street, purely to service B.M.A.'s public relations requirements. Julian Rogers was the "man on the spot", Julian later becoming Sales Director of British Midland Airways.

The first sign of a problem within the Company was hinted at early in February when it was confirmed that the Company had too few aircraft to do too many jobs, and that there was the possibility of sub-contracting the Jersey-Teesside service to a new carrier on the scene—Progressive Airways. At the same time Michael Bishop said that rumour-mongers were deliberately attempting to undermine the services provided by B.M.A. from Teesside. Some rumours even suggested that the Company were to cease operations on the London service at the end of March. The rumours were described as "utter rubbish".

There was one grain of truth in the rumours in that the Company in fact did not have the 1-11 capacity to maintain that type on the Teesside-London service and remain in the Inclusive Tour market. As a result of this, the 1-11's were withdrawn from Teesside scheduled service operation at the end of March and replaced by Viscounts, but still operating a direct London service. There were many people who thought this to be the death-knell of the service, but all were to be proved wrong. Today the service is operating on a four times a day basis and it is proved that it is reliability and frequency of service that the traveller requires, and this is very true of the business traveller. After all, the 1-11 only cut some ten minutes from the Viscount timings, an insignificant amount really on such a short sector.

The placing of the Viscount on the London service now meant that a shortage of Viscounts began to make itself felt, and so a good hard look at the whole scheduled service network was examined under a microscope, with the result that the Leeds-Glasgow service was withdrawn at the end of March in order to provide capacity for Teesside. It was a pity that this event had to take place, especially in view of the tremendous effort put in in previous years by many people on that route. The last service from Leeds was operated by Captain Cramp in Viscount 815 G-AVJB, and on arrival in Glasgow he was presented with a Haggis by the British Midland Airways Glasgow staff. The final service into Leeds arrived at 1800 G.M.T. and the crew were treated to a party at the White Swan in Yeadon village that night, by the B.M.A. Leeds staff. All of the staff at Leeds/Bradford were disbanded, one of the ground handlers going to B.M.A. Jersey for the summer whilst the Station Manager, Mr. Trevor Thomas, transferred to the charter sales department of the Company at East Midlands. Dan-Air took over the route and are still operating it using 748's.

Part of the impending troubles for the Company from the sales viewpoint began to make itself manifest early in the New Year, this being due to poor rates being obtained for the 1-11's on Inclusive Tour services. This was in stark contrast to the news realeased at the same time of the Company's profit of £99,532 (from a loss of £110,616 the year before) for the year ended 30th September 1970.

The Company's first U.S. station was set up on 1st March when Andy Handford, S.D.O. at B.M.A.'s Manchester base, flew to Seattle as Station Manager, ready for the coming summer when a Company Boeing would fly in every thirty hours from the U.K. The first flight from Seattle via Keflavik to East Midlands landed at Castle Donington on 28th March. The same day it was announced that the Company's second Boeing 707-321 G-AYBJ (which was handed over to the Company on 29th December 1970), would be arriving at East Midlands on Thursday 31st March. Four days after arriving at Stansted, "BJ" was operating its first commercial service for the Company by flying out to Jamaica empty to bring back a London based evangelical group with strong Caribbean connections. On board the flight, commanded by Captain John

Blackman, was a camera crew from Movietone News and also the Company's own Caribbean cabin staff. A film was shot for inclusion in a Central Office of Information story in a Commonwealth newsreel, and was subsequently distributed in two editions to more than twenty countries for both T.V. and newsreel consumption.

A first-class row blew up in May when a major U.S. tour operator, American Charter Company, reluctantly forced the Company to transfer its U.K. trans-Atlantic terminal from Castle Donington to Stansted, due to the lack of immigration officials at the airport, and the lack of currency exchange facilities. In a statement to the press Mike Bishop said that the East Midlands Airport had thrown away its chance to become an important terminal for international air traffic. The Company was extremely disappointed and very concerned about events since the Boeing flights from Seattle to Castle Donington had started two months previously. A strong commercial effort had been made to transfer the trans-Atlantic operations to the main base airport for obvious reasons, and there had been nothing but problems. A lot of foreign visitors had gone to the airport and received a distinctly bad impression. Both British Midland Airways and the Airport Authority had stood to profit if the service had remained at Castle Donington, both financially and in the long-term. The sums of money involved were not small, as the airport would have made a minimum of £50,000 in landing fees alone, apart from the prestige involved. The Company stated that there would not be any expansion of British Midlands Airways operations at East Midlands until services improved.

The main problem, not entirely the airport's fault, was because one immigration officer, who had to travel all the way from Hull, was supposed to deal with 186 passengers of every nationality. In addition the airport bank opened only twice a week and, of course, this was completely inadequate.

On Friday, 21st May, the inaugural 707 service from Manchester to Ostend operated. On board were 130 holidaymakers from Manchester and Liverpool on this the Company's first international scheduled service using jets. Included in the 130 were 37 members of the Liverpool Association for the Disabled, whilst members of Manchester Corporation Airport Staff and other non-airline staff members of Manchester Airport were guests of the Company for an afternoon's trip to Ostend and back. The Company particularly wanted to offer the flight to the non-airline staff at the airport who do so much to help give service to B.M.A.'s passengers, but who do not normally have the opportunity of flying as guests of an airline themselves. A very nice gesture, greatly appreciated by such staff as airport police, firemen and so forth. With a fair number of empty seats available, it did not cost the Company anything at all to invite these guests, but the gesture had been made and accepted. A great piece of Public Relations work on the part of the Managing Director, whose idea it had been.

The biggest aircraft ever to have been handled by the Company to date arrived at East Midlands Airport on Saturday, 5th June, 1971. Registration number N301EA, the aircraft was the prototype, Lockheed 1011 Tri-Star, returning to California after being present at the Paris Air Show. The stop-over at Castle Donington was to show the workers at the Rolls-Royce engine factories at Derby the aircraft into which their RB.211 engine had been installed. The aircraft did not present any handling problems directly, but indirectly it caused some chaos as passengers travelling on the Company's services (and for that matter the aircrews operating these services) could not get to the airport on time due to the terrific queues of people and cars trying to get a glimpse of the new wonder.

More positive signs that a deterioration in financial returns was on the way became apparent when the 9th July it was announced that the Company were experiencing a "disappointing summer". News was also given that a loss would probably be turned in after the deduction of depreciation and interest charges. Peter Cannon revealed that after flying a good year in 1970 British Midland Airways was having a disappointing summer and, if the trend continued until September 1971, it would not produce a profit after depreciation and interest charges. However, the Company were strong in management and cash, which should correct the situation in 1972.

Then, in very early September, it was announced that a loss of £1,650,000 was to be expected (it was in fact £1,671,733). The Company's latest budgets and the likely outcome for 1972 were to be examined by the accountants Peat Marwick Mitchell. A forecast of changes in operations with greater emphasis on scheduled services and more selectivity in charter business was made, so that maybe once again good could come out of evil, for here was the beginning of a policy of retraction from the Inclusive Tour business with consequent greater involvement in scheduled services, a policy which, in the winter fuel crisis of 1973/74, was to pay great dividends. There can be little doubt that the Rolls-Royce crisis seriously affected traffic returns on the East Midlands-Glasgow service, and rising world prices at that time particularly fuel prices (in reality insignificant when compared with the very high price rises in 1973/74) brought about a fall-off in charter flights and particularly low rates for those flights that were undertaken. Another contributory factor was the amount of positioning flying that had to be undertaken. In 1971 very few tour operators operated from the East Midlands (the Channel Islands being an exception) and so the 1-11's in particular had to position empty to Luton, Manchester, Birmingham, Bristol or Cardiff. Additionally the lease-purchase agreements on the three BAC 1-11's were of such a nature as to push the rate requirements up to a point where, to obtain an economical return, the rate was too high to attract many operators. Although it was not appreciated at the time, all of these factors were adding up to the need for an almost total emphasis on scheduled services in the long run. One could heave a sigh of relief that this was so at the beginning of 1974, but that is for later.

In contrast to the gloom brought about by the foregoing, it was "all systems go" at Teesside, where the London service was going great guns. The magical 1500 passengers a week had been achieved in spite of the 1-11 being replaced by the Viscount (although the service was by now operating on a three-times-a-day basis), and all monthly figures, except June, had shown a substantially higher number of passengers using the service than the corresponding month in 1970.

For example, 5,181 passengers used the service in August as compared with 4,573 in August 1970). As a result of this most heartening trend, it was decided during the coming winter not only to keep the service at the same frequency as the summer schedule (it was customary up to this point to cut back winter services), but also to mount a weekend service in addition, operating one morning return service on Saturdays, and an afternoon return service on Sundays. It was also hoped to put a 1-11 back on the service for the 1972 summer season, but in fact this was not to be.

Vancouver to East Midlands non-stop, that was the record set up on Sunday 5th September by one of the Company's Boeing 707's. The 4,800 mile flight normally called in at Keflavik, Iceland, but favourable winds allowed the flight to carry on towards Stansted, its scheduled destination. However, there the weather was poor and so East Midlands was selected as the alternate. It was the first time the Company had made the flight non-stop, and it was also the first flight into Castle Donington direct from Vancouver.

The day after the 707 flight above, British Midland opened its first facility at London Heathrow, when a ticket and enquiry desk was opened. All passenger and aircraft handling continued to be carried out by B.E.A. For some time now it had been considered necessary to carry out self-handling at the airport as soon as possible, but obtaining accommodation at Heathrow was more easily talked about than achieved, and it had taken long enough to obtain just this ticket desk. Still, it was a start, and the rest would come later.

In preparation for the 1972 season, Mike Bishop announced several new Continental routes on 8th December, but with his by now customary warning to "use them or lose them" accompanying the announcement. The routes were East Midlands to Brussels and Frankfurt (both via Birmingham), and Amsterdam (direct), a new mid-week Isle-of-Man service in addition to the weekend services, a "substantial increase" in the service to Jersey and Guernsey, and the re-introduction, after a year's absence, of weekend services to both Newquay and Ostend. The Amsterdam service, commencing April 3rd, would be every Monday, Wednesday and Friday, whilst the Brussels/Frankfurt service would operate Mondays, Tuesdays and Thursdays. These services, said Mike Bishop, were an indication of the renewed emphasis on the viable development of scheduled routes, particularly where the Company already had a strong regional representation. In addition to these announcements, television backup advertising was to be used for services out of the areas concerned. By using Midland I.T.V. it was possible to concentrate the effort, and these were backed up with conferences and agents' materials. The sales force, too, was sharpened, and the campaign split into two parts, one covering the period mid-December and January, the other covering mid-March to mid-May. The whole new policy now was to develop as a Midlands-orientated regional carrier, particularly revolving around Birmingham and the East Midlands.

Commensurate with the new route announcements, a slightly restyled livery was announced. Still retaining the house colours of light blue and dark blue, a broad light blue cheat line now ran straight through the window-line on all three types in use, and a wide white line separated this from a dark blue lower line, wide enough on the Boeing 707's and B.A.C. 1-11's in fact to accommodate the name "BRITISH MIDLAND". On the Viscounts, the name still remained above the window line, but the registration letters were now in dark blue letters on the light blue cheat line aft of the passenger door.

So ended yet another year, again an eventful time, but also one of bitter disappointment at the way profits and traffic had dropped. The one good thing was that Minster had by now stated that in spite of the £1.67m loss they intended to continue to back the Company.

Fleets as at 31st December 1971:—

Boeing 707-321	G-AYVE, G-AYBJ
Viscount 815	G-AVJB
Viscount 831	G-ASED, G-APND, G-APNE
B.A.C. 1-11 (523)	G-AXLL, G-AXLM, G-AXLN

1972

Having announced its intention of concentrating on scheduled services and running down the inclusive tour activities, the Company now had to find increased aircraft capacity to live up to its declared undertaking of entering the Continental scheduled services market early in 1972. With this in mind, therefore, Board sanction was sought and obtained to finance the purchase of two more Viscount 810 Series aircraft, but at the very beginning of the year there was no clear-cut idea of where the aircraft were to be obtained from.

In the latter part of November 1971, Mike Bishop had travelled to Tel Aviv on business and before leaving London Heathrow had purchased a copy of 'Flight International' purely with something to read en route in mind. In the "Aircraft for Sale" column was an advertisement that was to profoundly change the course of British Midland's path, and which prompted one speculative remark in a newspaper column that the Company was to acquire South African Airways entire fleet of Viscounts at a price of £750,000. The true story is as follows:

The advertisement read by Mike Bishop did indeed refer to the sale of the entire S.A.A. Viscount 813 fleet, and, having concluded his business in Tel Aviv, Mike made his way South to Johannesburg.

On arrival disappointment reigned supreme when S.A.A. state that, contrary to the content of the advertisement, the Viscounts were to be sold as a fleet complete with spares, and not separately. This presented quite a problem for cash was only available for the two already authorised aircraft. However, completely unabashed, this amount of money was offered for the entire fleet of 813's. Imagine the surprised look that surely must have appeared on Mike Bishop's face when the offer of £98,000 plus £37,000 for the entire Viscount spares holding was accepted.

This latter figure was later raised to £42,000 but to now include the Viscount 813 flight simulator (i.e. the simulator was purchased for £5,000 and was in fact still being operated by S.A.A. at that time)'. Now that the financial side of the deal had been concluded, a,vast amount of work lay ahead as may be appreciated. One question asked was: what were the Company going to do with seven extra Viscounts when only two more were envisaged? Mike Bishop was asking himself the same question too. Fortunately (for British Midland Airways) Channel Airways ceased operations and B.M.A. acquired some of their routes so that the extra Viscounts were very quickly put to good use. In addition the existing fleet was sold, G-AVJB (815) going to Kestrel International, based at East Midlands, as were Alidair, who took delivery of G-ASED (831). Arkia of Israel purchased G-APND and G-APNE (831's), although 'NE' was retained by British Midland Airways until September.

George Morrell, B.M.A. Chief Buyer, journeyed to Johannesburg two weeks before Christmas 1971, accompanied by Tony Topps, Chief Inspector, and Mike Baker, Planning Manager, together with an Air Registration Board representative Ray Atwood, to carry out a survey of the seven aircraft and to make arrangements for their return to the U.K.

On Tuesday, 18th January, the first two aircraft, G-AZLP with Captain Court in command, and G-AZLR with Captain Stevens in command, departed Johannesburg via Blantyre, Nairobi, Khartoum, Benina and Nice, arrived at the East Midlands Airport at mid-day on the 28th January. Subsequently GAZLS, G-AZLT, G-AZNA, G-AZNB and G-AZNC were ferried back to the East Midlands.

When one considers that all of these ferry flights were undertaken using a Flight System completely new to all crews concerned, and in the winter months too, it may be appreciated what a good job was done.

Now that the aircraft were back at the East Midlands, the Engineering Division had the enormous task of converting them to Company and U.K. A.R.B. standards, involving the removal of the complete radio installation from each aircraft and the installation of a new radio station to meet the more exacting European requirements. The design was carried out by Scottish Aviation who supplied a working party, whilst B.M.A. Engineering carried out the installation at a cost of £25,000 per unit.

In addition, all airframe structures and components were inspected for corrosion, cracks, etc. and a complete check cycle carried out. Each instrument panel was re-vamped to comply with A.R.B. requirements, and the brake units on each wheel were modified to latest standards to achieve the maximum takeoff weight permitted (South African Airways maximum take-off weight was considerably lower than at present, due to unmodified main brake units).

Whilst all this basic engineering work was in progress, the original S.A.A. paint was removed and the British Midland colour scheme applied. A tremendous effort was put in by all concerned and the end product on each aircraft was certainly worth all the effort, and the Engineering Division could be justly proud of their achievement. Roy Harben would have been proud to observe the same high standard of engineering he had insisted upon in his own days.

Next, once again, it was the turn of Captain Court and the Viscount training staff to implement the enormous training programme required to convert not only the existing Viscount crews onto the 813, but also crews retraining from the B.A.C. 1-11 (about which more later) and the new intake crews joining the Company. Captain Cramp gave ground courses for the crews, varying from two-day "differences" courses for crews already flying the Viscount, through to one-week courses for ex 1-11 crews and two week courses for new entrants to the Company, whether they were Viscount-endorsed or not. When crews were released by Cramp from the ground school, Captains Court and Shaw carried out the flying training programme. The average conversion flying time was in fact 2½ hours.

In parallel with the foregoing of course, all other departments of the Company were "hard at it" working to effect a smooth entry into service of these new aircraft. One problem encountered very early on was the cabin layout. Unlike the existing fleet with toilets at the rear, the 813's had toilets amidships, in-line with the propeller discs and thus, to give a seating capacity of 78 in common with the 831's meant that the seat-pitch was quite short and very soon passenger complaints were forthcoming. As a result of this, one row of seats was removed, reducing seating capacity to 73 but improving seat pitch, and very favourable passenger reactions were now obtained. The work-load on Reservations in re-allocating the then 78 full-loads were of course considerable. In addition the cabin layout brought P.C.F. (Passenger-cumFreight) problems, as the toilets left only a small area forward, giving reduced cargo volume. With Cargo Division selling hard this was a problem too.

The Operations Department were similarly working hard, with Operations and Training Manuals to be written and produced. Ted Kynnersley, Operations Superintendent, had a race against time to get the correct load computers produced. One particular problem he had was that due to the rate at which the aircraft were coming out of the Engineering Division and into service, the aircraft would be weighed one day and into service the next, leaving him 24 hours to produce all the A.P.S. (Aircraft Prepared for Service) loading data. Quite a job.

All seven 813's were in service by June 1972, and the smoothness with which they entered service was a credit to all staff concerned. British Midland had a good-sized Viscount fleet to be proud of.

In late summer 1972, Julian Rogers left I.P.R. to take up a marketing post in industry, his place being taken by John MacGregor. With John now as the guiding line, B.M.A. News really began to take on shape whilst Cramp continually exerted pressure to get each issue out on time. B.M.A. News was a tabloid newspaper in form and content and Cramp and MacGregor began a series of features in addition to the ones already mentioned, which were continued in each issue until the Summer 1973 issue which was the last to be produced by the pair. The intention had always been to produce the magazine "in house" but it was not until the Autumn 1972 issue that the first production was printed in the Company's own print shop on off-set litho equipment. All of the plate-making had been carried out by a trade firm who then supplied the plates to the Company. The result was a first class product and a credit to the print shop.

In August, 1973, Julian Rogers returned to the Company as Marketing and Sales Director and, with the intention of setting up an "in house" P.R. system, I.P.R. were given notice of termination of contract and so John MacGregor departed from the scene. At the same time, Captain Cramp now had more work than he could really cope with and so he, too, departed as Editor of "B.M.A. News", a new P.R.O., Miss Pat Harris, becoming Editor. Under her leadership the next issue of the magazine appeared in January 1974, but not as a completely sales orientated publication, the staff requirements being met by producing a monthly staff magazine entitled "Outline", which in itself was development of a magazine produced by Terry Liddiard for his "Outlying" stations. This too was produced by Pat Harris.

To return to 1972 however, with the introduction of more scheduled services on the now increased Viscount fleet, several 1-11 crews, as has already been mentioned, were transferred back to the Viscounts. With the poor return of Inclusive Tour work it had become necessary for one 1-11 to be dry-leased to Court Line, leaving just two 1-11's to carry on the Company's own Inclusive Tour work.

In early February, the U.S. Civil Aeronautics Board named B.O.A.C., Air India and B.M.A. in a suit filed in Brooklyn alleging illegal charter operations. The facts behind this rather alarming situation arose out of the almost impossible task of trying to enforce the rules on trans-Atlantic charter flights, in which passengers who travelled on so-called affinity group charters were required to have been fully paid-up members of the club or association with whom they were travelling for at least six months. The onus of checking the bona fides of passengers travelling on any particular flight fell on the carrier, and not on the person who was in fact organising the charter flight. The requirement was almost impossible to impose, for how could any carrier check out the credentials properly? However, both the C.A.B. in the U.S. and the C.A.A. in the U.K. carried out snap checks on passenger lists of aircraft about to depart east or west from the U.S. or U.K., with the result that many flights were cancelled leaving passengers stranded both sides of the Atlantic and often with the hapless airline having to operate across the Atlantic empty. Any wonder that B.M.A. made a loss. In addition, because flights were discovered to be "illegal", Government, mainly the U.S., filed suits and imposed fines. The passengers, in the meantime, invariably walked round the corner and travelled quite often on a scheduled carrier.

On 1st February another British independent airline, this time Channel Airways, went to the wall and an official receiver was appointed. On 25th February it was announced that the Company had purchased for £100,000 part of the Channel Airways network of services, viz: Southend to Jersey/Guernsey, Bournemouth to Jersey/Guernsey, and Stansted to Jersey/Guernsey. The staff and accommodation at Southend were retained although a British Midland

Airways Station Manager, Mr Reg Curwen, Senior Duty Officer at Glasgow, was appointed. In the event, after A.T.L.B. licence hearings, the Company was given the Stansted and Southend licences, but the decision over Bournemouth was given to Dan Air.

Before the licence hearings at the Air Transport Licensing Board, services from Southend (and Bournemouth) were operated under an exemption from the Board. The first scheduled service to be operated by the Company from Southend departed on schedule on Thursday, 2nd March, and, having arrived at Jersey, was quickly turned round to operate the 1315 Jersey to Hurn service, returning to the island at 1515 with 26 passengers and some freight. The aircraft concerned was Viscount 831 G-ASED (this was just before it's departure for sale to Alidair).

The acquisition of the Channel Airways routes and staff meant in fact that the Company's first station at Guernsey was open, for up until this time British United (Channel Islands) Airways had handled all B.M.A's movements, but with the increased traffic due to the Channel movements, it now became economically viable to operate a Company station in its own right. Mike Torrode, Channel Station Manager remained at his post to become B.M.A. Station Manager, Guernsey.

One other facet of the Channel Airways failure was the availability of training aids. Whilst lecturing some ex-Channel aircrew, Cramp was delighted to learn that there were a lot of training aids that Channel had used being put up for bid at Stansted. Hurrying down by car the following day he found, to his great delight, many sectioned components from the Rolls Royce Dart engine; wall diagrams for the engine complete with easel; a complete Vickers-produced Viscount training aids mobile "classroom" consisting of fully coloured systems diagrams together with systems and Dart engine; coloured wall diagrams for the B.A.C. 1-11 and 35mm slide transparencies for the 1-11. The result of this find was that British Midland now have a Viscount course available which is second to none, including the ability to give Dart engine courses "in house". This, coupled with the Viscount simulator shortly to come into use meant a first class trained pilot to such an extent that the Company was now "selling" the facilities to other carriers for their pilot training.

Two events occurred in March which were of importance to the Company insofar as sales and traffic were concerned. On 15th March, it was announced that the Belgian and West German authorities had granted traffic rights between Brussels and Frankfurt for the service that was to begin on 10th April. This was the first instance of a British Independent carrier being given *fifth freedom* rights i.e. allowed to pick up traffic in a foreign country destined for another foreign country, between these two countries for a scheduled service. The other event was the appointment, announced on 24th March, of Clarkair as B.M.A's representative on the Baltic Exchange, to help fill the increased capacity now available, particularly on the charter side. The sales drive commensurate with the new Company policy was about to begin.

Part of the new sales energy abounding were the inaugural flight arrangements for the new Continental routes, all associated with Britain's entry into the Common Market.

The first inaugural was on Friday, 7th April, when Viscount 831 G-APNE flew the first East Midlands-Amsterdam service. The press party on board made it known upon their return that the service facilitated direct air connections from Castle Donington, via Amsterdam, to more than 50 cities throughout the world such as Cairo, Bangkok, Freetown, Karachi, Kuwait, Leningrad, Moscow, Montreal, Singapore, Tel Aviv and others. The flight, scheduled for 90 minutes each way, in fact knocked 15 minutes off each leg, much to the delight of all on board.

The second inaugural was the Brussels/Frankfurt route, which departed on 10th April. With civic dignitaries on board. A civic reception was held in Brussels, at which it was announced that the service could very well be operating on a five-day week basis "very soon". In fact the five times a week frequency came about on September 4th. B.M.A. was represented on the V.I.P. list by Mr. J. Hodgson and Mr. Mike Bishop.

A further "step into Europe" by the Company was taken when on 11th April the Civil Aviation Authority heard an application by British Midland Airways for an East Midlands/Paris (Le Bourget) service. The hearing was the first to be heard (B.M.A. making history yet again) by the new C.A.A., and was presided over by the new Authority Chairman, Lord Boyd Carpenter. The C.A.A. had hoped that its first case would be a relatively simple one, so they must have been taken aback somewhat when four airlines, B.E.A., Dan Air/Skyways, Sagittair and Air Freight, opposed the application. The licence was granted in the Company's favour on 14th June.

Tim Walden, representing the Company at the hearing, submitted that as a result of a survey in connection with services for businessmen from East Midlands to Amsterdam, Brussels and Frankfurt, a demand for services to Paris and other areas in France had been found. In answer to the survey into the demand for a service to Paris, 2,100 firms in Sheffield, Derby, Nottingham and Leicester had answered, showing that in a year approximately 4,000 return journeys were made to France, 80 per cent of them to Paris. More than three-quarters travelled by air, and almost all went from London. In the first year, 5,014 passengers would be required to break even.

As a further evidence of a pressure sales drive, a new innovation was announced by Mike Bishop on 20th May, but this time it was in connection with the Jersey services. From Monday, 22nd May, it became possible for travel agents to determine where accommodation was available in the Island by ringing the local B.M.A. office in Birmingham, Bournemouth, Coventry, Luton, Southend, Stansted and Teeside. Mr. Bishop said "Jersey is an immensely popular holiday destination for all the regions British Midland Airways serves, and our carryings to the Island have shown such an increase that we want to ensure that there is sufficient hotel and guest house accommodation available readily for passengers who still wish to travel to the Island this summer but have not yet made bookings".

Figures made available for April 1972 showed that the Company's carryings to Jersey had doubled when compared with April 1971 (8,307 as against 4,153). This figure was achieved *before* allowing for 7,183 passengers on the Southend and Bournemouth routes carried as a result of Channel Airways' demise. The total carryings were therefore 15,490 in April 1972 as compared with 4,153 in April 1971. This growth in traffic to the Channel Islands underlined the Company's undertaking to tourism authorities in both Guernsey and Jersey, to vigorously develop traffic in the early season from all originating points in the British Midlands network. The new hotel scheme would further strengthen links between the Company and the tourist industry in the Islands and would stimulate additional business.

On June 14th, the U.S. Civil Aeronautics Board announced that three U.K. airlines, Dan-Air, Lloyd International, and British Midland Airways, would require prior approval from the Board for charter flights to the U.S., the order coming into effect on 15th July. All three carriers were accused of violating U.S. regulations which basically required that passengers travelling on charter flights to the U.S. should have been bona fide members of the group organised for purposes other than for travel for at least six months, that the flight should not be advertised and that a return fare based on the true cost of hiring the plane should be paid in advance.

British Midland Airways described the order as "harsh legislation", and took the step of consulting the Company's attorney in the U.S., Paul Reiber, who as it happened was in Europe at that time. Mike Bishop said "We are surprised at the move because we have in fact been in touch with the C.A.B., and a meeting of British Midland Airways and the C.A.B. was scheduled for this week to look at matters of mutual interest". What particularly surprised the Company was that the move should take place whilst discussions were under way. A great deal of screening of passengers had been undertaken in an effort to ensure that passengers were bona fide travellers in the required sense, as the Company had itself cancelled flights which could have given cause for concern.

An application by British Midland Airways for an injunction against the C.A.B. order was heard in the Federal District Court in Washington D.C. on Thursday 6th July and was successful, making it the first foreign airline ever to obtain an injunction against the C.A.B. Mike Bishop said on 10th July, "Governments on both sides of the Atlantic and air carriers all recognise that the present regulations for these flights are inadequate and new rules, which are currently being drafted, should be introduced as soon as possible. We sought the injunction because we felt that we were able to demonstrate that in spite of the difficulties in interpreting the present rules we had made substantial efforts to operate within them".

The new rules which were currently being drafted and to which the Managing Director referred were, of course, the Advanced Booking Charter (A.B.C.) rules which everyone hoped would solve the problem, but as 1973 was going to show, they only helped the scheduled service carriers and not the charter carriers.

The Chairman of the Civil Aviation Authority, Lord Boyd Carpenter, visited the Company on Friday 15th September, accompanied by a small group of Authority officials, the visit being his first in a programme of familiarisation with regional airlines and airports. A party of five senior Company executives, headed by Mr. Peter Cannon, Chairman, Mr. Michael Bishop, Managing Director, and Mr. John Wolfe, General Manager, welcomed Lord Boyd Carpenter to the Company headquarters. The first part of the programme was a specially organised film presentation of the Company's activities showing development and growth of the scheduled service network, and the inclusive tour and charter operations.

The Chairman of the Civil Aviation Authority inspecting British Midland Airways maintenance facilities at East Midlands Airport. Left to right: J. Smith, Technical Director, P. Cannon, B.M.A. Chairman, Lord Boyd-Carpenter, P. Murland, B.M.A. Director, and M. Bishop, B.M.A. Managing Director. (Raymonds).

After the film show, a tour of the Operations Department, and the engineering division facilities followed, before being entertained to lunch, after which a tour of the Airport had been arranged. At the conclusion of the visit, the C.A.A. Chairman thanked all concerned for the comprehensive programmes made available to the visitors, which he said would be of great value in his study of regional operations and the special problems they faced.

In a Company accouncement made on 28th September, the issued share capital of B.M.A. was increased to £5,034,500. These arrangements were made to provide additional funds for the further development and growth of the Company's overall operations, and in particular for the continued development of scheduled services, which operation had been one of the

131

success stories of 1972 with passenger traffic up by a significant 50 per cent over 1971. The new investment not only raised to 96.5 per cent of the share capital in the Company owned by Minster Assets, but emphasized the financial stability and strength that the Company had within that group.

As had been mentioned earlier, modern aircraft maintenance is based on a progressive system, designed to keep the aircraft down-time to a minimum. This system came in with modern, expensive jet equipment, and the Viscount did not come into this category. However, the amount of down time spent on the Viscount, particularly when grossed up on a fleet of twelve aircraft, can be very considerable indeed, and so it was the B. M. A. Engineering Division set about to rectify this situation by devising a progressive maintenance system for the Viscount.

The care and dedication that Engineering give to aircraft maintenance was a matter taken with great pride, and it was a unique Viscount reliability programme that was introduced. The programme reflected all B. M. A's specific needs in maintenance record-keeping practices, and the extent of the statistical and data-processing required was successfully negotiated with the C.A.A. as an entirely individual programme.

Central to this reliability concept was that it included all aircraft parts. The "hard time" life was removed from the majority of components other than those, the failure of which could cause serious results remained with a life-limiting factor.

Although it was recognised that component failures in an aircraft system do occur, upper limits to the rates of failure were established in order to maintain pre-determined standards of airworthiness and serviceability in each system. This involved the Company in keeping extensive records of failures and hours flown and, by those means, a determination of Mean Time Between Failures (MTBF), or its reciprocal, the Failure Rate, was achieved.

Information was collected, co-ordinated, analysed, and presented in a manner which readily portrayed the data for instant reliability determination. These figures were compared with either data supplied by the manufacturer in the case of new aircraft, or data collected over previous years where older aircraft types were concerned. By now, sufficient experience had been accumulated to formulate a precise pattern of procedure, and it was considered that this programme was necessary for the future development of Viscount operations.

The indications were that this type of programme could provide B. M. A. with a much closer and more spontaneous system for determining aircraft in-service performance which, in turn, would enable the airline to achieve a higher level of economic exploitation of the equipment. The programme also provided the C.A.A. with a closer knowledge of the reliability of the aircraft in service.

Thus it may be seen that the Company had made a magnificent step forward in its Viscount maintenance programme, an achievement which no other Viscount carrier, including the nationalised Corporations, had made and of which B.M.A., and in particular the Engineering Division, can be justly proud.

Viscount 813 undergoing maintenance at the Company's Main Engineering Base at East Midlands Aiport.

After waiting three years (to the day) since the opening of London-Teeside service, a B.M.A. check-in desk was made available at London Heathrow, and on Wednesday 1st November, the first passenger checked in direct with the Company instead of with British European Airways who, up until that time, had been handling all of the Company's requirements at Heathrow. The Station Manager was Chris Calderbank, who up until 1st October had been Station Manager, Manchester. The month of October was taken up by Chris in advertising for and interviewing applicants for new staff, and with trying to make some sense out of the chaos he was presented with at Heathrow. Even now, no airline offices were available at Heathrow, and it was not until early 1974 that office accommodation finally became available. Anyhow, at least the thin edge of the wedge was in, and how much nicer it was to be able to deal with one's own passengers. B.E.A. of course still provided ramp services and engineering facilities, but load control was now B.M.A's own responsibility.

On 31st October, the new hearing by the U.S. Civil Aeronautical Board into issues arising from alleged affinity group rule infringements by the Company was opened in the U.S.A. It will be remembered that the C.A.B. had imposed an order on B.M.A. requiring details to be filed of passenger lists on U.S. charters 21 days in advance of departure, that the Company had successfully appealed in the U.S. courts against the way in which the C.A.B. had handled the affair, and that the courts ordered a re-hearing by the C.A.B. It was in fact the first time a foreign airline had successfully sought an injunction against the Board, and under it the C.A.B. was told to give its reasons for imposing the 21-day listing order.

The preliminary hearing was heard on 31st October, with the full hearing following later on. Mike Bishop told the appeal court that the C.A.B. decision

Mike Bishop, Managing Director, with Chris Calderbank, Station Manager receiving the lease documents for the new London-Heathrow Accommodation. (Neil Maurer-Photography).

had been unfair because it had not given reasons for imposing its order. In addition B.M.A. had tried hard to keep within the affinity rules. Mike Bishop commented, "The C.A.B. has quite bluntly said to us—and in our hearing at the appeal court—that in 1972 it was going to have a purge on British carriers and their commercial profit in the U.S." "This is discriminating and has been one of our main causes for concern" he added. He alleged that the C.A.B. itself had been booking people on B.M.A. flights, and then turned round saying the Company had carried illegal passengers. "We believe this was unfair and unjust" he added. During the "war of attrition", as Mike Bishop called it, the Company stopped flying into New York.

After the preliminary hearing, judgement was deferred until the main hearing which took place in Spring 1973, when the Company were judged guilty of carrying illegal passengers and a "fine" of U.S. $50,000 imposed which was paid, following which B.M.A. were absolved from any further liability.

At the very beginning of November, and following the search for an airline with experience of operating successful scheduled services and an established record of developing new routes, Sudan Airways selected British Midland to operate its "Blue Nile" international jet services. The Sudan Airways Chairman, Mr. Mohammed Abdel Bagi, was partly instrumental in the choice, for, whilst the Company was engaged on the Nigeria contract in 1968/69, Mr. Bagi had been in Nigeria on a United Nations mission and had heard good stories. Indeed he had received recommendations from the Nigerians about the good service British Midland Airways had provided, and he had remembered them.

This very important contract, signed at the beginning of November, was the largest ever placed with the Company for its Boeing 707 fleet. Initially the contract ran until the end of 1973, but was later re-negotiated and extended to June/July 1974. The initial contract was valued at £3.3m, to be paid in U.S. dollars, and involved providing aircraft, crews, technical and management assistance, and a training programme for flight deck and cabin staff.

Mr. Peter Cannon, B.M.A. Chairman and Mr. Mohammed Abdel Bagi signing the Sudan Airways Contract. Standing—left to right: Mr. C. Murland, B.M.A., Michael Bishop, B.M.A., Mr. El Amir, Sudan Airways. (Neil Maurer photography)

The route system, radiating from Khartoum, serves Addis Ababa and Nairobi, Jeddah, Cairo, Beirut, Tripoli, Athens, Rome and London. B.M.A. aircraft, in Sudan Airways livery, also undertook charter flights and Presidential flights for President Numeri, President of the Sudan.

Commenting on the new contract, Mr. Bagi said "Sudan Airways has been evaluating both the short and long-term requirements for the provision of

135

international air routes serving the Sudan, and the most,economic and beneficial method of re-equipping the airline with more competitive aircraft (Comet 4's were previously operated) and improved services. The arrangements with British Midland Airways will provide the transition from our current operation to much larger aircraft".

Michael,Bishop added, "In addition to providing aircraft and crews for the basic operation, we shall also be undertaking a comprehensive training programme at our main base at the East Midlands Airport for Sudan Airways staff. This will include flight and cabin crews, engineers, flight operations and traffic personnel and accounts staff". In fact, flight and cabin crews were trained at Castle Donington, plus some flight engineers, but ground engineers, operations, traffic, and accounts staff never did materialise apart from one or two very isolated individuals, which was a great pity for B.M.A. were really looking forward to training these staff and still feel confident that a good job could have been done in this respect.

Several B.M.A. specialists travelled to Khartoum to give advice on the Boeing 707 operation to Sudan Airways staff, in particular to the flight operations planning staff, knowing full well that Sudan were going to purchase and operate their own 707's eventually, and it was genuinely felt that assistance here could help.

To return to 1972 however, the Company let it be known in mid-November that it had applied to the C.A.A. for a London-Exeter and/or Newquay service to commence on 1st April, 1973, at a frequency of up to 14 flights per week. Now it so happened that at the time Mike Bishop was considering the route, a Cornish businessman, Mr. Kenneth Bacon, Managing Director of Marriott Magnetics of Ponsharden, near Falmouth, was becoming painfully aware of the poor communications between Cornwall and the rest of the country. Frustrated by the poor road and rail links, he wrote to British Midland suggesting they started regular services between London and Cornwall. In replying to Mr. Bacon that the Company were already considering the route, Mike Bishop asked Ken Bacon if he knew the names of any potential users of such a service. Mr. Bacon, whose company exports much of their products, went one better and wrote to nearly 300 companies in Cornwall and West Devon, asking them if they would use such a service. On the strength of 55 favourable replies the licence application went in to use Royal Air Force St. Mawgan, near Newquay, as the terminal airport and to which, of course, holiday services from other points operated for some time.

The licence hearing took place in January 1973 and was successful, the route being operated for the first time on Monday April 30th, 1973.

In accordance with the terms of the Sudan Airways contract, the first group of six Sudan Airways air hostesses arrived at Castle Donington at the beginning of December for training on the Boeing 707 aircraft. As it turned out they were, in fact, the only party to go to the East Midlands Airport for any training. As the girls were guests of the Company at the time of the annual Christmas party, all six were invited along and came escorted by the B.M.A. Chief Hostess,

136

Miss Maureen Wilson, and Training Stewardess Miss Mary Foster.

Now that the Sudan contract was about to tie up all 707 capacity, the number of charter flights undertaken by the long-haul fleet was soon to diminish rapidly, although there remained a few flights for which contracts were signed before the Sudanese contract even showed itself on the horizon.

To end 1972 on a pleasant note, and to remain with the 707 fleet, B.M.A. New York were given, in December, approval from U.S. Civil Aeronautics Board to advertise the largest group of Tour Group Charters (equivalent to British Advance Booking Charters, and supposedly the answer to the affinity group charter problems previously discussed) announced up to that time. Although a number of major American airlines were also actively interested in T.G.C's, on this occasion Bill Allan, Sales Manager U.S. for B.M.A., found himself a pace-setter.

The B.M.A. package consisted of a 19-flight programme of charters for Air Travel Group Charters of Arlington, Virginia, to fly from Washington and Baltimore to London between 24th May and 27th September 1973. Mr. Forbes Huffman, head of Air Travel Group Charters, said all participating agents would be offered commission arrangements, and the flights would depart and arrive on Thursdays, drawing business not only from Washington and Baltimore, but throughout southern and eastern Pennsylvania, Virginia, West Virginia, Indiana, Maryland, Georgia and other States as far West as the Mississippi

Whilst selling this service, Bill Allan was confronted by one agent with the remark that "B.M.A. is old fashioned". However, it was meant in the nicest possible way, for it was this top New York agent's conviction that B.M.A. was one of the few airlines that can still give personal service. Of particular note was the record of on-time departures and good service by cabin staff. Certainly this last point was upheld when, for the third Christmas running, the Toronto Metro Teachers Association stated that they had thoroughly enjoyed their Christmas flight to the U.K. despite delays caused by appalling weather in Canada at the time. The B.M.A. custom of putting up Christmas decorations in the cabin once again proved immensely popular.

Fleets as at 31st December 1971:—

Boeing 707-321	G-AYVE, G-AYBJ
Viscount 813	G-AZLP, G-AZLR, G-AZLS, G-AZLT, G-AZNA, G-AZNB, G-AZNC
BAC 1-11 (523)	G-AXLL, G-AXLM, G-AXLN

1973

1973 was to be a year of cautious development in the schedule service sphere, whilst still implementing the policy of eventual withdrawal from the inclusive-tour field of activity and concentrating on scheduled services.

The Brussels/Frankfurt service was already operating on a daily frequency; the Amsterdam route was to increase to a daily service from April; the Teesside service was going back to four time a day from 1st April (it was three-times a day service in the winter), and was to remain as such even in the 73/74 winter; the Newquay, Strasbourg and Paris scheduled services were to be mounted, and finally a new Belfast-Jersey service was to be operated in 1973.

Clearly all of the foregoing would require more capacity in the way of Viscounts, and a huge sales campaign was going to be required to sell all this new service to the public. Firstly then, the aircraft capacity.

Sitting on the apron of the East Midlands Airport were three Viscount 814's belonging to a now-defunct German operator, Nora Air Services. A fourth 814 was also lying at Kessel-Calden in Germany. Mike Bishop purchased these four aircraft. The three aircraft at East Midlands had in fact been impounded by the airport authorities for non-payment of outstanding landing and parking fees. Captain Dave Court, Viscount Fleet Captain, flew to Frankfurt on 16th February in order to bring the fourth aircraft, D-ANAD, back from Kessel-Calden. Upon arrival there he found his departure from the airfield barred by various light aircraft which had been parked around the aircraft. However, after some slight manoeuvring the Viscount was finally moved, and it took off for the delivery flight to Castle Donington.

It was hoped that all four aircraft would be in service quickly, but it was discovered that the amount of corrosion on the aircraft was far greater than had been realised, in addition to which all of the servicing and maintenance histories of the four were mysteriously not available. The amount of re-work for the corrosion problem plus the fact that all component lives had to be recommenced, in some cases necessitating a check followed by another immediate check, meant that the throughput of each aircraft in the hangar was not as quick as the Engineering Division had hoped for, so that at the beginning of the 1973 summer season the Company were short of aircraft.

Another load to fall on the Engineering Division was the re-entry into B.M.A. service of Viscount 815 G-AVJB, which the previous year had been sold to Kestrel International. At the end of 1972 however, Kestrel had gone into liquidation and B.M.A. had foreclosed on the mortgage they had on "JB". It now remained for this aircraft to be repaired externally, re-furnished internally (as of course had to be done on the four 814's) and given a maintenance check, before entry into service.

With all five aircraft in service, the Company now had a well balanced fleet. The 813's were all flight-system equipped, whilst the 814's/815, were basically the same as the 813's (there were some very minor differences), but without the benefit of a flight system.

The second half of the requirement already referred to was the sales drive. It may be pertinent at this point to go back in time two years and explain the new energy and type of sales campaign that was already being waged. When M. D. Bishop was appointed Managing Director, he was instrumental in appointing Chetwynd Street, Leicester branch, as the Company's advertising agency. Under the leadership of Mr. Richard Lewis, a new and changed advertising policy was drawn up and approved by M. D. Bishop. The first practical result of this new energy appeared at the end of 1971, when a number of conferences of travel agencies throughout the regions of interest were held, the Midland Region "conference" being held at the "Talk of the Midlands" night club in Derby, which B.M.A. took over for the night. At this "conference" the travel agents presented were made to feel that British Midland were selling their services through the Travel Agency world. Each agency guest was handed a glossy red folder as he/she walked in through the doors, the folder containing point-of-sales display material. The folder explained, in vivid terms:—

"We may not be the largest airline on your books but your clients would never know the difference".

For 1973 a similar promotion was carried out, once again using a, social evening as a means of gathering and entertaining the travel agents, at the same time introducing the coming sales campaign to them. Various get-togethers were organised all over the country and once again the "Talk of the Midlands" in Derby was used as the venue for the Midlands Region, with Bob Monkhouse as the star entertainer.

For 1973 a new film had been made which featured an opening door revealing in turn shots of Jersey, Amsterdam, Brussels, Frankfurt, Paris, Dublin and other destinations, urging prospective passengers to "see your travel agent—he has the details". With each destination the announcer gave the flying time in minutes, and the slogan (developed later on in 1973) was "British Midland Timesavers". Timesavers stickers and mugs were given away lavishly throughout the travel trade, as were pads of notepaper with a Timesaver calender at the top of each page. All in a most impressive campaign. At £100,000, it's cost made quite a contrast with the £11,500, for 1964/65, too.

Another aspect of salesmanship and Company image, particularly where an airline is concerned, is the ground staff and cabin staff uniform, and in this respect B.M.A. were no exception. For the past three years the girls' uniforms had been orange in colour, but a new design was called for in support of the new image being created for 1973. Four different designs were entered, three being the work of a professional dress-designer, the fourth being the work of the Chief Hostess, Miss Maureen Wilson. At the management meeting in the early part of the year four girls modelled the new designs and the management committee were unanimous in their choice of Miss Wilson's design, although a few alterations were embodied.

The basic colour of the new uniforms was an attractive Sherwood green for hats, coats and tunics. Beneath the jacket was a lemon-yellow blouse with a striped stand-up collar in orange, yellow and green. A new Jacqmar scarf carried the same colour motif. There was a further link with Sherwood Forest in the "Maid Marian" tunic.

The ground and air crew girls wore the same basic uniform, but the cabin staff were identified by wings attached to their B.M.A. badges, and in addition they had short-sleeved blouses as distinct from ground girls who wore long sleeves. One of the cabin staff, Miss Andrea Shortland, was entered by the Company in the Miss Air Fair competition at the Biggin Hill Air Fair and was judged second to Miss India, so obviously the new design was welcomed by the trade and travelling public.

One of the first successes scored with the Sudan contract was the Company's participation in the annual pilgrimage by the Moslems to Mecca. The Company and Sudan Airways had both participated in the flights to Jeddah before, but 1972/73 was the first time that Sudan Airways had been able to mount such a massive lift with the newly available help from British Midland Airways. Flights to Jeddah operated mainly from Khartoum, but also included Fort Lamy in Chad, and Accra. As a result of the operation, the Chairman of Sudan Airways, Mohammed Abdel Bagi, sent the following telegram to Michael Bishop on the 16th of January:—

"Now that the first round of the Pilgrim Flights—the biggest of its kind in the history of Sudan Airways—has been completed satisfactorily, I hasten to send whole-hearted congratulations to all,those who contributed to its success".

Three days later it was announced that the Company had been appointed General Sales Agents in Europe for Sudan Airways. It was added at the time that both airlines would share a development programme in European countries, not only to create closer links between Europe and Sudan, but also to develop further British Midlands own traffic potential on scheduled services linking East Midlands with Amsterdam, Paris, Brussels and Frankfurt. Countries in which new sales offices were to open, on a joint basis, were Holland, Belgium, West Germany, France, Switzerland, Italy and Greece. Unfortunately it was not to be and the General Sales Agency agreement was restricted to the U.K. only. Sales organisations were set up in Amsterdam, Brussels, Frankfurt, Paris and Strasbourg, but the Italian, Swiss and Greek Sales Offices never did materialise which was a pity, for mutual assistance in growth could have resulted for both carriers.

Another important development that took place in the New Year was the appointment to the Board of Directors of three managerial staff. They were Mr. John Wolfe, general manager, Mr. Stuart Balmforth, company secretary and financial director, Mr. A. J. Smith, head of engineering and maintenance.

On a less happy note, Viscount G-AZLR suffered a mishap at the end of a positioning flight from Leeds/Bradford to Birmingham on the 19th January. As the aircraft touched down the port main undercarriage collapsed and the Viscount skidded along the runway before finally coming to a halt, but with its tail still blocking the runway. There were, fortunately, no passengers on board, only the two crew plus an extra, positioning Captain, and all three unhurt. After an intensive investigation it was decided that the undercarriage had not been properly locked down, but no blame was attached to the crew for the mechanical indicator showed the gear to be down and locked. What was not known was that the indicator had been frozen solid during its overnight stop at Leeds/Bradford, and had broken during undercarriage retraction thus giving a false indication. After some two weeks out of service the aircraft was back flying again.

It was announced at the end of January that the Minster (and B.M.A.) Chairman, Peter Canon, had travelled to South Africa on 5th January for "indefinite leave", mainly due to ill-health brought on by pressure of work. In the meantime, the annual financial report was issued which showed that the Company had made a loss of £846,000 in 1972, which when £443,000 of interest waived by Minster was added, became £1,289,000. This situation was immediately seized upon by various individuals and groups as a pointer to the downfall of B.M.A.

Mr A. R. G. McGibbon, deputy Chairman of Minster, was appointed Chairman of British Midland Airways, and in a personal address to the staff, stood by Minster's declared intention of seeing British Midland into profitability. It was accepted that the major factor in the £846,000 loss was the short-fall in revenue from the long-haul 707 operations.

Confirmation that the Company was to pull out of the I.T. market and concentrate on the scheduled services was given by Mike Bishop when he talked of the financial year's loss to the press. The sale of two B.A.C. 1-11's was in an advanced stage, but one (still on lease to Court Line) would be retained "to give the capability to come back if we want to".

Seat rates for the air travel element of an Inclusive Tour package had been squeezed to an unacceptable low, and now it was B.M.A's intention to "stand on the sidelines" until the tour operating industry sorted itself out.

The contribution from 707 services was down on budget by some £850,000, primarily because of the "highly demanding political and commercial factors which prevailed in our long-haul business in the peak earning season to the U.S.A. and Candada". Mike Bishop forecast that 707 operations would be put back on their feet, now that 5,000 hours annual utilisation had been guaranteed for the two aircraft, under the Sudan Airways "Blue Nile" contract. This left 1500 hours of 707 operation to market, utilisation which would become available when the aircraft lay over in the U.K. at the weekends.

The main thrust would now be on scheduled services, which alone would produce a £400,000 profit in the current year and contribute handsomely to the overall forecast of modest profitability for 1973.

The 1-11 deal was the part exchange of two 1-11's with three Handley Page Dart Herald Series 214's from Trans Brasil in Sao Paulo. Currently, the two 1-11's were leased from British Aircraft Corporation (Holdings), but B.M.A. would be the title holder when they were sold. The deal, which had been on and off and was now on again (the Brazilians had increased the amount of money they required for the Heralds, but this had now been sorted out), and one 1-11 was to go in April and another in November. Efforts in finding buyers for the 1-11's had been adversely affected by a weak market and a standstill in the growth of the worlds airlines. The fact that the British Aircraft Corporation themselves had four new aircraft awaiting buyers, plus one repossessed 1-11, as well as American Airlines with 27 earlier model 1-11's up for sale, did not help the Company's 1-11 disposal problem at all. However, it was ultimately achieved and now the largest burden of all had been removed.

Two agency and press receptions in quick succession took place in February, one in Belfast on Monday 19th, and one in Newquay on Wednesday 21st. The Belfast reception was to announce the commencement of the new Belfast to

Herald G-ASVO en route from Sao Paulo.

Jersey service for holidaymakers, due to commence on Saturday, 19th May, and to operate every Saturday and Sunday in the Summer. Northern Ireland travel agents who had previously experienced difficulty in obtaining space on existing internal services, warmly welcomed the news.

The Newquay reception, held in the Bristol Hotel, Newquay, was similarly warmly welcomed by both travel agents and Cornish businessmen. Mike Bishop, announcing the new service, stated that it was (as usual) on a "use it or lose it" basis, and that the service would not be reviewed for eighteen months, at which time, if it was not paying, it would be withdrawn. Apart from Mr. Bacon, previously mentioned re. the Newquay service, David Mudd, M.P. for Cambourne and Falmouth was also at the reception and he paid tribute to Mr. John Pardoe, M.P. for North Cornwall for the enthusiasm he stirred among Cornish M.P's for the project. "He played a first-class role in making this a reality instead of a pipe-dream" he said.

The Company was now planning an investment of between £250,000 to £300,000 over the eighteen months in direct operating costs, in order to make the Newquay service pay, and it would now be waiting with baited breath to see if, as one Cornish newspaper correspondent put it, the Cornish would stick to their word and use the service. By 1974 the service was going very well.

Another "first" for B.M.A. occurred on 24th March when His Excellency President Gaafar Mohamed Numeri, accompanied by Mrs. Numeri, arrived at London Heathrow for a State Visit. He flew in a B.M.A. Boeing 707 and the aircraft, commanded by Captain John Blackman, 707 Fleet Captain, taxied to a halt at the stand reserved for the Royal Family and Visiting Heads of State and Dignitaries, thus becoming the first British independent carrier to use the stand.

The President departed in the same Boeing on Sunday, 31st March to Belgrade. As part of the new agreement with Sudan Airways, the Company's London Office was transferred from Saville Row to new premises at 52 Curzon Street, W.1., early in April. The office was intended to be a joint British Midland / Sudan Airways office, the first of seven to be brought into operation as a result of the General Sales Agreement with Sudan Airways.

April in 1973 really was a month for new flights—three to be exact. Monday, 2nd April saw the first of the East Midlands to Paris (Le Bourget) services depart, the route being operated daily except Saturday, with the Friday departure in the evening as was the Sunday service, this to give prospective holidaymakers a long weekend in Paris (if they could afford it!).

Monday, 30th April saw two inaugurals, the first of course being the long-awaited and much publicised Newquay service. It was the long term intention to operate the route with the Herald, but for the first ten months it was to be the Viscount which would be used. Initially a daily service, it was to go to a twice-daily frequency in November.

The third service to commence in April, also on the 30th, was the London-Strasbourg route, its inception being due to the European Parliament being resident in Strasbourg. The aircraft which operated the service was in fact the one which originated in Newquay in the morning, operating Newquay-London-Strasbourg-London-Newquay. Not a bad utilisation really.

The London-Teesside service hit new heights when, on 31st May, the number of passengers carried in one month topped the 9,000 mark for the first time since the route was operated by B.M.A. in October 1969. The achievement represented a 221% rise over the October 1969 figure, not a bad accomplishment by any yardstick. Up to the end of May the number of passengers carried in 1973 was in excess of 36,000 and it was hoped to exceeed the 100,000 mark by the end of the year.

On 8th June, Viscount G-BAPG was landing at East Midlands Airport, but when the nosewheel touched the runway a loud bang was heard on the flight deck and the nose dropped. It was later found that the nose undercarriage support "A-frame" structure had failed, and allowed the leg to collapse rearwards. The failure was found to have been initiated by metal fatigue.

Nobody on board the aircraft, on a normal scheduled service from Glasgow, was injured, but damage was caused to the nose undercarriage structure, the base of the front pressure bulkhead and surrounding fuselage belly skin.

August 1st saw the welcome return to British Midland of Julian Rogers, this time as Director responsible for marketing, advertising and public relations. Julian, aged 32 at the time, was previously the Company's public relations officer when still employed by I.P.R. in London, it will be remembered.

One of Julian's first "projects" as marketing director took place in the Albany Hotel, Nottingham, over the weekend of 15th/16th September, when a conference and sales course was held. The training programme included recordings on video-tape. Newquay station manager Peter Barnes was filmed making a "presentation" to Trevor Thomas, charter department. European as well as U.K. sales staff and station managers took part in the conference, which was opened and closed by Mike Bishop. The conference was highly successful and was appreciated by all who attended. The educational benefits were enormous, and it certainly marked the beginning of a whole new approach to the Company's concept of marketing.

About this time, 1st October, the three Dart Heralds acquired from Trans Brasil were coming into service after a complete overhaul by the Engineering Division, including the installation of a complete new radio station, similar to the one fitted to the South African Viscount 813's. The test-flight of G-ASVO, the first to enter service on 17th October ended with the police, firemen and Derbyshire Royal Infirmary's Flying Squad being alerted when the nose-wheel developed trouble (in fact an electrical fault). Needless to say, the aircraft landed quite safely.

Whilst on the subject of the Herald, it will be remembered that the 1-11's had now been phased out of service (the last service was in fact on 24th September) and the crews were now about to be employed on the Herald fleet—Captain Peter Austin, 1-11 Fleet Captain, in fact became Herald Fleet Captain, with Captain "Titch" Clarke as his deputy. A completely new Operations Manual had to be written by them from scratch, but with a fair amount of help from Captain Dave Moores who at one time had been earmarked to run the Herald fleet.

It is a tribute to all concerned, engineers, Fleet and Deputy Fleet Captain, Chief Hostess, Route Planning Manager, and many others, that the amendment to the Air Operators Certificate for the "new" type was obtained without a hitch.

The Company's policy for 1974 was announced at the beginning of October by Mike Bishop, when he said that B.M.A. would spend the next two years (1974 and 1975) building up traffic on the existing network rather than open up new routes. At the same time all inclusive tour operations outside the scheduled service network routes would be dropped. The last route expansion planned was for an extension of the East Midlands-Amsterdam route to Dusseldorf (this was in fact turned down by the C.A.A.).

With direct reference to the East Midlands region, the question was being asked of businessmen—"Business in Brussels, Frankfurt, Amsterdam or Paris? Just set up an appointment and hop on a plane at East Midlands Airport in the morning, and you'll have plenty of time for your meeting and be back again in the same evening". As an independent airline based outside London, the future of B.M.A. depended on the rate of growth of the provincially based service which could be established in the catchment areas concerned. If more people flew B.M.A. and used the existing services, this would generate the revenue to allow further development of new routes and provide better quality frequencies on the routes already being operated.

A significant recent feature of this development was the Company's emphasis on continental services. There was (and is) a growing demand from Midlands businessmen that they should at least have the option of direct continental services. Regrettably, it is a well-known fact of life in the airline industry that there tends to be a lobby for a service long before there is any likelihood of it being economically viable. This comes from the relatively few passengers who would use the service frequently. However, a new service rarely becomes truly viable until it is made use of casually by the bulk of the business community, most of whom may only use it occasionally.

In the case of East Midlands, there was not only the problem of building up awareness of new routes, but also the need to combat a shattering lack of awareness of what must be one of the finest provincial airports in the country, the East Midlands Airport. Right in the centre of the East Midlands region between three major conurbations of Derby, Nottingham and Leicester lies an airport without congestion, and having first class facilities for first class domestic and international services with world-wide connections, yet the impression is gained that it is virtually unknown even by the people who pay for its up-keep.

Over the years of operation, the business community with a more adventurous spirit had used the airport for their flights within the United Kingdom, notably to Glasgow, Belfast and Dublin and, as Continental services became available, further afield.

A device which helped in route development was the combined use of the East Midlands Aiport and Birmingham Airport for route development, coupled with a combination of continental destinations. Thus one of the major continental services started as an East Midlands/Birmingham/Brussels/Frankfurt operation in April 1972. Just over a year later the stage was reached where the two continental services could be split and fly separately East Midlands/Birmingham/Brussels, and East Midlands/Birmingham/Frankfurt, with day return facilities on each route.

The Paris and Amsterdam routes, whilst not sharing destinations or origination points, had built up a steady franchise with the local business community. The decision to use the reduced off-peak aircraft requirements during the winter months to allow day return facilities on these gave the Midland business community a chance to vote with its feet and vote with its freight.

If the business community demonstrated its need for these services over the winter months, then consideration would be given,to the introduction of full double daily services in the coming spring.

"It is a case of use the extra frequencies or lose them," said Mike Bishop.

During the summer, and following one or two incidents, mainly involving the Viscount fleet, it had been decided, as a policy, to increase the training given to crews. As a result of this decision an advertisement was place in the aeronautical press for a simulator/ground instructor, and so it was that on 1st September, Mr. Peter Hill joined the Company in this capacity. The intention was that the simulator bought from South African Airways for the Viscount 813, and which was by now installed, should be programmed for C.A.A. approval to carry out bi-annual checks, and that when this approval was obtained, every four working days a complete crew, i.e. Captain and First Officer, would be withdrawn from line flying and undergo at least two days technical refresher training in the classroom, followed by two days on the simulator, culminating in a bi-annual check, at which point the crew would be released to the line and new crew brought in.

To remain with this story for a moment, a simulator engineer, Mr. David Whitfield, joined the Company on 1st January, 1974, and C.A.A. approval was obtained in July that year.

It will be remembered that Captain Cramp had been editor of the Company house journal "B.M.A. News" for some time, but his last issue was in August 1973. When Julian Rogers joined the Company as Marketing Director he (or rather his department) took over the responsibility for B.M.A. News and also for a Traffic Department staff "magazine" called Outline (for the Outlying stations) and, in particular, Miss Pat Harris, who joined the Company on 1st October as Pubic Relations Officer, was given the personal responsibility for the production of the two items. Pat had previously been a director of Granby P.R. International Limited, a Leicester based public relations consultancy, and had held P.R. posts in industry and advertising.

November 1st, besides seeing in the increased scheduled services promised for the Winter timetable, also saw the appointment of three Sales Managers on the Continent. Mrs. Renate Rothwell, formerly in the U.K. retail travel trade, was appointed Brussels-based sales manager for Belgium; Mr. Bill Campbell, formerly London-based manager for Group Travel and Finance Services (U.K.), was named sales manager for the Strasbourg area; Mr. Blair Allen was appointed sales manager for Holland, based in Amsterdam, and was formerly seven years with Avianca Colombia as commercial sales manager U.K. and Eire. It was hoped that these three key staff would increase the operations in Europe.

Two other major events occurred in November, the first being an extension to the Sudan Airways contract to continue it up to June and July 1974. The terms of the contract were re-negotiable in order to take into account increased operating costs, but at least the extension meant the continued employment of the Boeing 707 fleet.

In October, the war in the Middle East involving Israel, Syria and Egypt gave cause for the oil producing countries to increase the price of crude oil and at the same time announce a cut-back in supplies. As a result of this far-off conflict, prices began to rise all over the world, not least in Western Europe, with the result that airfares began to rise, and in early November B.M.A. announced that air fares could rise as much as 7%. Little did we know of what was still to come.

As the war progressed, cut-backs in oil deliveries increased, whilst the price doubled and doubled again. On 4th December the Department of Trade and Industry announced that airlines would be allocated, for the period 21st November to 31st December, 90% of their total fuel uplift for October 1973. Remember this information was given out on 4th December. Chaos reigned supreme, as the saying goes. Obviously something had to give and the consequence was a cut-back in some of the scheduled services. What a blow to an airline that was striving desperately to make a come-back and cut its losses, with a policy of developing scheduled services. Owing to the method of rationing introduced when the announcement was made the Company had already run out of fuel in some places, such as Belfast, whilst at other airports there was an allocation of fuel, large amounts in some cases, which were of absolutely no use at all.

At the beginning of October, the Operations Manager had welcomed with a sigh of relief the appointment of Squadron Leader Ron Young, A.F.C., as Assistant Operations Manager. Ron, an ex Air Support Command Examining Unit navigator, was going to prove almost indispensible in the Operations Department. However, due to the enormity of the fuel problem within one month of joining the Company he found himself controlling all the fuel supplies and distributions, so that the Operations Manager, Captain Cramp, found himself virtually back where he started, is without an assistant. Fortunately this state of affairs did not last too long and the fuel rationing in the U.K. ended on 1st April 1974, but not before airfares had had to be increased by 20%, (so much then for the original forecast of 7%).

Another innovation introduced by the Company was Midland Overseas Tours, a wholly-owned subsidiary of B.M.A. with Mr. Trevor Thomas as manager, based at the East Midlands Airport. M.O.T. was brought into being to create and promote both outbound and inbound package tours on any of the Company's services which had both the capacity and a suitable fare structure, but lacked support from external agencies. An example of a package tour devised by M.O.T. was one based on the London-Strasbourg service. For £35, bed, breakfast, evening meals and ski-lift pass were provided. The flight departed London on Friday morning and returned Monday afternoon. In conjunction with the local tourist board's Passeport de Strasbourg (free entry to museums, free coffee and aperitifs), the new package was hailed by one critic as "What the entertainment business calls a big attraction". It certainly was the way to sell empty seats.

Another aspect of the fuel situation, which people outside of the airline business did not consider when thinking of an airline, was the effect it had on ground equipment. Ground Power Units and Air Start Units were particularly affected by the shortage of diesel oil. With only 1,000 gallons of diesel oil allocated for the month of December it was almost an impossible situation. G.P.U's could not be used some of the time because there was no fuel, and this meant Viscounts and Heralds having to do starts on their internal batteries, often leading to "hot-starts" on the Dart engines with an accompanying small amount of damage to the engine, acceptable in itself but all leading to a lower engine life and an increase in overhaul costs.

The first Herald of the three to arrive from Brazil, G-BAVX went into service on 9th November. This aircraft began flying on route proving on the Belfast and Dublin service, before finally replacing the Viscount on the Newquay service on 1st April 1974. Now the winter timetable had been printed showing the Herald block times, but one passenger arriving at London from Newquay on the Viscount and not knowing all the background was heard to comment,

"This is the only airline I've ever flown on that arrives on schedule". Nobody mentioned the obvious benefits of the faster Viscount's operating on Herald schedules.

So ended yet another year.

The fleet as at 31st December was:—

Boeing 707-321—	G-AYVE, GAYBJ
Viscounts 813—	G-AZLP, G-AZLR, G-AZLS, G-AZLT, G-AZNA, G-AZNB, G-AZNC.
Viscount 814—	G-BAPD, G-BAPE, G-BAPF, G-BAPG
Viscount 815—	G-AVJB
Herald 214—	G-BAVX (in service) G-ASVO, G-ATIG (the last two still to enter service on 31.12.73)

1974

The New Year started under a dark cloud. The fuel crisis was still upon us, and the political situation was far from good with the prospect of a long-drawn-out miners' strike on the horizon. What with the increased price of aviation fuel, tour operators were having to place a high fuel surcharge on charter flights, and the holiday airlines were having a rough time with cancellations from people who could not afford the fuel surcharge.

Later on, when the country went on a three-day week during the miners' strike the situation from these carriers' point of view went from bad to worse and some never really recovered.

Within British Midland however, there was a form of jubilation that at long last the Company was not in the same boat as most other independent airlines, and thanking its lucky stars that the Company's policy to get out of the inclusive tour market and concentrate instead on scheduled services had been taken and implemented in the nick of time.

As a pointer of things to come (it was hoped), in January the Teesside-London service carried over 10,000 passengers in the month, the best so far. Mike Bishop announced that, commencing 1st April a fifth service would be introduced on the Teesside route, starting from London instead of Teesside, and that for 1975 the possibility of a Teesside-Gatwick service was being considered.

Another good sign in the Company's fortunes was heralded on 7th February when Mike Bishop officially opened the Company's new Paris office at 18 rue de la Pepiniere. He pointed out that the soundness of B.M.A's policy in emphasizing the importance of good links between capital cities and the Provinces had been demonstrated by the increasing of the domestic services. The Company believed there was a great demand for services from Provincial centres in the United Kingdom to European capitals, and it also felt that there was a tremendous potential for tourism in the East Midlands and that the new Paris office would be making every effort to introduce the region to French holidaymakers.

Manager of the new Paris office was Monsieur Jean Stergard, who had spent several years in the travel business as manager in France of Skyways Coach-Air, L'Agence Republique and recently with Rousseau Aviation.

The continuing rise in costs of almost everything one touched, and in particular the cost of aviation fuel which at times was rising faster than the price of petrol motorists were paying at garage pumps, prompted most U.K. airlines, British Midland included, to apply for domestic fare increases of up to 20%. These increases were granted by the C.A.A. and came into effect on 1st April, almost coinciding with the withdrawal of the Viscount on the Newquay service and its replacement by the Herald, all of course originally intended but carried out a little late due to the difficulty in getting spares for the Heralds, thus delaying their in-service date (only two Heralds were in service at the end of April, G-BAVX and G-ASVO). These two facts brought forth ribald comments from some passengers whom the Company now considered as "regulars", but what alternative was there in view of these massive increases in fuel costs? Unfortunately, for the Company, the British Rail fare over the same period did not go up at all and the net result was a definite fall-off in traffic on the route, sufficient to delay the introduction of the by now well-advertised third service.

At Birmingham, and after negotiations lasting over three months, the Company finally clinched a contract securing the handling at Birmingham of the world's newest scheduled service and national airline, Air Malta. Appointing B.M.A. as agents, Air Malta said that they had been impressed by the obvious keeness shown by everyone involved in the discussions, the efficiency produced in very difficult working conditions, the excellent impression given to passengers by the Company's public check-in area, but most of all by the recommendations received from other airlines handled by B.M.A. at Birmingham.

Another feather in the Company's cap was the winning of a handling contract for BAC 1-11 of British Airways Channel Island Division. Quite a change for B.M.A. to be handling British Airways; it was usually the other way round.

One final piece about the Traffic handling department was the fact that at Teesside on 4th April, for the first time, an all-female shift took over the whole B.M.A. station. In fact the situation was highly unusual in airline circles in any event, and says a great deal for the high quality of the traffic staff concerned.

One result of the Arab-Israeli conflict, with its ultimate fuel crisis for the countries of Western Europe, was the rapid increase in the rate at which the search for North Sea Oil was carried out. As a result of this oil companies which were carrying out the search, and in particular those who had "struck it rich" off Scotland, were extremely busy flying men and materials to the Scottish main bases of Aberdeen and Sumburgh in the Shetlands. In a way this turned out to be a god-send for B.M.A., as four Viscounts which it was originally intended to lay-up in 1974 (remember the decision to only use eight Viscounts on scheduled services) would now be put to use in these "oil contracts".

The situation the Company now found itself in was a reversal of just before Christmas for now both Viscount and Herald crews had to be recruited and trained. Part of the Viscount crew training was to have been done on the

Viscount 813 simulator, for which C.A.A. approval had been sought. However, when the inspection team came to the East Midlands Airport to carry out the approval inspection, they turned it down, much to the disappointment of the simulator engineer, Dave Whitfield. Now it should be pointed out that never before had the Company been involved in a simulator and no guidance was given as to what was expected of the machine, so that the calibration was carried out to Redifon's (the manufacturer) specification. Unfortunately what was wanted was a specification more akin to one of the Viscounts.

In the next four weeks, Dave Whitfield, Peter Hill (instructor) and Jack Lane of Redifon, worked like slaves to rectify the faults, sometimes putting in as many as ninety five hours work in a week. At the next inspection, the list of "complaints" had been reduced from thirty-one to four, but still the approval was not forthcoming until finally obtained in July 1974.

British Midland now had what must be the finest set-up in Viscount training in the country, nationalised undertakings included, and this is a tribute to the training staff who set up the organisation, and to the Company for providing the material and equipment for doing it.

As the year progressed it became obvious that the hoped for increase in traffic on the Newquay service was not forthcoming and so the introduction of the third daily service was cancelled. However, to cater for an anticipated increase in traffic over the summer holiday period, and bearing in mind the inability of the Herald to carry round-trip fuel from London to Newquay and return plus a full passenger load, the Heralds were withdrawn from the route on the 1st June and the Viscount re-appeared, much to the delight of the business commuters.

1st April saw the usual changeover in airline circles from Winter to Summer services, and British Midland was no exception. Of particular importance was the doubling in frequency of the East Midlands to Dublin service from once daily to twice daily. To avoid a dramatic increase in capacity offered, however, the Herald was placed on the route. At the same time a new sales representative was appointed in the Republic of Ireland, Mr. Martin O'Rouke, who took up residence in Dublin.

Another frequency increase innovated on 1st April was the introduction of the fifth daily service on the Teesside route, but this time the service departed from London to Teesside, departing at 0720 from Heathrow. However, neither of these frequency increases proved their worth, and when the winter services came around again in October they were dropped.

One month later, on 1st May, one of the longest serving Station Managers with the Company, "Viv" Woodhams, Station Manager at Birmingham, retired, and went to live in Cornwall. "Viv" had handled Derby Aviation's traffic at Bournemouth in the "old days" when with Jersey Airlines, and had been "acquired" when the Company bought out Midland Airport Services in 1962. "Viv" was also responsible for providing much of the information appertaining to Birmingham contained in this narrative.

Thursday, 18th July, 1974, was a big day in the history of the Company, for it marked the 21st anniversary of the Company's first scheduled service. It will be remembered that on Saturday 18th July 1953, Captain Eric Lines had operated a de Haviland Rapide on the Derby (Burnaston)—Wolverhampton—Birmingham (customs clearance) to Jersey service. In 1974 Captain Lines again flew the scheduled service from East Midlands to Jersey, but this time in a Herald. To mark the occasion, a reception was held at the East Midlands Airport attended by the Chairman, Managing Director, Director, Senior Management, Captain and Mrs. E. W. A. Lines and the press. Passengers on the service were given free drinks and took part in another reception on arrival in Jersey.

At the end of July, the contract with Sudan Airways finally came to an end. There can be no doubt that the operation had succeeded in putting Sudan Airways back on the international scene. Passenger and freight returns were up and the schedule keeping had been improved beyond all measure. All of this benefitted not only Sudan Airways but British Midland as well in the shape of further contracts to come, based on the reliability that was now becoming associated with the name "British Midland".

One Boeing 707, G-AYVE, was withdrawn from the Sudan early in July and was quickly re-furbished with 189 passenger all-economy seating, and repainted in British Midlands own colours. This last act was a tonic in itself for all of the B.M.A. staff, enabling them to see one of their Boeings back in the Company's livery after such a long time. There was one difference in the paint scheme however, and this was a statement to the effect that the aircraft was "On Contract to British Caledonian Airways". The contract lasted for three months, at the end of which time the Company had once again "left its mark" for a job well done, particularly in the sphere of schedule keeping. Certainly at the end of the contract B.M.A. was viewed by B/CAL with a healthy respect. The routes flown for B/CAL were UK (Gatwick, Manchester and Prestwick) to Canada (Toronto, Ottawa, Vancouver), U.S.A. (Oakland), West Africa (Accra, Lagos) and East Africa (Nairobi).

At a General Management Committee meeting in mid-1974 it had been proposed and accepted that the practice of giving awards to long-service employees should be re-instated (the practice had ceased in 1965), and so it was that on 2nd August Mr. Tony Topps, Chief Inspector and Quality Control Manager in the Engineering Division, received his gold watch for 25 years service from Michael Bishop, Managing Director.

Tony joined the Company in 1949 at Wolverhampton under the Air Schools umbrella, later transferring to Burnaston. In 1960 he was appointed Deputy Chief Inspector and became Chief Inspector in 1970.

In early August Court Line Aviation, the big holiday package tour operator, went into liquidation, causing much consternation throughout the travel industry. B.M.A. were not directly affected, but indirectly the collapse initiated the eventual closing of B.M.A's Glasgow station. The loss of the handling revenue from its movements at Glasgow where B.M.A. had handled Court Line, coupled with the loss of revenue from the collapse of Donaldson International whose movements had also been handled by B.M.A. at Glasgow, now resulted in a total revenue loss such that the unit was no longer viable and subsequently it was closed in January 1975.

One excellent spin-off from the Donaldson collapse insofar as the Company was concerned was that Iraqi Airways, who had been wet-leasing two 707's from Donaldson, now found themselves short of capacity, and so it was that 707 G-AYBJ found itself finishing the Sudan contract, being quicky re-furbished to 189 seat all-economy configuration and repainted in British Midland colours with this time "On Contract to Iraqi Airways" as an addition. 'BJ' departed East Midlands Airport for Baghdad on the evening of Saturday 10th August, with Captain R. Hardy, 707 Deputy Fleet Cpatain, in command. The contract lasted just over three months, and so B.M.A's colours were seen at such places as Moscow and Delhi, as well as Baghdad, although most of the flights were from Baghdad to London.

To remain with Boeing 707's for a while, a decision had been taken at Board level to make the 707-321's more attractive to would-be operators who wished to lease the aircraft, by carrying out a complete internal and external refurbish as soon as the opportunity arose. It was recognised that, with the Pratt and Whitney JT4-12 turbojet engines fitted on the 321, fuel consumption was high and therefore range a little restricted, making it somewhat of a liability for cost-conscious operators. Against this of course was the fact that the book value was quite low, and this helped the situation in a running cost problem. To make the aircraft really attractive however it was essential to get away from a "charter aircraft" interior and make it acceptable to a full-fare schedule service operator and his passengers.

At the end of September therefore, when 'VE' had completed the British Caledonian contract, Aviation Traders (Engineering) Ltd. at Stansted Airport, accepted the aircraft in for overhaul and refurbishing. All bulkheads were covered in redwood veneers, new seats were installed, and fuselage walls and ceiling redecorated to give a "wide-body" effect. A lot of money had been spent, but it was felt worthwhile and was an indication of the professionalism that abounded throughout the Company commencing with the Board of Directors.

Returning to the main story once again. Julian Rogers as Marketing Director, announced in mid-August that, commencing 1st September, the Company would introduce a "spouse special" fare enabling the wives of business men travelling to the Continent to accompany their husbands, with the wife travelling at half fare. The Company promised to be "most discreet" in cases of the "wives" turning out to be girl-friends or secretaries. In addition to the half fare rate for the wives, the Company had arranged free hotel accommodation with several Continetal hoteliers. B.M.A. was the first airline to arrange such a package deal for businessment. Another first for the Company.

In another attempt at good marketing, British Midland, in conjunction with Holiday Inns, the world's biggest hotel group, staged a sales conference in the Holiday Inn at Leicester on September 5th. The aim this time was to "sell" the Provinces as a conference location, in particular to Continental businessmen. Sales managers from Amsterdam, Paris, Frankfurt and Brussels attended the conference. Mr. John Stringler, Holiday Inns Conference Sales Manager for the U.K., stated that the target was to market an airline-hotel conference package in Europe for "around £45" a head.

Considerable market research had been carried out, and the cost of a 3-day conference in Paris was found to be in the region of £65. The potential in the U.K. Provinces was therefore tremendous, for not only were the basic overheads cheaper but shop prices were lower in comparison with the Continent. Bearing in mind that very often wives accompanied husbands on these conference trips, the shopping element was of considerable importance.

Towards the end of 1974, the world economic situation, and the economic situation in Britain in particular, began to make itself felt in the aviation industry. One result of all this gloom was the cutting out of several services by British Caledonian, and included in this cut-back was the London (Gatwick)—Belfast trunk route. British Midland jumped in immediately and offered to take up the route, providing a continuous service to the public. So it was then that the last B/CAL service to Belfast operated on Thursday, 31st October, 1974, and B.M.A. began operations on the service the following day, 1st November.

The route started off very quiety at first with passenger loads in single figures, but ultimately began to improve considerably. The service was well and truly welcomed by N. Ireland travel agents, and by the N. Ireland Government, who went to great lengths to make this point known and to assist in many ways.

Another good route, right from its inception, had been the Teesside-London service. At the end of October 1974 the number of passengers carried in the first ten months of that year was 98,459, so that before November was through, over 100,000 passengers had used the service, and it was hoped to top the 120,000 mark before the year's end.

Returning once again to the Newquay negotiations that had been going on for some considerable time with both the Royal Air Force at St. Mawgan, and the Esso Petroleum Co. Ltd., who supplied the Royal Air Force at the station with fuel. The net result of these discussions was an agreement in principle for Esso to supply the fuel for civilian use to the R.A.F. bunkers, whereupon B.M.A. would provide a bowser which in turn would be supplied from the R.A.F. bunkers, this concession being upon the understanding that the arrangement would cease when a civilian bunker became available. During the protracted negotiations, Restormel Council took up a suggestion put forward by Michael Bishop that British Midland should operate the Newquay Civil Air Terminal at the airport acting as agents for the council. After many committee stages, agreement on this point was finally reached and on 1st December, the Company officially took over the Civil Air Terminal. One of the first tasks to be undertaken by Terry Liddiard, Route Facilities Manager, in conjunction with Peter Barnes, B.M.A. Station Manager Newquay, was to apply for a licence for the Terminal Building bar, open during normal licencing hours, and with a hot buffet operating so as to coincide with all arrivals and departures.

To supplement the Terminal Building bar at St. Mawgan, on Friday 13th December Terry Shad applied for and won a licence to develop a fully licenced airport hotel at his "Little Carloggas", only 500 yards from the Terminal. This in itself could only help to develop public interest in the facilities at Newquay Airport.

Just before Christmas, a VC10 of East African Airways Corporation had been involved in an incident at Nairobi airport when it slipped off supporting jacks whilst undergoing routine maintenance. The result of this for B. M. A. was an urgent request to provide capacity on East African's scheduled services, and so 707 G-AYVE was dispatched post haste and the contract took the aircraft away until April 1975. Routes were London to Nairobi, Seychelles, Rome and other points.

Now it had been decided at a Board meeting that too much capacity was held by the Company, so a new leasing company was formed to "sell" the two Boeings, all three Heralds and four Viscounts, it being felt that eight Viscounts were ample for the anticipated traffic on the scheduled service network in 1975. It had also been decided to advertise the new company and its aims in a four-page colour supplement in "Flight" just before Christmas. In the event this advert was not required and did not appear.

The fleet as at 31st December 1974 was:

Boeing 707-321	— G-AYVE, GAYBJ
Viscount 813	— G-AZLP, G-AZLR, G-AZLS, G-AZLT, G-AZNA, G-AZNB, G-AZNC
Viscount 814	— G-BAPD, G-BAPE, G-BAPF, G-BAPG
Viscount 815	— G-AVJB
Herlad 214	— G-ATIG, G-ASVO, G-BAVX

1975

Captain "Joe" Sharpes, based at Teesside, let the New Year in for the Company with a zing when, on New Year's Day, he clocked up the fastest ever commercial flight between London and Teesside, and this in the humble Viscount.

The flight time of just 38 minutes beat even the fastest time set up by jet aircraft when they were used on route. The published flight time is one hour and ten minutes, and whilst the scheduled time was being virtually cut in half most of the Teesside-bound passengers were unaware that they were on a record-breaking flight. As Joe Sharpes said "We had everything going for us and the flight went so quickly I didn't have time to let the passengers know what was happening. I was just able to wish them a quick Happy New Year".

The record was made possible because for once a direct track was possible between London Control Zone Boundary and Teesside Airport. Normally the flight would have remained on the U.K. airways system, and it was on this "long distance" of course that the published schedules were calculated. On 1st January 1975 however, there was only a light passenger load, and all of the military flying areas were inactive being New Years Day, so that it became obvious that there was an excellent chance of the direct routing.

In sharp contrast to the above (if the pun can be excused) the economic situation in the country and indeed the world, was quite gloomy and in January share prices fell to an all-time low. Obviously the well-being of the Company had to be critically looked at by the Board. The result of this in-depth investigation made itself manifest early in January when it was decided to cut the Viscount fleet to nine units, withdraw the Heralds from service and augment the Boeing fleet in view of the long-haul market situation.

The final in-service flight of the Herald within B.M.A. took place on Sunday, 16th February, when the service from Jersey landed at East Midlands. All further Herald services were carried out by Viscount aircraft. The Heralds were put up for lease or preferably sale and there were many enquiries.

The outlook for the Boeing fleet at the beginning of 1975 seemed quite hopeful. 'VE' was still operating for East African Airways and would be until early April at least, whilst 'BJ' was flying for the Bangladesh national carrier. Other good enquiries were on the horizon from a number of promising sources, hence the transfer of four crews from short-haul fleets (the First Officers came from the Viscount fleet). If all went well additional aircraft capacity would be required for the summer, so negotiations were made for the dry-leasing of another 707-321 should the need arise. Hopeful indeed.

The reduction in the Viscount operation to nine aircraft was not as bad as at first seemed, but in order to offer an explanation it will be necessary to return for a moment to the summer of 1974 when the Turkish Army invaded Cyprus and successfully divided the island. In the conflict Nicosia airport was badly damaged, and with it virtually all of Cyprus Airways fleet was destroyed. Those aircraft which were repairable could not be moved as the front line passed through the airport, and the United Nations troops were in occupation. To all intents and purposes Cyprus was now devoid of all communications apart from a few small ships plying to and fro. The Turks opened an old wartime airfield and operated Fokker F27's to Turkey. The Greek-Cypriots did not have any such services open to them. The only airfield available in the Greek area was the Royal Air Force base at Akrotiri, but for obvious political reasons this base could not be used as a civilian airport for Greek-Cypriot use.

As a result of the situation in Cyprus, the General Manager of Cyprus Airways, Mr. Samsos, approached British Midland in September 1974, with a proposal to lease one, possibly two, Heralds to operate from a re-furbished wartime fighter strip at Paphos in the south west corner of the island, to Athens, Beirut and Tel Aviv. Whilst the Herald performance for Paphos strip was being evaluated, the Route Planning Manager, Mr. Jim Barry, decided to evaluate the Viscount 813 on the same routes under the same conditons. The result was a good one and this was conveyed to Cyprus Airways who decided to drop the Herald and accept the Viscount. Apart from the better payload, a large number of Cyprus Airways crews had the Viscount endorsed on their licences and thus could be utilised to fly their own services.

Shortly afterwards the Paphos project was dropped and a request made to evaluate another old war time strip at Lakatamia, just four miles from Nicosia. At this point two B.M.A. directors, Mr. A. J. Smith, Technical Director and Mr. J. Wolfe, General Manager and Director, travelled to Cyprus by courtesy of the Royal Air Force, landing at Akrotiri (where Army intelligence branch immediately "arrested" them both and questioned them for some time as to their reasons for entering Cyprus—this after travelling with the Foreign and

155

Commonwealth Office clearance to fly on a service aircraft had been obtained). Upon returning to the U.K. (again via the R.A.F.) they brought with them large-scale charts of the strip and its proposed extensions. Once again a considerable amount of work was carried out in evaluating the operation, and International Aeradio Ltd. drew up aerodrome plates for the strip. Once again the project was dropped.

In October, Captain D. Court, Viscount Fleet Captain and Captain P. Austin, then Herald Fleet Captain, flew to Beirut and then proceeded by coastal steamer to Larnaca. However it was not the sunshine cruise that some of their colleagues thought that it was going to be for them. When they first boarded the ship they found that the sea was too rough to put to sea, and when, finally, the voyage began, both Court and Austin found themselves as "deck cargo" sitting on deck in deck-chairs, with a blanket around themselves for the 15 hour voyage, as all the below-decks accommodation had been taken up.

Upon arrival in Larnaca both pilots were taken to see yet another proposed airstrip, just outside the town. Once again it was another wartime airstrip, this time being used as a town rubbish dump, and the main runway concrete was cracked right across at one point. Having investigated the strip, including possible radio aid sites, both returned to the East Midlands Airport where, once again, a complete evaluation was carried out, and International Aeradio made further plates of the airfield. Once again the project seemed to die a natural death.

In mid-January 1975, quite suddenly the contract was signed and Cyprus Airways Chief Pilot, Captain Sam Melling arrived at East Midlands Airport to take the Viscount 813 technical course, followed by a simulator course and line training on British Midland's own route network.

Two Viscount 813's were withdrawn from service, G-AZLR and G-AZLT, and the paintwork revised. "British Midland" was painted out on the fuselage and replaced by "Cyprus Airways", and the whole tail was repainted, this time in light grey but with the Cyprus Airways motif emblazoned on it.

At 2100 on Wednesday, 5th February, 1975, both aircraft departed from East Midlands for Cyprus and services from Larnaca to Athens, Heraklion (Crete), Beirut and Tel Aviv were commenced on Monday, 10th February.

The Cyprus lease was to continue on a relatively long-term basis as a dry lease, so that for the immediate future the Viscount problem was near enough solved.

To return to the economic measures being undertaken at the beginning of 1975, in addition to the new fleet dispositions just described, further measures were taken. With three Heralds and three Viscounts now removed from the scene, fewer maintenance staff were required, and so forty engineers were made redundant.

Further economic measures were the making redundant of six sales staff, and the closing down of B.M.A. stations at Southend and Glasgow, the handling being transferred to handling agencies at those airfields. As explained previously, at Glasgow the loss of the Court Line and Donaldson International traffic now made the continued operation of the station an uneconomic proposition. With the withdrawal from service of the Heralds the oil contracts at Aberdeen were abandoned and of course the small traffic unit maintained by the Company there was withdrawn.

The exceedingly vicious war which had raged in Vietnam for many years finally came to a somewhat dramatic end in 1975. Not unnaturally there were many South Vietnamese who wished to escape the Communists, but additionally there were many orphan children in danger in the country. In an endeavour to airlift 150 such children out to the United Kingdom the Daily Mail newspaper chartered a Company 707-G-AYVE on 4th April, 1975, on behalf of Project Vietnam Orphans and the Ockenden Venture, both charitable organisations. Fuel was provided free by B.P. and the aircraft was flown by an all-male crew, it being thought unwise to ask any air hostess to operate into war-torn Saigon.

The crew, commanded by Captain "Freddie" Burkett, were Senior First Officer Harry Reed, Senior Engineering Officer Ted Baker, Navigating Officer Pete Wighton, Stewards Lionel Roberts, Mike Davis, George Guy and "Patch" Partridge, and ground engineer Roy Pawson, left London on a normal British Airways flight to Bombay, to await the aircraft being flown by Captain John Blackman. Also on board the outboard flight were the editor of the Daily Mail, Mr. David English, plus a train of doctors and nurses.

In Saigon about 100 children had been brought to the airport in buses, but outside the perimeter they were stopped as Vietnamese authorities claimed that the 1500 quota of orphans permitted to emigrate had already been filled. More telephone calls followed between the airport authorities and the Ministry of the Interior. All this time the children were waiting in the buses in which the temperature was more than 100°F.

Finally the Ministry over-ruled the airport emigration control and the children were free to board, but still the buses remained at a standstill because emigration insisted that minute checks be made on all of the 17 Doctors and Nurses who were attending the children on the buses.

Another hour passed and still the paper-work went on at a snails pace. All the time people were pleading for speed. The distress of the children in the buses was becoming a severe medical problem. One spastic girl had to be rushed into the airport building to be doused with water because of heat exhaustion.

Finally, after three hours of waiting, permission was given and the buses were allowed through to 'VE'. The on-board doctors and nurses were waiting to greet them. Up in the forward part of the cabin a miniature operating theatre had been set up just in case. Intravenous drips were tied up for cases of dehydration. Dressings, drugs, baby foods, nappy pads—all contributed to the flight by well-wishers in Britain—were set out throughout the aircraft. Swiftly the nursing team settled the babies into position and began giving them water to overcome the effect of the three hours in the stifling heat of the buses.

Captain Burkett started the engines and then, at the very last minute, came another objection from the authorities. Officals arrived and claimed yet again that the orphans had not received Vietnamese Government permission to leave.

157

One told Captain Burkett that he would not get A.T.C. clearance to leave until the officials were satisfied that the children were entitled to leave.

Inside the aircraft the temperature rose to 110° F as for 15 minutes Mr. English argued on the tarmac with the officials. More officials arrived. Finally Mr. English agreed to sign five forms some of which were then counter signed by Mr. Hunt of the British Embassy who had himself been arguing for some six hours non-stop.

Mr. English was told he would have to stay in Siagon, but after officials had radioed the tower that flight BD757 was authorised to take-off, he re-boarded the aircraft in the general confusion. Captain Burkett gunned the engines, swung onto the runway and made an immediate take-off.

Once the aircraft gained altitude and the air-conditioning began to work, the children began to settle down and the nurses started changing them and putting on fresh clothing. Doctors began their medical checks and on-the-spot diagnoses.

The doctor in charge, Dr. Griffin, of Chislehurst, Kent said that the general condition of the babies was not good. There was one baby who looked as if it might not survive. It certainly would have died that day if it had been left in Saigon. The Sister who was looking after it, Elizabeth Lamb, was absolutely brilliant.

Dr. Griffin continued, "It's really remarkable. My own view is that at least six of these children would have died in the next 60 hours if they had been left in Saigon.

"The Cabin crew of this aircraft have performed in a manner that can only be described as magnificent. Because of the danger, no stewardesses were on the last leg into Saigon. The four male stewards worked non-stop with the medical teams, changing nappies cuddling screaming children and feeding them. They have behaved fantastically—it has been the equivalent of having four extra nurses aboard this aircraft".

By the time the aircraft landed at Heathrow these four stewards had been on duty 29 hours, for they volunteered to continue to work even after the relief crew came aboard at Bombay on the return flight.

Once again the staff of British Midland had risen to the challenge and had endeared themselves to the people they served. So also had the medical team on board. The nurses finished the trip dead on their feet, absolutely exhausted and burnt out.

In point of fact the flight turned out to be the only British aircraft to rescue children and was in fact the last aircraft of any nation to rescue orphans before the war in Vietnam finished.

The Company's "Instant Airline" theme, whereby aircraft together with crews, engineering back-up and operational support formed a package deal and were leased to any potential airline, really began to pay off in April 1975, when seven airlines in the Middle East Africa and Europe used the new leasing services.

The biggest single contract was for the leasing by Syrian Arab Airlines of two Boeing 707's for routes radiating from Damascus to European and Middle East capitals. This one contract alone was worth £2.5m, and was initially for a period of one year commencing May 1st 1975. Similar, short term contracts were also placed with Zambia Airways, East African and Sudan Airways. Cyprus Airways, who it will be remembered, were helped to "get off the ground" in February, placed an order for a third Viscount 813, adding another £500,000 to the total. Air Anglia and British Island Airways added a further £250,000 when they each leased a Herald for the summer season. The total earnings announced on 17th April came to £4,000,000. To cope with the 707 requirement two more of these aircraft, G-AYVG and G-AZWA were added to the fleet, both of which were ex-Donaldson.

The 1974 annual report for Minster Assets, issued in June 1975, showed that British Midland had turned in an operating profit of £20,146, compared with an operating loss of £442,809 for 1973. However, when interest on loan repayments was added to these figures a loss of £754,108 and £217,497 was recorded for 1973 and 1974 respectively. However when the international picture for the world's airlines was taken into account B.M.A's record for 1974 was quite an achievement and indicated yet again that the Company was in fact pulling itself up by its own bootstraps in order to climb back into the black again. 1975 was to show an even better result.

The Viscount simulator approval renewal became due at the end of July and Dave Whitfield, the engineer, worked very hard with Peter Hill, Chief Ground Instructor, to have everything on top line for the C.A.A's inspection. In an endeavour to improve the flexibility of the simulator, Whitfield had designed, built and installed a modification enabling complete generator failure to be simulated and this worked very well indeed, particularly as the equipment had not been built to achieve this in the first place.

The approval inspection went very well, and the approval certificate was upgraded to permit the renewal of instrument ratings to be carried out on the simulator. One criticism however was the absence of a stall warning "stick-shaker" and it was a condition of renewal that this modification be installed forthwith. Once again Dave Whitfield set to and designed and installed the equipment even though it was never anticipated by the designers that this would be required.

In early July there was issued what was tantamount to a policy statement, and it came in two parts. In the first case some independent operators and the State airline used some very strong language after the chairman of British Caledonian had made a statement about the "second force airline" coupled with a suggestion that a Government stake in B/CAL would be a sign of commitment to the "second force policy". Mike Bishop said "I disagree with the confrontation which Adam Thompson has started. The independents and British Airways can live together in a sensible framework of legislation. However, the independents and British Airways should be complementary rather than competitive. If you're in the business of being competitive with the State airline you'll get a bloody nose".

The second case was a statement by Mike Bishop to "Flight International" in which he said that the Company would fly at least eight Viscounts on scheduled services into Europe until at least 1985 and possibly 1990. The Viscount 810 series in use were all built around 1958, and the Company and the British Aircraft Corporation were giving attention to ways of extending the aircraft lives.

Two Viscount 814's, G-BAPF and G-BAPD, were sold to Skyline Sweden in September. That Company's Chief Pilot, and some of his crews attended the B.M.A. ground school on 14th August, taking delivery of the two aircraft on 5th September and 16th October (SE-FOX and SE-FOY respectively).

Yet another big and significant wet-lease "instant airline" contract was announced on 1st September. Starting on 16th September one Boeing 707 would commence flying for M.A.S., Malaysian Airlines System, on routes radiating from Kuala Lumpur to Hong Kong, Taipei and Tokyo, and also to Sydney and Melbourne. Two weeks later, on 18th September, it was announced that P.I.A., Pakistan International Airlines had agreed to a £½m lease for their routes radiating from Karachi.

By now the "instant airline" concept was catching on so fast that it was necessary to acquire a further two Boeing 707's, and so it was that G-AYXR was delivered to the Company on 22nd August and flown from Miami via Anchorage, Alaska to Hong Kong for modifications and refurbishing, whilst G-BAEL was ferried by the same crew under Captain Freddie Burkett from Miami via Castle Donington to Hong Kong for the same engineering work to be undertaken.

In mid-September the travel industry was somewhat surprised when, as if to emphasize the statement made by Mike Bishop in July a joint announcement by British Airways and British Midland Airways was made introducing a substantially improved air service between Birmingham and London Heathrow, subject to approval by the C.A.A. From 1st November, it was intended that B.M.A. would provide three return Herald services a day on the route, whilst British Airways would continue with a single return service a day. The main benefit of this service was the ease with which passengers, both business and holidaymakers, could make the frequent direct connections out of London with British Airways flights and other airlines' services to dozens of destinations all over the world. Similarly, businessmen and other visitors arriving from abroad would find it much easier to be able to reach Birmingham and the Midlands without spending time making surface connections. The advent of the new National Exhibition Centre at Birmingham had indeed made the route very attractive. It was anticipated that in the first year alone B.M.A. itself would get 50,000 passengers to make the service viable. In fact, in just over six months the passenger loads were so good that on exhibition days a Viscount had to be put on the route in addition to the 50 seat Herald which normally operated the service. There were many who would have to eat their own words later about this service, those who said it would not be a route in six months, let alone a winner.

One of the most interesting aspects of the new service was the reality that the privately owned sector of industry could work, and work successfully, with the State owned carrier, even to the extent of both carriers co-ordinating their respective efforts to this end. The first flight of the new service operated on Monday, 30th November, 1975.

The half-yearly financial figures released on 24th October were very encouraging. On turnover, up from £4,225,000 to £5,776,000, the operating loss was reduced from £291,000 to £166,000 in the six months ending 30th June. Borrowings from Minster Assets had by now been repaid. Passenger traffic carryings on the scheduled service network had increased by 2.1% and this was largely responsible for the improved financial position, and pointed to a good profit for the year.

November was the anniversary of the taking-over of the Belfast/Gatwick service when B/CAL dropped the route in 1974, and to mark the first birthday a reception was given by the Company to the travel trade and press on 4th November at the Russell Court Hotel in Belfast. At the reception it was announced that in the first year of operation 60,000 passengers had been carried and a net profit between £25,000 and £50,000 had been made. Mike Bishop also announced that "cut-price flights" might be available in 1976 if B.M.A. were able to renew its licence on the route.

The amount being talked about insofar as the C.A.A. was concerned was only a differential of £2, but Mike said at the reception that he would like to see a "substantial difference", talking of a round-trip fare in the region of £25 as opposed to the existing full fare of £44. In fact a fare differential of the magnitude hinted at never became reality.

To round off a highly successful year, figures released at the year's end showed that the Birmingham-London service had carried on the first two months of operation just over 5,000 passengers, and in doing so confounded many gloomy prophets in the aviaton industry who had predicted a very lean period before the National Exhibition Centre opened. How wrong they were:

The fleet at the year's end was:—

Herald 214   —G-ATIG, G-ASVO, G-BAVX
Viscount 813   —G-AZLP, G-AZLR, G-AZLS, G-AZLT, G-AZNA,
                 G-AZNB, G-AZNC
Viscount 815   —G-AVJB
Boeing 707-321 —G-AYBJ, G-AYVE, G-AYVG, G-AZWA, G-AYXR,
                 G-BAEL

1976

A New Year's present came to Britain when on Thursday, 15th January, 1976, Michael Bishop accepted an American aviation "Oscar", the only foreign airline to be so honoured in the 1975 presentations which took place on that date in the Plaza Hotel, New York.

The annual Airline Industry Awards, sponsored by a leading U.S. air transport publication, "Air Transport World" were presented in eleven categories, and the award to B.M.A. was in the contract services section and recognised the worldwide sales campaign and operation of the "Instant Airline" leasing service. Mr. Richard Lewis, managing director of Chetwynd Streets (Midlands) Ltd., of Leicester, the Company's advertising agents, accompanied Mike Bishop to New York for the award presentation.

The Teesside-London service which had done so well since taking over the service from Autair in 1969 apart from a small drop in passenger carryings in December 1975, really broke all records in March 1976 when, for the first time, over 12,000 passengers in the month were carried, the actual figure being 12,272. The previous record had been 10,290, set in January 1974. Many of these extra passengers had flown due to a rail strike but as Ashley Sharpe, the Teesside Station Manager for B.M.A. said, "We are obviously delighted. Of the extra passengers who flew with us because of the rail strike, a small but nevertheless significant number have continued to fly".

March also saw the arrival at the Company's training school at the East Midlands of six British Airways Viscount Crews, who attended a short course for the Viscount 813's which the Corporation were to lease to replace their Viscount 700 series on the Prestwick shuttle route for the Trans-Atlantic service, connecting Belfast, Glasgow, Edinburgh, Aberdeen and Carlisle with Prestwick. Currently flying the Viscount 806 with British Airways, the crews spent four days studying the technical differences between the two variants and carrying out simulator exercises.

On 1st April the London (Heathrow)—Strasbourg service, which had run for two years, was dropped through lack of support. Another significant change to appear in the summer 1976 timetable, effective from 1st April, was the doubling of the Amsterdam service which now departed East Midlands at 0750 and 1700 daily Monday to Friday, returning from Amsterdam 0945 and 1855, so that this partly offset the dissapointment felt on the Strasbourg service.

Also on 1st April, Mr. George Morrell, Puchasing Stores Manager with the Company for 20 years, retired.

New leasing contracts started on 1st April too, when two (subsequently three) Boeing 707's began work for Tunis Air, with a contract worth initially £2.5m. Additionally four other major airlines, Kuwait Airways Corporation, Malaysian Airlines System, Pakistan International and East African Airways, placed orders for the "Instant Airline" varying from one month to six months to provide summer supplementary capacity on their own routes.

Wednesday, 21st April saw the publication of the financial report for the year ending 31st December 1975, and very encouraging the report was too. The following is an extract:—

	Year to 31.12.75 £'000	Year to 31.12.74 £'000
Turnover	14,816	10,668
Trading profit before tax	477	20
Interest to parent Company	(57)	(237)
Nett profit before tax	420	(217)
Tax	NIL	NIL

All arrears of dividends in respect of the 9½% convertible cumulative preference shares amounting to £200,949, were paid on 31st December, 1975. No ordinary dividend is recommended.

Reporting to shareholders, the Chairman, Mr. A. R. G. McGibbon, said "It gives me very great pleasure to report a profit for British Midland Airways of £420,000 before taxation. This is easily your Company's best ever performance and is all the more creditable for having been achieved in a year which by universal consent was one of the most difficult ever experienced by the airline industry throughout the world. On your behalf I would like to thank everyone involved throughout the Company for their hard work in making such an achievement possible".

On the 18th May the Company announced that it was seeking C.A.A. approval for an extension of the discount fare on the Belfast-Gatwick route. A differential of £2 per one-way trip already existed on the route at certain times of the day, but the Company wanted this extended to other times, and also intended to push for a widening of the differential between London (Heathrow) and London (Gatwick). Mike Bishop, in making the announcement, stated that B.M.A. had a responsibility to ensure that business remained profitable. Fare increases, be warned, could be counter-productive. It was not the Company's intention to start any sort of rate war with British Airways who operated Belfast-Heathrow. Both had a role to play in the market for air travellers between Northern Ireland and the rest of the U.K.

A further Arab country joined the ever-growing list of countries using "Instant Airline", when Libyan Arab Airlines, the national flag carrier of Libya, leased a Boeing 707. Libyan Arab was the seventh Arab customer to use the service, and since its inception in 1973 a total of £11,000,000 had been earned, mainly in U.S. currency.

Having announced on more than one occasion that the Company was to reintroduce medium-range jets onto the scheduled service network, it came as no surprise to the industry when, on Monday 28th June 1976, Michael Bishop announced at a press conference at St. George's Hotel, Teesside Airport that the great day had at last arrived. What did surprise everybody though was the choice of the McConnell Douglas DC9. The aircraft would be the first of its type to be operated by a British carrier and would in fact remain on the American register for the first nine months or so whilst certification to British requirements was accomplished. In view of all this, and the intention to operate the new aircraft on the Teesside-London route in the first instance, it was necessary to obtain a C.A.A. waiver. The aircraft DC9-14, C/N 47048, registration N65358 originally YV-52C operated by Avensa, would be hired initially from McDonnell Douglas and contracts were exchanged on Friday 18th June 1976. Powered by Pratt and Whitney JT8D fan engines with a range of 1250 miles, extra utilisation would be achieved by carrying out Inclusive Tour flights from Teesside during the hours of darkness.

Making the introduction Mike Bishop said "This is the first time we have introduced a new aircraft outside the East Midlands. If the operation is successful we hope to introduce more aircraft in 1977. The first to operate from

163

the East Midlands will be in 1977. We are especially pleased at renewing our association with Douglas Aircraft Corporation, whose famous earlier product the DC3 (Dakota), together with the Argonaut, played such a significant role in the original development of our airline".

The aircraft was undergoing a pre-delivery overhaul at Phoenix, Arizona at the time the announcement was made, and was due to be delivered on 25th July, but that was later put back to 10th August.

The Chairman of the Teesside Airport Committee, Councillor Bill Emerson, was particularly pleased at both the announcement and the apparent timing, for only a few days earlier the Department of Trade had announced that Teesside Airport was not to be developed in view of Government estimates of traffic growth there. He described the advent of the new jet as "the first wedge in a fight against the report" which favoured development of nearby Newcastle Airport instead. "We intended to drive home the first wedge to the Department to show it where it has gone wrong in its forecast for Teesside" he explained.

The introduction of the DC9 meant an absolute hive of activity within the Company. There were Operational Manuals to be written, training schedules to undertake, route evaluations to be made, load/trim sheets to be introduced, engineering back-ups to be laid in train, and a host of other requirements to be taken into account.

The training of the Aircrew was undertaken by K.L.M. Royal Dutch Airlines, in Amsterdam, and the first course of pilots returned from their three-week course with K.L.M. on Monday, 26th June, being immediately replaced with the next course together with Peter Hill, Chief Ground Instructor, who would undertake any future aircrew courses. K.L.M. would also undertake the routine engineering requirements until such time as the aircraft was transferable to the British register.

Captain Jim Shaw transferred from the 707 fleet to become DC9 Fleet Manager, with Captain R. Wise as his deputy. Captain Neil Bromiley became Viscount Fleet Manager and Captain "Nass" Tatalias, Herald Fleet Manager.

Again the Teesside figures rocketed into the record charts in June, when 11,531 passengers were carried, justifying Mike Bishop's decision to make the Teesside-London route the introductory one for the DC9. Similarly it was also announced in July that the Birmingham-London service had seen an increase in carryings of 100%. The result of this latter increase was an agreement by the Company with British Airways to increase the frequency from four to five flights a day, excluding that provided by British Airways themselves, from 1st September, subject to C.A.A. approval. Who said that State-owned airlines and Independents couldn't live side-by-side? There was also more to come.

On 4th August Mike Bishop outlined the Company's plans for 1977, the emphasis being on the build-up of services from Birmingham rather than the East Midlands, the splitting of the Birmingham-Brussels-Frankfurt service into its two components to provide a Birmingham-Brussels and a Birmingham Frankfurt service, and the operation of the Birmingham-Copenhagen service, successfully acquired from Alidair some time previously, but never operated.

The Copenhagen service ran into trouble later on in the year when, although announced by the Company as about to be operated (the first flight was planned to depart Birmingham on Monday, 31st October), the Danish Government refused licencing permission on the grounds that the bi-lateral agreement between the two countries was satisfied by the services provided by Scandinavian Airlines System (S.A.S.) and British Airways, and that there was insufficient traffic to justify a route between Birmingham and Copenhagen. However it was believed that the real reason lay in pressure from SAS which did not want competition on its Manchester service. British Midland felt that the National Exhibition Centre would of itself generate sufficient traffic for the service. The British Government backed B.M.A. and banned SAS services to Manchester and Glasgow, whereupon the Danes accused Britain of using blackmail tactics. In the event the service was never operated by BMA, but perhaps again it was an ill-wind because the following year the licence was used in a "swop-session" with British Airways when the Company agreed to take over B.A's Liverpool services.

The DC9 arrived at the East Midlands Airport on the 27th August, having been flown in from Arizona by a KLM crew. It's introduction into service was to be delayed some three weeks or so in order that certain engineering work necessary to commence the task of bringing the type onto the British Register could be undertaken. The decision had been taken to re-commence the naming of Company aircraft, a practice dropped when the Argonauts were put into service, and so N65358 became the second aircraft to bear the name Dove Dale and the Derbyshire coat of arms. The first service flown by Dove Dale took place on the 27th September as planned on the Teesside route.

In spite of all the excitement and enthusiasm abounding with the DC9 aquisition, an air of gloom found its way into the hearts of all staff when in mid October the first six months trading figures for 1976 reported a loss of £436,000, despite a reminder that it was still anticipated that a profit for the year would be returned, the figure claimed being £420,000.

The first pilot to retire on pension from the Company did so on 16th October, he was Captain Eric Lines, who had by then completed 26 years service with BMA. He received two silver goblets and a silver tray from his colleagues, and the Company gave him a farewell dinner and gifts at a reception in Nottingham later in the month. Captain Lines had started when the Company was Derby Aviation, flying Rapides on charter work and War Office contract, including operating the first scheduled service flight (to Jersey) in 1953, the inaugural Glasgow service in 1957 and had flown every aircraft type operated by the Company with the exception of the Boeing 707 (and of course the DC9, which came too late for Captain Lines to take the conversion course).

As part of a rationalisation programme, together with a desire to withdraw from the London-Newquay service yet at the same time keep faith with the undertakings given to the Cornish people not to leave the service high-and-dry, it was announced in early December that Brymon Airways had applied to take over the service from British Midland, and if C.A.A. approval was forthcoming, then a Herald would be purchased by Brymon from the Company to operate the service. The C.A.A. approval did appear and ultimately the service (and the Herald) were transferred to Brymon Airways on 1st January, 1977.

To the great shock of many people, particularly the employees, it was announced just before Christmas that, due in the main to a substantial decline in the "instant airline" business, big cut-backs were to be announced after Christmas, including the instant grounding of three B707's, the redundancy of some 250 staff, mostly engineers and administrative staff, and the possible closing down of one or two outstations. The 707 grounding was not so drastic as would at first appear, as the last aircraft to be acquired were done so on an hours-flown lease contract, and therefore if they were not flying then no costs would accrue (other than parking fees, but then these were quite expensive in themselves). Later, due to costings produced the number of engineers involved in the redundancies was reduced from 173 to 90, but still a large number of other staff finally did go.

One other result of the cut-backs was the taking-over of the Birmingham and East Midlands to the Isle-of-Man services by Dan-Air using Hawker Siddeley 748's.

Not a very happy ending to the year.

The fleet at the years end was:—

Herald 214	— G-ATIG, G-ASVO, G-BAVX (IG being sold to Brymon Airways)
Viscount 813	— G-AZLP, G-AZLR, G-AZLS, G-AZLT, G-AZNA, G-AZNB, G-AZNC
Viscount 815	— G-AVJB
Boeing 707-321	— G-AYBJ, G-AYVE, G-AYVG, G-AZWA, G-AYXR, G-BAEL
Douglas DC9-14	— N65358

1977

Early in the New Year, and as part of the Company's "recovery programme", Viscount 815, G-AVJB finally departed from the Company having been sold to Jersey's own airline Intra. This now meant that only the seven Viscount 813's remained.

To strike a happier note and again to prove that an ill-wind blows some good, a contract was signed, quite quickly, in Nairobi in early February. The background was as follows. East African Airways, supported by a consortium of Kenya, Tanzania and Uganda, had gone into liquidation following its failure to meet many debts and the subsequent grounding of its fleet in London and repossession of the Super VC10's by British Aircraft Corporation. After one week of inactivity the Kenyan Government decided to set up their own airline, Kenya Airways, and British Midland were approached to provide two B707's linking Nairobi and Mombasa with London, Rome, Frankfurt and Zurich.

166

With only forty eight hours notice the first aircraft had been prepared, including painting in Kenya Airways new colours by Ernie Robey, the Company's "wizard with the paint brush", and positioned to London Heathrow to operate flight KQ515. Captain Ron Hardy, Boeing Fleet Manager flew G-AYXR out of Heathrow, where a small crowd of Kenyans had gathered to see it depart. Upon arrival at Nairobi at 0850 on 5th February, Hardy made a pass over Nairobi to show off the new airline and then landed at Embakasi Airport to a fantastic welcome by the Kenyans. The waving bases at the airport were overflowing, and assorted teams of traditional dancers lined the apron until the crowds broke through the police cordon and thronged right round the aircraft.

For BMA the decline of East African Airways had brought new business and a ray of hope. Also on the 7th February it was announced that another two B707's had been leased to Kuwait Airways Corporation. The first aircraft was delivered on 1st March with second being flown to Kuwait on 30th March. Although aircraft had been leased to Kuwait before, the new contract now brought to 24 the number of airlines, all I.A.T.A. members, to use the "instant airline".

Kenya Airways later on in March leased a third 707, bringing to five the number of Boeings being used, so the nosedive the Company had begun to experience at the beginning of the year had now been reversed. Good news indeed, but a long way to go yet.

For many years now the island of Guernsey in the Channel Islands had been resisting jet aircraft landing at the island's airport, this resistance being due to a desire to prevent noise problems and also the fear that large numbers of greenhouses, of which the island had thousands, would be broken or damaged by the vibration. Two airlines, British Airways and British Island Airways had both warned Guernsey that the time was fast approaching when the jet ban would have to be lifted, and now BMA approached the islands with a similar warning plus a request to carry out proving flights with the DC9. As the DC9 was fitted with the relatively quiet American manufactured JTD-9 engines, whilst the other two carriers used Tridents and BAC 1-11's respectively, both fitted with the noisier Spey engines, it was odds-on that Mike Bishop's request would receive a better audience than the others. Certainly the island would have to alter its views quickly in the future or stagnate into a backwater insofar as any future progress in aviation was concerned.

1977 was time for a change of cabin staff and ground receptionist uniform and the month of April saw its introduction. Out went the green Maid Marian uniform, and in came a fresh, classic style, chosen for simple elegance and hard wear. The colour chosen was mink and to complement their suits the girls wore short-sleeved V-necked, striped blouses in shades of tangerine, dark brown and coffee. The raincoats were also in the mink shade, set off by long scarves in the same pattern as the blouse. Brown patent leather court shoes, matching handbags with gilt trimmings and mink shade hats in a Robin hood style completed the ensemble.

Mid-April saw the final financial figures for 1976 issued and, as predicted they were pretty gloomy. The anticipated pre-tax profits nose-dived from

£420,000 to £90,000, on a turnover up from £14.8m to £18.6m. The chief problem turned out to be the leasing division, but hopefully those days were now gone.

As if to offset the above gloom, it was revealed that, possibly due to the introduction of the DC9 the Teesside-London route had again broken all records when 12,666 passengers used the service in March, and yet again in April when 12,877 passengers were carried. Similarly, the Belfast-Gatwick figures had reached 60% more than the same period in 1976. At a Belfast reception Mike Bishop revealed the figures and said he hoped to receive authority from the C.A.A. to increase the daily frequency from three to four flights, replacing the Viscounts with DC9's.

In the early hours of Saturday 9th July, Boeing 707 G-AZWA en route from Beirut to Kuwait with Captain Barry Hattem in command and First Officer Bob Coker and Flight Engineer Dave Brown as his technical crew, was hijacked by armed Palestinians, who demanded the release of 200 prisoners in an Arab jail. The aircraft was allowed to land at Kuwait, where some of the passengers were freed, but the crew, together with the remaining passengers, remained all day in the aircraft standing in the blistering heat. Later on a Kuwaiti highranking police officer, a South Yemeni diplomat and a Palestinian commando representative boarded the aircraft in exchange for the hostage passengers. All were expecting to be flown to Aden with the hijackers. Captain Ron Hardy, 707 Fleet Manager, First Officer Harry Read, and Chief Flight Engineer Jim Hawkins were standing by to relieve Captain Hattam and his crew and to everybody's delight the hijackers allowed the substitution to take place. Two stewardesses, Cynthia Hobson and Judith Croasdell displayed cool courage when they noticed two other hostesses walking towards the aircraft and persuaded the hijackers that the two necomers were part of the relief crew and were allowed to leave. As they walked towards the terminal building the other girls suddenly turned in the direction of another plane. It was a nervous moment for Cynthia and Judith for they knew that the hijacker's guns were pointing at their backs and they didn't know how the hijackers would react. The girls just kept on walking very slowly, and nothing happened.

Later the aircraft took off ostensibly, for Aden where landing permission had been granted, but hours after the take off the Boeing landed in Damascus, where once again negotiations began. At one point negotiations broke down and the aircraft, fully fuelled, was about to take-off once again, with orders to fly to Tripoli, but the hijackers could not agree and so it taxied back to its original position, where one of the hijackers left the aircraft and talked directly to the Palestinians and Syrians, and apparently agreed to a plan to overpower the leader "Abu Sayed". He returned to the Boeing which again began taxying as if to take-off, but inside the hijackers disarmed their leader and surrendered.

The news of the end of the hijacking was radioed to the incident control room established at Castle Donington, Mike Bishop said "We are very proud of the crews. It's all very well to say hijacking is an occupational hazard but it's a great menace". So ended British Midland's first (and only it is hoped) hijacking.

In order to improve reservation facilities the company signed a £350,000 contract with British Airways to link up with B.A's computer system BABS. The contract, initially for three years, would link-up with the world-wide BABS system and would involve the initial installation of 25 video display terminals and three medium-speed printers in nine separate locations covering BMA's major telephone sales, space control and ticketing offices. Instant access from East Midlands, Birmingham, Teeside, London and Channel Islands areas would be provided to the British Airways computer complex at Heathrow. In signing the contract (in which BMA became the first independent airline to be linked into the British Airways system), Mike Bishop said "The signing of this agreement demonstrates further the co-operation which exists between ourselves and British Airways". The system came "on-line" on Monday 12th December.

By this time, August, it had been decided to replace some of the fuel thirsty B707-321's fitted with pure-jet engines, with less-thirsty fan-engines, so that two B707-320C aircraft, one acquired from British Caledonian Airways, and one from World Airways, an American carrier, came into service, one going to Kuwait and the other to Kenya Airways. Additionally another DC9 this time leased from Finnair, was put into service, mainly to enable an extension of jet services to take place.

On 12th September the first DC9 "Darley Dale" inaugurated the type on the Belfast-Gatwick route, cutting the time from 1 hour 30 mins to 55 minutes. The fare used on the jet-service was the same as that when the Viscount was used. Now this may not sound much of a historical item, but for some time BMA had been doing battle to reduce fares against a lot of opposition from British Airways (one of the few areas where conflict with the airline was happening), and had achieved a fare differential on the Belfast-Gatwick route of £5 single compared with the Belfast-London Heathrow route, this after an unsuccessful appeal against the decision by B.A.

A similar state of affairs existed on A routes to Guernsey, where BMA had successfully negotiated a 20% discount fare provided bookings were made at least four months in advance. The result had been a rise in passengers from 11,673 to 13,289 over the same period last year, whereas British Airways and British Island Airways both lost traffic in the first six months of the year following an increase in fares. BMA had all in all been pursuing a policy of reducing fares for quite some time, much to the delight of the travelling public.

The first six-months trading figures, announced on 11th October, showed a pre-tax profit of £111,000, a big turn-round from 1976, when a loss of £499,000 was recorded. Hopes,were high that the twelve-month figures would again show a healthy return.

Thus ended yet another very interesting year, one commencing with big redundancies and finishing with what was hoped to be a nice operating profit, not to mention an additional DC9 and the exchange of some older Boeing 707's for fan-engined 707's.

The fleet at the end of the year was:—

Viscount 813   — G-AZLP, G-AZLR, G-AZLS, G-AZLT, G-AZNA,
                 G-AZNB, G-AZNC
Viscount 814   — G-BAPE, G-BAPG
Boeing 707-321 — G-AYBJ, G-AYVG, G-AYXR, G-BAEL
Boeing 707-324C — N370WA, G-AZJM
Douglas DC9-14 — N65358, OH-LYB

1978

As the year dawned the long-standing row with the Danes over the Birmingham-Copenhagen route developed into a major disagreement, with S.A.S. seeking traffic rights at Hong Kong, as well as rights from Scandinavia into "oil-city" i.e., Aberdeen, all being thrown into the arena. In this anniversary year in the Company's history it was a pity that it had to open this way.

1978 was an anniversary year indeed, being the fortieth birthday of the foundation of the Company, the thirtieth birthday of the first fare-paying passenger flight by Derby Aviation, and the twenty-fifth birthday of the Company's first scheduled service.

As if to celebrate such an anniversary year on Wednesday, 4th January, Mike Bishop announced that an application had been made to operate services from Glasgow and Liverpool to Cork, this being the first hint that B.M.A. were interested scheduled service-wise in Liverpool. "It's part of a strategy" he stated, going on to say that "Liverpool is a new area of interest to us. We feel there's something to be done there. There is a potential for Liverpool Airport". This new strategy, together with the solving of the Birmingham-Copenhagen service to everybody's satisfaction was later to be of immense importance to B.M.A.

Another "first" occured in the opening weeks of "anniversary year" when Mr G. Pinkerton of Quorn, Lincolnshire, made history for the Company by being the first passenger to have his reservation handled by the new sophisticated computer reservations systems, and was given a complimentary ticket to mark the occasion. The date was 18th January.

Also effective on 30th January, and perhaps indicative of the Company's progress, were increases on other routes, notably the East-Midlands to Amsterdam to be three times daily, a daily Birmingham to Amsterdam, a twice daily Birmingham to Brussels, and a twice daily East Midlands to Brussels.

Not allowing the grass to grow under his feet, Managing Director Mike Bishop flew into Liverpool on 25th January as the only passenger in B707-321 G-AYBJ, making one of its last flights for B.M.A. before being sold to a buyer in Miami, Florida. The flamboyant arrival at Liverpool Airport was to meet members of the airport committee in private talks, followed by an announcement of future BMA plans for Liverpool to airport staff, before announcing these plans to the Press. The announced plans were big indeed; BMA were prepared to base three Viscounts and one DC9 at Speke. Five daily flights to London were envisaged, together with two to Belfast, three to the Isle of Man, one to Dublin, four to the Channel Islands and one to Glasgow. Summer services could provide more flights on the Cork, Channel Islands and Isle of Man routes. Additionally it was hoped to operate regular scheduled services from, Speke to Paris, Frankfurt, Amsterdam and Brussels.

In the midst of all this British Airways were given an ultimatum by Liverpool Airport operating authority—use the licences you have or give them up. The concern by the airport authorities was understandable, for the facility was losing £1.6m per annum, and the attraction of BMA possibly opening up all the proposed new services if BA did not increase existing services was a real carrot. Mike Bishop said "It is quite clear that traffic from Liverpool has been unnecessarily depressed and held back. There has got to be a fresh start and a new style of operation". More was yet to come.

A new "instant airline" lease was announced on 10th February, when details of the contract were released. Two Boeing 707-320C fan-jets were to be operated for the Yemen Airways Corporation, the national flag carrier of the Yemen Arab Republic. Initially the contract would run until the beginning of 1980 to provide scheduled services linking the Yemen with neighbouring Middle East countries and a new service to Europe, serving Paris and London. BMA would supply aircraft, crews, engineering and ground support, as well as extending the new computer reservation facilities, together with marketing and sales assistance. The contract was worth £8.4m.

At the same time as the Yemen deal was announced, an extension of the Kuwait Airways Corporation was also made known, to the value of £1.9m. The two contracts together gave the Company its biggest-ever order book for the "instant airline" service.

Another innovation on the horizon was the application to the C.A.A. for a ten-year licence linking Birmingham and East Midlands, to commence on 1st April if approval was forthcoming. The ability to operate such a connection had been around in the days of Derby Airways, and although occasionally referred to, had never seriously been applied. The object was really to provide income on a sector which Company aircraft operated many times a day, very often with empty seats, and although primarily to provide an inter-connect with services originating at the two points, no doubt some passengers would use the service for itself and at least provide a modicum of income.

At the beginning of April, the financial return for 1977 was announced, and very encouraging it turned out to be, especially when one considers that that year had commenced with massive redundancies. The pre-tax profit was up from £90,000 in 1976 to £1.47m. Turnover jumped by over £7.5m to stand at £26.27m. The profit was 3-5 times higher than the previous best year when it was £420,000 pre-tax. The success of 1977 was attributed to stronger scheduled services from both the East Midlands and Birmingham, with an 11% growth over 1976. Aircraft had been better utilized and had produced more profit. The overseas leasing service had a successful year, particularly when compared with the disastrous beginning, and had exceeded expectations. Another factor had been when fifteen months earlier BMA had asked the CAA to allow lower fares experimentally on some routes, as it was felt that this would attract more passengers and increase profits, particularly on the Channel Islands routes. It had proved successful and was reflected in the good financial returns, and now the Company were to ask the C.A.A. to extend the scheme to Brussels, Amsterdam, Paris and Frankfurt routes.

Monday, 3rd April, saw the first of the year's anniversaries being celebrated, when the Mayors of Derby and Nottingham delivered birthday cakes to the Lord Provost of Glasgow to make the twenty first anniversary of the Glasgow service. The anniversary flight was operated by a Douglas DC9 aircraft, compared with the first flight in 1957 which was operated by another Douglas aircraft, the DC3, G-ANTD with Captain E. W. A. Lines in command. Quite a change.

The fortieth anniversary of the foundation of the Company (as Air Schools Ltd in 1938) was celebrated at a luncheon given by BMA in the Savoy Hotel in London. Guests included the former Chairman and Managing Director Wing Commander H. A. Roxburgh and Mrs Roxburgh, Mr Robin McGibbon, present Chairman of BMA and Minster Assets, Mr Michael Bishop, Charles Murland, director BMA and Minster, and Stuart Balmforth director BMA. Proposing the toast to BMA Mr J. M. Lawrie, director general of the Air Transport Users Committee and a former member of the Civil Aviation Authority, said "The motto 'The Friendly Independent' was very good". He added that he associated BMA with the buccaneers of aviation.

On 11th May the results were announced of talks conducted in conditions of absolute secrecy with British Airways over the future of Liverpool Airport, although a Press report leaked out the previous Monday, 8th May, had already given both staff and public the main points of the agreement. The plan was for British Airways to pull out of Speke completely, allowing British Midland to take over all existing BA routes out of Liverpool, but also to extend the network as already explained. BA staff would be given the option of transferring to BMA, remaining with BA but work elsewhere or to take a voluntary redundancy. In return for all this BMA would "swop" certain routes with BA; including the controversial Birmingham-Copenhagen route (thus solving everybody's problems in this regard), and subject to C.A.A. approval which in the event was forthcoming.

As B.A. had made substantial losses with its Liverpool operation, and B.M.A. with its lower overheads could make a go of the routes radiating from there, together with the fact that B.A. were in a better position, politically, to operate the Birmingham to Brussels and Frankfurt services (it was apparent at this point that foreign carriers were about to "climb on the back" of these BMA developed services, and B.A. would be in a better position to ride out the competition than BMA), the move was very shrewd and, properly handled, should prove of benefit to all concerned, not only BMA but B.A., and Liverpool and Birmingham Airports. Furthermore, in 1979, there was a strong possibility that a "bump" in the main runway at Manchester would see the closure of that airport whilst the bump was ironed out, in which event both BMA and Liverpool Airport would reap extra benefits. Who knows? One thing was sure however, and that was Mike Bishop's meaning when he flew into Liverpool again (this time in a DC9 named Merseyside) on 12th May with his by-now oftsaid slogan "use it or lose it", for if the travelling public did not use the services, he would most certainly cut the cord far faster than British Airways had done.

Yet another "instant airline" leasing contract came on 20th July with a requirement to lease three Boeing 707's to Air Algerie, two in passenger configuration, the third as a freighter. The contract, worth £8m was announced at the same time as a further requirement for one B707 freighter to go to Pakistan International Airways. The whole leasing fleet was now fully committed.

News of momentous proportions was announced on 21st July. Minster Assets were to dispose of British Midland Airways at a price of £2.875m to three executive directors of BMA, Mike Bishop (Chairman and Managing Director), John Wolfe (General Manager and Director) and Stuart Balmforth (Financial Director) a private American citizen, Dr. Robert F. Beauchamp of California, (who has substantial interests in finances, building, insurance and farming) and Mr. Grahame Elliott. The three executive directors, aquiring 75% of the issued share capital, ensured that control remained in British hands. Minster Assets were given a firm intention by the new owners to continue and develop the existing business of BMA. Assurances were also given that the interest including pension rights, all of BMA employees would be safeguarded. So now BMA was truly independent.

The news would not affect the planned "swap" in Liverpool with B.A., official approval for which had been given by the C.A.A. on 14th July, with the effective date being Monday, 29th October.

As October and "swap day" drew near, the Company started a massive advertising campaign with the slogan "The new Liver Birds are coming to Liverpool". The Liver Birds theme could apply both to the turquoise and blue liveried aircraft, or to the hostesses specially picked for their good looks, who would be on duty at the beginning of October to sell BMA tickets. The whole campaign was aimed at persuading some of the 300,000 passengers who fly from Merseyside through Manchester every year to switch to Speke. One setback not expected was a strike of Post Office engineers engaged in installing the land-line connecting the BMA Liverpool number with the computer in Derby and Heathrow. It meant an inevitable delay in providing the service, but it was hoped to complete in time to assist in early bookings and sales. In fact the line was connected in time and the computer ticket booking system became operational on 30th September.

The introduction of the DC9 onto the Teesside-London service, coupled with the inaugurationm of the Heathrow to Central London Underground link, had resulted in a further traffic growth on the route, culminating in a record 13,136 passengers in August 1978. Looking to further future growth on the route, Mike Bishop announced on 26th September that he was looking for U.K. certification of the DC9 Series 30 aircraft, carrying 120 passengers, which if successful he would look to put on the route in place of the present 85 seater Series 10. He also hinted that BMA may be looking to the stretched 165 seat version for the 1980's. Reference was also made in the same statement to the possibility of a Teesside-Gatwick Link possibly in early 1980, subject to C.A.A. licencing approval.

In mid-October the Station Manager of BMA's London Heathrow base left that station to become Station Manager Liverpool, and so inherited a fistfull of headaches inevitable when a major change of carriers is involved, and this change was most certainly the biggest such swap in British Civil Aviation History. It was a pity that a factor which nobody could avert delayed the first of the Company's Liverpool-London services—fog, but two hours late the "big change was under way at last".

As 1978 drew to a close it was nice to reflect upon the events that the Company had been involved in during its forty year existence; the build-up and management of Derby's first Municipal Airport at Burnaston; the training of 14000 pilots during the Second World War, including the,initial training of the country's first glider pilots; involvement in packaging and heavy earth-moving equipment; the build-up of passenger services to the point where the Company had been directly responsible for the creation of a major new airport, the East Midlands Airport; the development of regional and provincial air services from and to points where these services are now an essential part of the community viz Teesside-London, Newquay-London, Liverpool services to all points; the first,foreign air-carrier to take-on the American C.A.B. and win a High Court action against that body; the only foreign carrier to win an American aviation "Oscar" in 1975; the champion of lower and not higher fares wherever possible; the proof that small but efficient smaller carriers can live side-by-side with nationalised giants and can indeed do so in almost complete harmony.

This then has been the story of that forty years, a story of ups and downs, heartbreaks and at times near bankruptcy, and the welding together of a great team to overcome all of these odds and to emerge in 1978 as a great independent airline. Captain N. Roy Harben D.F.C. would most certainly be proud if he could see the young man that his brain-child has grown into. Great oaks from little acorns do indeed grow.

The fleet at the year's end (and the end of forty years) was:—

Viscount 813	— G-AZLP, G-AZLR, G-AZLS, G-AZLT, G-AZNA, G-AZNB, G-AZNC
Viscount 814	— G-BAPD, G-BAPF, G-AYOX
Viscount 836	— G-BFZL
Boeing 707-321	— G-AYVG, G-AYXR
Boeing 707-324C	— G-AZJM
Douglas DC9-14	— G-BFIH, OH-LYB
Boeing 707-338C	— G-BFLD, G-BFLE
Boeing 707-373C	— N370WA

This appendix lists all of the scheduled services ever operated by the Company, and is taken from available timetables commencing 1958 and continuing through to the Winter 1978/79 timetable. Some of the services were in fact only operated once per fortnight, e.g., Derby to Calvi, but nevertheless these services were public and not just available to Inclusive Tour Operators. Other services shown are "bread & butter" routes and have operated throughout the year and every year.

Some services were operated from Derby (Burnaston), some from East Midlands after the move across in 1965, whilst others were operated from both airfields. It is for this reason that both Derby and East Midlands have been listed, so that the true extent of the operations may be readily seen.

Under Birmingham and Derby it will be noted that Amsterdam is annotated with an (F) denoting the pure freighter service that was operated during the Winter 1964/65. The passenger service from East Midlands to Amsterdam now operates twice daily Monday to Friday, and daily at weekends.

The point of origin only has been listed, not the return service.

BELFAST to
Enniskillen, Jersey, London (Gatwick).
BIRMINGHAM to
Amsterdam (F), Barcelona, Brussels, Cork, Frankfurt, Guernsey, Isle-of-Man, Isle-of-Wight, Jersey, Luxembourg, Newcastle, Newquay, Ostend, Palma, Rotterdam, Teesside.
BRISTOL to
Amsterdam, Barcelona, Genoa, Luxembourg, Ostend, Palma, Perpignan, Valencia.
CAMBRIDGE to
Guernsey, Jersey, Ostend.
CARDIFF to
Amsterdam, Barcelona, Genoa, Luxembourg, Ostend, Palma, Perpignan, Valencia.
CARLISLE to
Belfast, Guernsey, Jersey, London (Gatwick).
COVENTRY to
Jersey.
DERBY (BURNASTON) to
Amsterdam (F), Basle, Belfast, Calvi, Carlisle, Cork, Dublin, Enniskillen, Glasgow, Guernsey, Isle-of-Man, Isle-of-Wight, Jersey, Luxembourg, Newcastle, Ostend, Rotterdam, Staverton.
EAST MIDLANDS to
Amsterdam, Barcelona, Basle, Belfast, Bergen, Bristol, Brussels, Cork, Dublin, Edinburgh, Enniskillen, Frankfurt, Glasgow, Guernsey, Isle-of-Man, Isle-of-Wight, Jersey, Leeds/Bradford, Newcastle, Newquay, Ostend, Palma, Paris, Rotterdam.

175

ENNISKILLEN to
Dublin.
GLASGOW to
Enniskillen.
ISLE-OF-MAN to
Belfast.
LEEDS/BRADFORD to
Edinburgh, Enniskillen, Glasgow.
LIVERPOOL to
Belfast, Brussels, Dublin, Frankfurt, Isle-of-Man, London (Heathrow).
LONDON (HEATHROW) to
Birmingham, Isle-of-Man, Newquay, Strasbourg.
LUTON to
Belfast, Dublin, Enniskillen, Guernsey, Isle-of-Man, Jersey, Ostend.
MANCHESTER to
Barcelona, Cork, Exeter, Isle-of-Wight, Newcastle, Newquay, Ostend, Palma, Teesside.
NEWCASTLE to
Glasgow
NORTHAMPTON to
Guernsey, Isle-of-Man, Jersey.
OXFORD to
Jersey.
SOUTHEND to
Guernsey, Jersey.
STANSTED to
Jersey.
STAVERTON (CHELTENHAM/GLOUCESTER) to
Guernsey, Jersey, Ostend.
SWANSEA to
Ostend.
TEESSIDE to
Isle-of-Man, Jersey, London (Heathrow).

```
                               1  5  1  6  1  6  1  6  1  6  1  6  1  6  1  6  1  6  1
                               9  9/ 9  0/ 9  1/ 9  2/ 9  3/ 9  4/ 9  5/ 9  6/ 9  7/ 9  8/ 9
                               5  6  6  6  6  6  6  6  6  6  6  6  6  6  6  6  6  6  6
                               8  0  0  1  1  2  2  3  3  4  4  5  5  6  6  7  7  8  8  9  9
EMA—Jersey                     X  X  X  X  X  X  X  X     X     X     X  X  X  X  X  X  X
Oxford—Jersey                  X
EMA—Guernsey                   X  X  X  X  X  X  X  X     X     X     X     X  X  X  X  X
EMA—Ostend                     X     X     X     X     X     X,    X     X     X     X     X
Birmingham—Ostend              X     X     X     X     X     X     X     X
EMA—I.O.M.                     X     X     X     X     X     X     X     X     X
EMA—Glasgow                    X  X  X  X  X  X  X  X  X  X  X  X  X  X  X  X  X  X  X  X  X
Birmingham—Jersey                    X     X     X        X  X     X     X     X     X     X
Birmingham—Guernsey                  X     X     X     X        X     X     X     X     X     X
EMA—Dublin                           X  X  X  X  X  X        X  X  X  X  X  X  X  X  X  X  X
Luton—Dublin                         X  X  X  X  X  X                             X        X
Luton—I.O.M.                         X
Northampton—I.O.M.                   X     X
Northampton—Jersey                   X     X        X        X        X
Staverton—Jersey                     X     X        X  X  X        X        X        X        X
Staverton—Guernsey                   X     X        X  X  X        X        X        X        X
Staverton—Derby                      X
Luton—Jersey                         X     X        X        X        X        X     X  X        X
Luton—Guernsey                       X     X        X        X        X        X        X        X
Cambridge—Jersey                     X     X        X        X        X        X        X        X
Cambridge—Guernsey                   X     X        X        X        X        X        X
Bristol—Ostend                       X     X        X  X  X        X        X
Cardiff—Ostend                       X     X        X  X  X        X        X        X
Leeds—Glasgow                              X  X  X  X  X  X  X  X  X  X  X  X  X  X  X  X  X
Bristol—Luxembourg                         X     X     X
Bristol—Palma                              X     X     X        X        X        X
Cardiff—Luxembourg                         X     X     X
Cardiff—Palma                              X     X     X        X        X
EMA—Calvi                                  X
EMA—Luxembourg                             X     X
EMA—Rotterdam                              X     X     X     X
Staverton—Ostend                           X     X     X     X
Swansea—Ostend                             X     X     X     X
EMA—Cork                                      X  X  X        X        X
Birmingham—Cork                               X  X  X  X
Birmingham—Luxembourg                         X
Bristol—Barcelona                             X     X        X        X        X
Bristol—Perpignan                             X
Cambridge—Ostend                              X     X        X
Cardiff—Barcelona                             X     X        X        X
Cardiff—Perpignan                             X     X
Carlisle—Guernsey                             X     X        X
Carlisle—Jersey                               X     X        X
EMA—Belfast                                   X  X  X  X  X  X  X  X  X  X  X  X  X  X  X
Carlisle—Belfast                              X  X  X        X
Derby—Carlisle                                X  X  X
EMA—Newcastle                                 X  X  X  X  X  X
Birmingham—Newcastle                          X  X  X  X  X  X
Birmingham—Barcelona                                X        X
Birmingham—I.O.W.                                   X        X        X        X
Birmingham—Palma                                 X     X
Birmingham—Rotterdam                             X     X
Bristol—Amsterdam                                X     X
Cardiff—Amsterdam                                X     X
Carlisle—London                                  X
Derby—Basle                                      X
EMA—I.O.W.                                    X     X        X        X        X        X
Luton—Ostend                                     X
Manchester—Barcelona                             X     X
Manchester—Ostend                             X     X     X     X
Manchester—Palma                              X     X                                   X
Northampton—Guernsey                             X     X
Bristol—Genoa                                          X
Bristol—Valencia                                       X
Cardiff—Genoa                                          X
```

177

```
                        6  1  7  1  7  1  7  1  7  1  7  1  7  1  7  1  7  1  7
                        9/ 9  0/ 9  1/ 9  2/ 9  3/ 9  4/ 9  5/ 9  6/ 9  7/ 9  8/
                        7  7  7  7  7  7  7  7  7  7  7  7  7  7  7  7  7  7  7
                        0  0  1  1  2  2  3  3  4  4  5  5  6  6  7  7  8  8  9
EMA—Jersey              X  X  X  X  X  X  X  X  X  X  X  X  X  X  X  X  X  X  X
Oxford—Jersey
EMA—Guernsey            X  X  X     X  X  X  X  X  X  X  X  X  X  X  X  X  X  X
EMA—Ostend              X     X     X     X     X
Birmingham—Ostend
EMA—I.O.M.              X     X     X     X     X     X     X
EMA—Glasgow             X  X  X  X  X  X  X  X  X  X  X  X  X  X  X  X  X  X  X
Birmingham—Jersey          X  X  X  X  X  X  X  X  X  X  X  X  X  X  X  X  X  X
Birmingham—Guernsey     X     X     X  X  X  X  X  X  X  X  X  X  X  X  X  X  X
EMA—Dublin              X  X  X  X  X  X  X  X  X  X  X  X  X  X  X  X  X  X  X
Luton—Dublin
Luton—I.O.M.
Northampton—I.O.M.
Northampton—Jersey
Staverton—Jersey
Staverton—Guernsey
Staverton—Derby
Luton—Jersey                     X     X     X     X     X     X     X
Luton—Guernsey                     X     X     X     X     X     X
Cambridge—Jersey
Cambridge—Guernsey
Bristol—Ostend
Cardiff—Ostend
Leeds—Glasgow           X  X  X
Bristol—Luxembourg
Bristol—Palma
Cardiff—Luxembourg
Cardiff—Palma
EMA—Calvi
EMA—Luxembourg
EMA—Rotterdam
Staverton—Ostend
Swansea—Ostend
EMA—Cork
Birmingham—Cork
Birmingham—Luxembourg
Bristol—Barcelona
Bristol—Perpignan
Cambridge—Ostend
Cardiff—Barcelona
Cardiff—Perpignan
Carlisle—Guernsey
Carlisle—Jersey
EMA—Belfast                   X  X  X  X  X  X  X  X  X  X  X  X  X  X  X  X  X
Carlisle—Belfast
Derby—Carlisle
EMA—Newcastle
Birmingham—Newcastle
Birmingham—Barcelona
Birmingham—I.O.W.
Birmingham—Palma
Birmingham—Rotterdam
Bristol—Amsterdam
Cardiff—Amsterdam
Carlisle—London
Derby—Basle
EMA—I.O.W.
Luton—Ostend
Manchester—Barcelona
Manchester—Ostend                X     X     X     X
Manchester—Palma
Nothampton—Guernsey
Bristol—Genoa
Bristol—Valencia
Cardiff—Genoa
```

Route	1958	59/60	1960	60/61	1961	61/62	1962	62/63	1963	63/64	1964	64/65	1965	65/66	1966	66/67	1967	67/68	1968	68/69
Cardiff—Valencia												X								
Luton—Belfast												X								
EMA—Enniskillen												X		X						
Glasgow—Enniskillen												X		X						
Leeds—Enniskillen												X		X						
Luton—Enniskillen												X								
Manchester—Cork												X		X						
Belfast—Enniskillen												X		X						
EMA—Amsterdam												XF								
Birmingham—Amsterdam													XF							
EMA—Bristol												X								
Enniskillen—Dublin														X						
Manchester—I.O.W.												X			X					
Manchester—Exeter												X								
Birmingham—Newcastle												X								
Birmingham—Teesside												X								
Manchester—Newcastle													X							
Manchester—Teesside														X						
Newcastle—Glasgow												X								
EMA—Leeds														X	X	X	X	X	X	X
EMA—Barcelona														X		X		X		
EMA—Basle														X				X		
EMA—Bergen													X							
EMA—Newquay															X		X		X	
EMA—Palma															X		X		X	
EMA—Edinburgh																		X	X	
Leeds—Edinburgh																			X	
Teesside—London																			X	
Birmingham—I.O.M.																				
Coventry—Jersey																				
Teesside—Jersey																				
Birmingham—Brussels																				
Birmingham—Frankfurt																				
Birmingham—Newquay																				
EMA—Brussels																				
EMA—Frankfurt																				
Manchester—Newquay																				
Teesside—I.O.M.																				
Southend—Jersey																				
Southend—Guernsey																				
EMA—Paris																				
Stansted—Jersey																				
London—Strasbourg																				
London—Newquay																				
Belfast—Jersey																				
Belfast—Gatwick																				
London—Birmingham																				
Liverpool—London																				
Liverpool—Brussels																				
Liverpool—Frankfurt																				
Liverpool—Dublin																				
I.O.M.—Belfast																				
Liverpool—Belfast																				
Liverpool—I.O.M.																				
London—I.O.M.																				

*For EMA read Derby (Burnaston)

|---|---|---|---|---|---|---|---|---|---|---|---|---|---|---|---|---|---|---|---|---|
Cardiff—Valencia																				
Luton—Belfast																				
EMA—Enniskillen																				
Glasgow—Enniskillen																				
Leeds—Enniskillen																				
Luton—Enniskillen																				
Manchester—Cork																				
Belfast—Enniskillen																				
EMA—Amsterdam							X	X	X	X	X	X	X	X	X	X	X	X	X	X
Birmingham—Amsterdam																				
EMA—Bristol																				
Enniskillen—Dublin																				
Manchester—I.O.W.																				
Manchester—Exeter																				
Birmingham—Newcastle																				
Birmingham—Teesside																				
Manchester—Newcastle																				
Manchester—Teesside																				
Newcastle—Glasgow																				
EMA—Leeds	X	X	X	X	X															
EMA—Barcelona																				
EMA—Basle																				
EMA—Bergen																				
EMA—Newquay						X		X		X										
EMA—Palma																				
EMA—Edinburgh																				
Leeds—Edinburgh																				
Teesside—London			X	X	X	X	X	X	X	X	X	X	X	X	X	X	X	X	X	X
Birmingham—I.O.M.			X		X		X		X		X		X							
Coventry—Jersey			X		X		X		X		X		X		X					
Teesside—Jersey			X		X		X		X		X		X		X					
Birmingham—Brussels				X	X	X	X	X	X	X	X	X	X	X	X					
Birmingham—Frankfurt				X	X	X	X	X	X	X	X	X	X	X	X					
Birmingham—Newquay				X	X	X														
EMA—Brussels				X	X	X	X	X	X	X	X	X	X	X	X					
EMA—Frankfurt				X	X	X	X	X	X	X	X	X	X	X	X					
Manchester—Newquay				X	X	X														
Teesside—I.O.M.				X		X		X				X		X		X				
Southend—Jersey				X	X	X	X	X	X	X	X	X	X	X	X					
Southend—Guernsey				X	X	X	X	X	X	X	X	X		X						
EMA—Paris				X	X	X	X	X	X	X	X	X	X	X						
Stansted—Jersey					X		X		X		X									
London—Strasbourg				X	X	X														
London—Newquay				X	X	X	X	X	X											
Belfast—Jersey				X	X															
Belfast—Gatwick																				
London—Birmingham													X	X	X	X	X	X	X	X
Liverpool—London														X	X	X	X	X	X	X
Liverpool—Brussels																				X
Liverpool—Frankfurt																				X
Liverpool—Dublin																				X
I.O.M.—Belfast																				X
Liverpool—Belfast																				X
Liverpool—I.O.M																				X
London—I.O.M.																				X

*For EMA read Derby (Burnaston)

NAME	FROM	TO	NOTES
Wing Commander N. R. Harben, D.F.C.	1938	14.2.47	Founder of Air Schools Ltd., & Chairman until he passed away 14.2.47
E. W. Phillips, M.B.E.	1938	December 1965	Original Managing Director
Mrs. R. Harben	1938	?	
Group Captain C. A. B. Wilcock, A.F.C., M.P.	March 1947	14.1.62	Chairman during this period. Passed away 14.1.62.
Wing Commander H. A. Roxburgh, A.F.C.	June 1947	7.1.65	Chairman 21.1.62 to 7.1.65. Managing Director 21.1.62 to 26.10.63 (joint with R. R. Paine)
R. R. Paine	July 1947	16.9.69	Managing Director 21.1.62 to March 1969.
L. Barley	July, 1947	?	
D. W. T. Sullivan	1948	2.6.69	Commercial Director
M. M. Agar	21.1.62	2.6.69	Company Secretary & Financial Director
F. A. Marshall	1.1.65	2.6.69	Technical Director. Joint Managing Director with R. R. Paine, June 1966 to 2.6.69
J. Castle	10.12.68	3.7.69	Minster nominee. Main architect of BMA / Invicta Merger.
D. Telford	5.3.69	2.6.69	Invicta
Wing Commander H. Kennard	5.3.69	25.7.69	Invicta
Captain P. J. Bruce-Souster	5.3.69	2.6.69	Invicta
J. Hodgson	5.3.69	16.6.72	Chairman during this period. Minster appointee.
M. D. Bishop	20.3.69	Current	Managing Director September 1969 to date, and Chairman.
Captain S. D. Fenton	20.3.69	17.12.69	Operations Director
H. Free	20.3.69	16.6.72	Minster Appointee
C. Murland	16.6.72	21.7.78	Minster Director
P. Cannon	16.6.72	16.7.73	Chairman during this period. Minster Chairman.
J. T. Wolfe	26.10.72	Current	General Manager and Director
S. F. Balmforth	26.10.72	Current	Company Secretary from 2.6.69. Financial Director.
A. J. Smith	26.10.72	August 76	Technical Director
A. R. McGibbon	16.7.73	21.7.78	Chairman until 21.7.78
J. Rogers	6.8.73	January 75	Sales and Marketing Director
Dr. R. F. Beauchamp	21.7.78	Current	
G. Elliott	21.7.78	Current	

Registration	Type	C/N	Into Service	Acquired From	Disposal and Other Remarks
G-AILL	Messenger 2a	6341	21/8/47		The first 'true' commercial charter for the Company flown by this Aircraft.
G-AJZJ	Gemini	6465			
G-AIUK	Rapide	6640	6/48	Kenning Aviation	To Kenya 3/55 as VP-KND
G-AKOV	Rapide	6612	8/50	Inter-City Air Services	To Kenya 3/55 as VP-KNC
G-AEAL	Rapide	6325	4/53	Hunting Surveys	Sold 3/56 as F-OAVE
G-AIUL	Rapide	6837	6/54	Keale Street Pottery Co.	Sold to A. S. Hubbard 3/57
G-ANTD	C47B Dakota	14969 26414 43-49153	18/4/55	C. E. Harper Aircraft Co. Ltd. Exeter	Sold to Cameroon Air Transport as TJ-ACF 17/10/68. Later to Air Anglia Norwich as G-ANTD. Now scrapped. Dove Dale.
G-AMGW	Marathon 1a	127	27/3/56	West African Airways	Withdrawn from service 25/7/60. Millers Dale.
G-AOGZ	C47B Dakota	16534 33282	1/6/56	Royal Air Force	Originally KN628, Field Marshall Montgomery's personal aircraft. Sold to Strathallan Air Services 1/4/67. Darley Dale.
G-AMHR	Marathon 1a	129	13/7/56	West African Airways	Withdrawn from service 18/7/60. Scrapped Burnaston 12/60. Monsal Dale.
G-APBC	C47B Dakota	15676 27121 43-49560	9/5/58	Transair Ltd. Gatwick	'Slab-sided' wing fillet-built from I-TRES 'Italian' fuselage, 'British' wings etc. Sold to Southwest Aviation, Shoreham, 30/4/68. Still in service. Derwent Dale.
G-AMEW	Marathon 1a	118	7/7/58	Ministry of Supply	Delivered 28/8/57 ex XA265 navigation trainer. Withdrawn 27/9/60. Scrapped Burnaston 1962. Not named.
G-AMSW	C47B Dakota	16171 32919	24/4/59	Cambrian Air Services	Crashed French Pyrennees 7/10/61. Fern Dale.
G-AMSX	C47B Dakota	16448 33916	24/4/59	Cambrian Air Services	Sold to Guyana Airways as VP-GCF 22/12/65. Peak Dale.
G-AOFZ	C47B Dakota	9131	16/2/60	Hunting Clan African	Ex VP-YON. Sold to Gulf Aviation 22/3/66. Main plane from R.A.F. Dakota KP267. High Dale.
G-AGJV	C47B Dakota	12195	9/3/61	B.E.A.	To Air Envoy 13/3/69. Millers Dale.
G-AKJH	C47B Dakota	13164	5/61	B.E.A.	To Gregory Air Services. Never bore the name British Midland. Monsal Dale.
G-ALHS	Canadair C-4 Argonaut	164	2/62	Overseas Aviation (C.1) Ltd.	Withdrawn 16/10/67
G-ALHY	Canadair C-4 Argonaut	170	6/62	Overseas Aviation (C.1) Ltd.	Withdrawn 6/11/67.
G-ALHG	Canadair C-4 Argonaut	153	18/12/62	Overseas Aviation (C.1) Ltd.	Crashed Stockport 4/6/67.
G-ALHN	Canadair C-4 Argonaut	160	—	Overseas Aviation (C.1) Ltd.	Both stored at Burnaston and broken up for spares 63/64.
G-ALHP	Canadair C4 Argonaut	162	—	Overseas Aviation (C.1) Ltd.	Reduced to spares
G-ALHV	Canadair C-4 Argonaut	367	—	Aden Airways	Ex VR-AAT. Acquired 12/63. Reduced to spares.
G-ASKK	Herald 211	161	1/2/65	Handley Page Ltd.	To B.U.A. (C.1) 15/2/67. Originally Series 202 as CF-MCK Maritime Central Airways, but did not enter service. Modified to 211 as PI-C910 and to Sadia as PP-ASU.
G-ATHE G-APWA	Herald 207 Herald 100	165 149	17/8/65 16/4/66	Handley Page Ltd.	Loaned by manufacturers until 15/9/65, during mods to 'KK'. On loan from Handley Page Ltd. Returned 30/9/66.
G-AODG	Viscount 736	77	10/1/67	B.U.A.	Crashed on landing in poor weather at East Midlands 20/2/69.
G-ASED G-APNE	Viscount 831 Viscount 831	419 403	12/2/67 3/4/67	B.U.A. B.U.A.	To Alidair 1972 To Arkia Air Transport 4X-AVE
G-AVJA	Viscount 815	336	2/6/67	Pakistan International	Crashed on training flight take-off Manchester Airport 20/3/69.
G-AVJB	Viscount 815	375	3/7/67	Pakistan International	Sold to Intra Jersey, Jan. 77 (having spent some time with Kestrel Aviation).
G-AWCV	Viscount 760	186	12/4/68	B.O.A.C. Associated Companies	Ex VR-AAN. WFU 1970
G-AWGV	Viscount 785	116	27/5/68	Alitalia	Ex I-LIRE. WFU 1970
G-APND	Viscount 831	402	20/1/69	B.U.A.	To Arkia Air Transport 4X-AVF
G-AWXI	Viscount 814	339	16/3/69	Condor Flugdienst	Ex D-ANOL. Written off London (Heathrow) Airport, 12/69, after engine fire.

Registration	Type	C/N	Into Service	Acquired From	Disposal and Other Remarks
G-AOCB	Visocunt 755	92	11/2/69	Transferred from Invicta	Both acquired 11/2/69 from Invicta. Scrapped 1/70
G-AOCC	Viscount 755	93	11/2/69	Transferred from Invicta	Sold to A. J. Walter 8/70
G-APPX	Viscount 702	73	4/4/69	B.O.A.C. Associated Companies	Ex VP-BBV. Sold to Air International.
G-APTD	Viscount 833	426	20/4/69	B.U.A.	Leased from B.U.A. until Nov. 1969.
G-AXLL	B.A.C. 1-11 (523FJ)	193	1/1/70	B.A.C.	New. Sold to Trans Brasil Nov. 1973. as PP-SDT
G-AXLM	B.A.C. 1-11 (523FJ)	199	12/2/70	B.A.C.	New. Sold to Trans Brasil Nov. 1973. as PP-SDV
G-AXLN	B.A.C. 1-11 (523FJ)	211	12/3/70	B.A.C.	New. Sold to Trans Brasil March 1974. as PP-SDU
G-AYBJ	Boeing 707-321	17597	19/4/70	Pan American	Ex N719PA. Sold to Jet Power Miami.
G-AYVE	Boeing 707-321	18083	3/4/71	Pan American	Ex N757PA. Sold to Skyways International Panama.
G-AZLP	Viscount 813	346	20/1/72	South African Airways	Ex ZS-CDT, built 22/10/58. Current.
G-AZLR	Viscount 813	347	20/1/72	South African Airways	Ex ZS-CDU, built 26/10/58. Current.
G-AZLS	Viscount 813	348	28/2/72	South African Airways	Ex ZS-CDV, built 18/11/58. Current.
G-AZLT	Viscount 813	349	28/2/72	South African Airways	Ex ZS-CDW, built 24/11/58. Current.
G-AZNA	Viscount 813	350	9/3/72	South African Airways	Ex ZS-CDX, built 20/12/58. Current.
G-AZNB	Viscount 813	351	9/3/72	South African Airways	Ex ZS-CDY, built 10/1/59. Current.
G-AZNC	Viscount 813	352	25/3/72	South African Airways	Ex ZS-CDZ, built 29/1/59. Current.
G-BAPD	Viscount 814	340	1/73	NORA Air Services	Ex D-ANAD, built 10/1/59. Current.
G-BAPE	Viscount 814	341	1/73	NORA Air Services	Ex D-ANIP, built 15/2/59. Current.
G-BAPF	Viscount 814	338	1/73	NORA Air Services	Ex D-ANUN, built 5/10/58. Current.
G-BAPG	Viscount 814	344	1/73	NORA Air Services	Ex D-ANIZ, built 4/59. Current.
G-ASVO	Herald 214	185	14/3/73	SADIA	Ex PP-SDG, built 1/9/65. To British Air Ferries
G-ATIG	Herald 214	177	18/4/73	SADIA	Ex PP-SDI, built 16/9/65. To Brymon
G-BAVX	Herald 214	194	19/4/73	SADIA	Ex PP-SDN, built 23/12/67. To British Air Ferries
G-AYVG	Boeing 707-321	17598	19/2/75	Continental Bank of Illinois	Ex N720PA. Current.
G-AZWA	Boeing 707-321F	17605	13/4/75	Continental Bank of Illinois	Ex N727PA. To International Air Leasers Miami.
G-AYXR	Boeing 707-321F	17608	13/1/76	Continental Bank of Illinois	Ex N730PA. Current.
G-BAEL	Boeing 707-321F	17602	28/8/75	Continental Bank of Illinois	Ex N724PA. To International Air Leasers Miami.
G-BCZR	Viscount 838	466	10/5/76	Field Aircraft Services	Ex 9G-AAU. On lease from Fields. Returned 7/76.
N65358	DC9-15	47048	8/76	McDonnell Douglas	Ex YV-52C Avensa; became G-BFIH 4/78. Dove Dale. Current.
N370WA	Boeing 707-373	19442	3/73	Leased from World Airways	Returned 12/12/78
G-BFLD	Boeing 707-338C	19625	3/4/78	Qantas	Ex VH-EAE. Current.
G-BFLE	Boeing 707-338C	19293	18/4/78	Qantas	Ex VH-EBT. Current.
G-AZJM	Boeing 707-324C	18886	14/3/73	B.C.A.L.	Current. Ex 3D-ACM.
G-AYOX	Viscount 814	370	13/10/78	Arkia	Ex D-ANAC, 4X-AVA. Current.
G-BFZL	Viscount 836	435	23/3/79	Royal Swazi	Current.
OH-LYB	DC9-14	45712	19/9/77	Leased from Finnair	Darley Dale. Renamed Merseyside. Current.
N48075	DC9-15	45723	15/2/78	Leased from Southern	Returned 30/9/78. Named Darley Dale.

Miscellaneous

Registration	Type	C/N	Into Service	Acquired From	Disposal and Other Remarks
G-ACLL	Leopard Moth	7028			Company hack. Sold.
G-AMDA	Anson 1a	N4877	22/7/55	Air Navigation and Trading Co.	Sold to Skyfame Museum 1961.
G-ARMI	Piper Apache	23-1980			Scrapped Burnaston 1961.
N701PA	Boeing 707-321	17674		Pan American	Flown from Miami 15/3/76 to be reduced to spares.
G-BAGB	Siai Marchetti	L20131-40			Personal aircraft M. Bishop/Dr. Beauchamp.

Registration Type	C/N	Into Service	Acquired From	Disposal and Other Remarks
Registration Type	C/N	Into Service	Acquired From	Disposal and Other Remarks
Registration Type	C/N	Into Service	Acquired From	Disposal and Other Remarks

G-AILL Miles Messenger 2A flew the first commercial charter for the Company. (N.D. Welch)

Percival Proctor 5 G-AHTE in Derby Aviation colours. (N.D. Welch)

Miles Gemini G-AJZJ. (N.D. Welch)

D.H. Rapide G-AIUK entered service in 1948. (M.P. Marsh)

D.H. Rapide G-AKOV was put into service in 1950. (M.P. Marsh)

Rapide G-AIUL did not enter service until 1954. (Newark Air Museum—N. Franklin)

Dakota G-ANTD wearing Derby Aviation titles 'TD' was the Company's first Dakota.
(Newark Air Museum)

G-AOFZ Dakota "High Dale" in the current 1960 livery. (N.D. Welch)

Dakota Freighter G-AKJH with the modified logo style. (N.D. Welch)

G-AGJV "Millers Dale" Dakota at Burnaston with scrapped Marathon and Anson in the background. (N.D. Welch)

Dakota G-APBC "Derwent Dale" with British Midland logo's at Newcastle. Woolsington Airport in December 1964. (Map)

Dakota G-AODGZ "Darley Dale". (N.D. Welch)

Miles Marathon G-AMGW "Millersdale" in Derby Aviation Livery 1956.

G-AMHR "Monsal Dale" the second Marathon—also in Derby Aviation Colours. (A.J. Jackson)

The third Marathon to join the Fleet was G-AMEW. It was acquired from the RAF and is seen here at Bristol Lulsgate Airport in Derby Airways Livery in 1960.

Canadair C4 Argonaut G-ALHY ex-Overseas Aviation, with Derby Airways titles in 1962. (N.D. Welch)

Derby Airways full two tone blue livery shown to effect on Argonaut G-ALHS. (Waller Studios Ltd)

Argonaut G-ALHY in British Midland Colours.

A cargo of cigarettes being offloaded from Argonaut G-ALHY. (Photo Vision).

G-ALHY being scrapped at East Midlands Airport in 1969.

190

Handley Page Herald G-ASKK in its smart new livery in early 1965, note the short lived "Flying Egg" motif on the engine cowling. 'KK' was British Midlands first Turbine Powered Aircraft. (Aviation Photo News/B. Stainer)

For comparison the mid 1970's livery is shown here on Herald G-BAVX.

G-AODG was the first Viscount operated by British Midland Airways. A 736 model it is seen here at East Midlands Airport in 1967. (L. Hudson)

G-AVJA Viscount 815 in 1968.

Viscount 814 G-AWXI served for only 9 months with B.M.A.

G-APNE Viscount 831 Ex British United Airways went to Arkia of Israel and is seen here in basic Arkia colours but with British Midland Titles. (Map)

Viscount 785 G-AWGV in a late 1960's B.M.A. livery. (L. Hudson)

Viscount 814 G-BAPE Ex Nora Air Services at Birmingham Elmdon in May 1977. (Map)

193

Viscount 815 G-AVJB.

Viscount 814 G-BAPD. (S.G. Richards)

Viscount 838 G-BCZR.

G-AVJB wearing The Kestrel International Livery.

G-BAPD in Skyline of Sweden colours and dual registration SE-FOX.

Viscount 813 G-AZLS in Cyprus Airways colours.

194

Viscount 831 G-APND at East Midlands Airport in 1969.

G-AZLP Viscount 813 Ex South African Airways in July 1977. (Map)

G-AZLR Viscount 813 Ex South African Airways at Birmingham, Elmdon in 1977. (Map)

Viscount 813 G-AZNA at London Heathrow. (Map)

G-AZNB Viscount 813 at Birmingham Elmdon in May 1977. (Map)

G-AZNC Viscount 813 Ex South African Airways. (L. Hudson)

BAC ONE-ELEVEN 523FJ G-AXLL B.M.A.'s first jet airliner. (BAC)

A rare shot of the three B.M.A. BAC ONE-ELEVENS together. (BAC)

G-AXLN BAC ONE-ELEVEN 523FJ. All three aircraft were sold to Trans Brasil in 1974.

Handley Page Herald G-ATIG wears "on contract to Air Anglia" stickers at Woolsington in March 1976. (Map)

G-ASVO Herald 214 came from Sadia in Brasil as did G-ATIG and G-BAVX. (Map)

G-BAVX the third of the Heralds operated by BMA in the mid 1970's. (Map)

Douglas DC-9-14 N65358 was the first DC9 to be operated by a British Airline and became G-BFIH "Dove Dale". (Map)

OH-LYB B.M.A.'s second DC-9, is leased from Finnair. (Map)

N48075 DC9-10 named Merseyside is seen here at Reykjavik in May 1978. (Map)

G-AYBJ the first Boeing 707 for British Midland. (Map)

G-AYVE like G-AYBJ was Ex Pan American.

Boeing 707-321 G-AYVG on lease to Libyan Arab Airlines is seen here at Luton in July 1979. (Map)

199

Boeing 707-321F G-AZWA in basic Kuwait Airways colours at East Midlands Airport in October 1977. (Map)

G-AYXR 707 321F in Kuwait Airways livery in 1978. (Map)

G-BAEL 707-321F in Pakistan International livery at London Heathrow in January 1976. (Map)

G-BAEL again, this time with Kenya Airways titles at Heathrow in September 1977. (Map)

G-AYBJ in the colours of Syrian Arab Airlines.

Nigerian Airways colours carried by G-AYVG at London Heathrow in January 1976. (Map)

G-AYVG with Malaysian Airline System Titles.

G-AYBJ again, this time in the colours of Kenya Airways at Heathrow in 1977. (Map)

G-AYBJ Boeing 707 in Sudan Airways Yellow Tail "Blue Nile" colours. (Map)

G-AYBJ in another Sudan Airways Livery at a later date.

Group Captain C.A.B. Wilcock A.F.C. M.P. Chairman from March 1947 to January 1962.

Wing Commander H.A. Roxburgh A.F.C. Chairman from January 1962 to January 1965.

F.A. Marshall, Joint Managing Director June 1966 to June 1969. (W.W. Winter Ltd.)

J. Hodgson Chairman March 1969 to June 1972. (C.R. Le Clercq)

P. Cannon, Chairman June 1972 to July 1973.

S.F. Balmforth Company Secretary from June 1969. Financial Director. (Raymonds)

J.T. Wolfe General Manager and Director since October 1972. (Raymonds)

A.R.G. McGibbon, Chairman July 1973 to July 1978. (Sound Stills Ltd.)

203

M.D. Bishop, Managing Director since September 1969 and current Chairman and Managing Director. (Christopher John)

D.H. Rapide instrument panel of the late 1940's and early 50's. (Hawker Siddeley)

Douglas DC9-14 Flight Deck—late 1970's.

A British Midland Boeing 707, for once in the company's own livery. (Layland-Ross Ltd.)

The interior of one of the British Midland "Instant Airline" Boeing 707's. (Layland-Ross Ltd.)

B.M.A. Boeing 707 in Sudan Airways "Blue Nile" livery. (Layland-Ross Ltd.)

707 G-AZWA in full Kuwait Airways colours. (Layland-Ross Ltd.)

BMA Boeing 707 wearing Zambia Airways titles over the livery of its previous operator, Donaldson International Airways. (Layland-Ross Ltd.)

East African Airways logo and motif on a BMA Boeing 707. (Layland-Ross Ltd.)

Bangladesh Biman logo and motifs on the ex-Donaldson 707. (Donaldson-Ross Ltd.)

G-BFLD in the basic white and decorative motif of Deta Linhas Aereas de Mocambique.
(Layland-Ross Ltd.)

208